The Small Investor Goes to Market

A Beginner's Guide to Buying Stocks

Jim Gard

Ten Speed Press
Berkeley, California

For Mom

Ten Speed Press
P.O. Box 7123
Berkeley, California 94707

Distributed in Australia by Simon and Schuster Australia, in Canada by Publishers Group West, in New Zealand by Tandem Press, in South Africa by Real Books, in Southeast Asia by Berkeley Books, and in the United Kingdom and Europe by Airlift Books.

Cover design and interior illustrations by Gerry O'Neill (gerryoneill@mindspring.com)
Interior design by Jeff Brandenburg, ImageComp

Library of Congress Cataloging-in-Publication Data

Gard, Jim
    The small investor goes to market: a beginner's guide to buying stocks / Jim Gard
    Includes bibliographical references and index.
      ISBN 0-89815-981-4 (pbk.)
      1. Stocks. 2. Speculation. I. Title.
    HG4661.G37 1998   97-39103
    332.63'22—dc21   CIP

First printing, 1998
Printed in the United States of America

1 2 3 4 5 6 7 8 9 10 — 02 01 00 99 98

Table of Contents

Acknowledgments

First, last, and always, Lynn, without whom there wouldn't be a book, or a family, or a house, or a garden, or a universe, or a past, or a future. Besides being the light of my life, she has, to put it briefly, done everything for months on end so that I could do this. Words fail me.

Others have made significant contributions. It is simply amazing, the number of people who will step up and offer help when one asks. This book could have been a lot longer and drier, but a few people read parts of the first drafts and offered their opinions and reactions. In particular, my sister Susan Kolesar and sister-in-law Carol Sunderman were early commentators on some tentative drafts and helped organize my thinking and plans. My buddy from the early times, Jim Ratliff, had particularly sharp and valuable guidance on improving my focus on the issues.

A friend in Chapel Hill, North Carolina, Mrs. Josephine Kuizin, was the kind of critic every writer needs. She did not waste my time or her own . . ."What is this? I can't understand this!" or "Nobody wants to read that junk." I believe every reader owes her thanks for making the final product something that would not waste the reader's time. Josephine is the kind of critic that a lot of writers need, if they could stand up to her.

And Lynn.

Other early readers, who all brought their own points of view to help sharpen mine, were Barry Munson, Hayden Childs, Patricia Hockmeyer, April Burgos, and Dawn Bennett. Each of them helped me to improve my understanding of my readers' needs.

Several companies were generous in helping me to gather data, examples, charts, or cartoon materials. Without their help the book would have been substantially less readable. None of these companies endorse any of the content of the book, but all of them have made contributions. Those helpful companies include AIQ, Inc., the American Association of Individual Investors (AAII), America Online, the American Stock Exchange, CompuServe, Dow Jones, First Call, Frank Russell and Company, Goodyear Tire and Rubber, *Investors Business Daily*, Morningstar, the National Association of Securities Dealers, the New York Stock Exchange, Norfolk and Southern Railroad, Procter and Gamble, Ruddick Corporation, Standard and Poor, Telescan, Inc., The Value Line, and Zacks Investment Services.

One who gets credit for attracting your attention to the book is the illustrator, Gerry O'Neill. He did the cartoons and the cover design for this and

The Small Investor. He has made major contributions to the appeal and success of both. And he is a good person to work with.

None of this would go very far without the support and confidence of my publisher, Ten Speed Press, and editor, Mariah Bear. When I wrote the acknowledgments for the first book, I had not seen the results. I did not know how good both were. Now I know, and I can say that Ten Speed Press does classy work, and Mariah brings it all together with grace and skill. It is a pleasure to work with her and her confederates.

And Lynn.

The beginning is the most important part of the work.

—PLATO, *THE REPUBLIC*

Introduction

Most individual investors are interested in the stock markets. Many of them realize that buying and selling individual stocks is tough business, but they are still interested. Even though most small investors should be investing mainly in mutual funds, the fascination with trading individual stocks just doesn't go away. No matter what their circumstances, investors are fascinated with the notion of buying a stock they have selected on their own, but a great many of them have no idea how to begin.

But is it wise to invest in individual stocks? Is it practical? For many people the answer is no, but for some, it may be yes. While the extra risks and work involved are simply not realistic for many small investors, and I would not encourage anyone to make this their prime investment strategy, this is a private decision for each investor. What I will encourage you to do, if you choose to buy individual stocks, is to learn and adopt some of the methods I detail in the following pages.

If you are considering selecting your own stocks, then one of the first questions you may have of professional money managers is "How do they do it?" There is no simple answer to that question. They all do it differently. There must be a thousand reasonable approaches to stock selection. Even the professional investors are not able to agree among themselves on the best method. So how do you decide? The answer is that you find something that you can manage and believe will work for you. If a stock selection method is too difficult, or simply doesn't make sense to you, then it won't work for you. But some other methods may be better.

So, you begin by adopting a method. Before Franklin D. Roosevelt was elected to his first term as president, he spoke about the country's need for action[1]. He said, "It is common sense to take a method and try it. If it fails, admit it frankly and try another." In the latest edition of his famous book, *A Random Walk Down Wall Street*[2], Burton Malkiel wrote, "While reports of the death of the efficient market theory are vastly exaggerated, there do seem to be some techniques of stock selection that may tilt the odds of success in favor of the individual investor." I am not going to encourage you to experiment in the stock markets, because that can be a hard school indeed; however, if you are going to try, don't just flounder around, take a method!

This book is not a guaranteed map to success and fortune. It is not a presentation of one method that is sure to make you a superior stock picker. It is not the last word on selecting individual stocks for your portfolio. It will help you decide whether to begin, and how.

There are some books and magazines that present what they claim is "the one true way." If those authors knew the one true method to fortune in the markets, then they would keep it confidential. If they let the cat out of the bag, and we all started following the one true method, then it wouldn't work any more. Some of the published methods are reasonable, and worth further study. Some are not. How do you know which are practical and worth your time and attention? That is the tough question. There is no clear and simple answer. There is no one best method for everyone. There are some methods that are practical for investors with a lot of experience, but not for others. Other methods may be suitable for investors who are comfortable with statistics. Still other methods are appropriate for investors who believe in technical analysis. Think about this process as if you were choosing your clothes, or your medicine. There are a lot of different products that are right for someone, but only a few of them are right for you.

My goal in writing this book is to show you several different approaches to buying stocks, and help you decide whether one or two of them might be good for your investing practice. That implies the related goal of helping you decide if it might be better for you to avoid this business altogether. Nothing in this book is intended to persuade you to begin, or continue buying individual stocks. But if you must, then consider carefully your methods and expectations.

---

[1] May 1932, Oglethorpe University.
[2] Very highly recommended for your further study.

Can you use this book? I hope so. Let me describe the intended audience. If you have a little experience or have read some introduction to investing, such as *The Small Investor,* and are considering taking on individual stocks, then this book should be a good starting point. You may choose to skip some sections if they seem too complex. I want to help you find what works for you; or, perhaps make an intelligent decision that none of this stuff works for you.

There is a lot of vocabulary introduced in the book that will help you understand the markets, and also gain more from reading the *Wall Street Journal* or watching CNBC. There is a rather extensive glossary at the end of the book to help you keep track of the terminology. It would be helpful and educational to buy a copy of *Barron's Dictionary of Finance and Investment Terms* and keep it close by while you read.

A final essential warning: Nothing in this book should be taken as a recommendation that you use these methods, or that you buy and sell stocks based on your own analysis. There are some people who would be better advised to stay out of that business. Most of us should consider using mutual funds as the major part of our investment plans. Many should use funds exclusively. However, if you must get into the rough sport, here's a little help.

"That one there . . . he's been investing without a method!"

I encourage you to let me hear (in care of Ten Speed Press) what you find useful or not, and what kind of particular challenges or success you have found in your personal investing. I will respond to as many letters as I can.

No one knows what he can do till he tries.

PUBLILIUS SYRUS, *MAXIMS*

Preliminary Remarks

This chapter introduces the most basic concepts of the stock market, such as, what are stocks? and where do they come from? Some readers may feel that they can skip this section, and others may like a low-key introduction.[1] If you paid your money, then take your choice. The basic concepts include

- the purpose of stock

- the origin and purposes of the stock markets

- common stock

- preferred stock

- compound growth

- reading newspaper stock listings

Stocks, and shared ownership of a business, are created when a company is ready to grow beyond the financial resources of the original owners. For example, say that a small publishing company, the Reading Riddles Publishing Company, had been going along with modest success for five years with the owner, Robert Reading, providing all of the capital and management. After a particularly strong year in 1996, when he published two best-selling cookbooks, Robert began getting more good new proposals than

---

[1] If you read *The Small Investor*, then you probably can safely skip this chapter.

he could handle alone. He decided that it was time to expand his business. He needed more staff, more management; larger operational space, more and newer equipment. Robert estimated that he needed $20 million to fund his expansion for two years. The current value of the business was $700,000 and his personal net worth was $450,000.

Reading might have been able to borrow the $20 million from a bank, but he chose instead to bring in new ownership to provide the new capital. He decided to reorganize his business into a publicly traded corporation and share the ownership. Robert established one million shares of ownership and offered them for sale in the public financial markets. (That is a long and complex process, but for our purpose just assume he got it done.) He sold the shares for $20 apiece to 450 buyers who each bought between fifty and 12,000 shares in January of 1997. He kept 60,000 shares for himself as repayment for his previous total ownership.

The one million new shares of ownership became the common stock of the corporation. Each new shareholder was entitled to a share of ownership of the company proportional to the number of shares she had bought. She was entitled to vote for the directors of the company, receive a part of the earnings—as approved by the directors—and sell her shares of ownership in the open markets whenever she wished.

Because the company had become a publicly traded firm, the United States Securities and Exchange Commission (the SEC) would require regular and timely public reporting of at least the following:

1. Quarterly and annual financial statements
2. Significant business news that might affect the value of the shares
3. Changes in major ownership[2] and the board of directors

Buying and Selling Shares

The people who bought the original shares of ownership made investments and hoped to receive a profit on their investments. Other people may have heard about Reading Riddles as an interesting new company, but they were not willing to buy the shares at first. Any of these people might become involved in buying and selling shares later. Let's look at a few examples, and see how they dealt with the stock:

---

[2] Major ownership means 5 percent or more of the stock.

Example 1: Betty had been a longtime employee of Reading Riddles who loved the company and had great confidence in Robert Reading. When she heard about the public offering she took $4,000 of her savings and bought 200 shares. For the first year, she did not receive any part of the earnings of the company because the directors decided not to pay any earnings to the shareholders. At the end of the first year, she needed the money to pay for her son's first year of college, so she asked a broker to sell the shares. The broker reported that the best price he could get at the time was $13.75 per share, and he charged her $175 for his sales commission. Betty got back $2,575 for her investment of $4,000.

Example 2: Jon Holding did not buy the stock at the initial public offering (IPO), but knew about the company and watched and studied them for three months. He then decided to buy 5,000 shares, which his broker said could be obtained at a price of $23 per share. Jon invested $115,000 to buy 5,000 shares. He held those shares for six years. The directors did not pay any earnings out to the shareholders in 1997, 1998, or 1999, but they decided to pay 5¢ per share in the year 2000 , 8¢ per share in the year 2001, and 11¢ per share in 2002. In 2002, Jon decided he wanted his money back to buy a boat. His broker told him that the current stock price was $27.50 per share. Jon sold his stock for $137,500. In the six years he also collected $1,200 in earnings dividends and paid $2,185 for the brokerage fees on two trades.

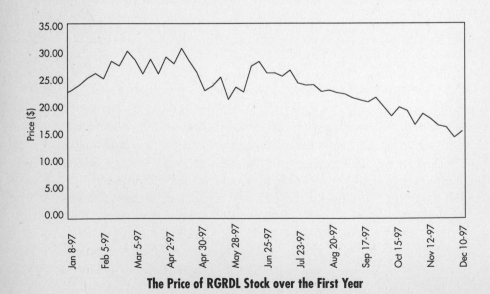

The Price of RGRDL Stock over the First Year

Example 3: Mary Lynn was an experienced and aggressive stock trader. She heard about the company's initial public offering and decided it looked like a good opportunity. She did not buy in the IPO, but did buy one month later for $25 per share. She bought 1,000 shares that cost her $25,000 plus a sales commission for her broker of $320. Over the next two months, the market price of the stock went as high as $29, but then it started falling. Two months later it was down to $22 and still falling. Mary Lynn called her broker and said to him, "Look, if this thing ever falls as low as $20, then sell me out at whatever price you can get!" Two days later, she was sold out at a price of $19.75, and paid another $300 in brokerage fees. She had a net loss on the experience of $5,870.

Market Prices

The three investors we observed all had different experiences with Reading Riddles Publishing Company stock. Their differing stories of success or failure are caused by many interrelated factors. All of the differences are due to the investor's own decisions and the ideas and actions of other investors. Look at the history of the stock from January 1997 to the end of the year.

In the first year after the IPO, several factors influenced the stock's share value. Early in the year, there was a lot of general investment interest in the publishing industry, in new small companies, and in Reading Riddles's new books. A lot of investors who had not bought in the IPO, started asking their brokers to get them into RGRDL (RGRDL was the stock market symbol for the new stock). People started offering higher prices for the stock, and the price went up as high as $29.

Prices varied from minute to minute. On Friday, March 22, 1997, at 11:37, there were four offers to buy a total of 4,000 shares, and the highest price offered was $28\frac{7}{8}$ (i.e., $28.785, or $28 and 78.5 cents). At the same time, there were two offers to sell a total of 3,200 shares: 2,200 shares offered at $29.50 and 1,000 shares offered at the market price (best available deal). That meant the stock market specialist could arrange a sale of 1,000 shares for $28\frac{7}{8}$, but the other 2,200 shares would not be sold just then.

At that time, the market price of RGRDL was $28\frac{7}{8}$ because that was the active trading price. It did not matter that someone else wanted to sell at $29.50 and someone else wanted to buy at $28.75. The only price that was active was the $28\frac{7}{8}$. The current market price is set and reset throughout every trading day. It is always the most recent price at which a willing buyer and a willing seller completed a trade.

Lesson: The price of a traded stock changes constantly. It is set at the price that the most recent buyer and seller agreed on a deal.

What happened to RGRDL in the second half of the year? They had great difficulty with the two major projects for the year. One author was eight months late in completing his manuscript, and the other became involved in a widely publicized scandal that severely damaged the market potential of his book.[3] Word got out. The public became disillusioned with Reading Riddles, and more people wanted to sell than buy.

On November 5, 1997, at 3:30, the price was $18 per share. At that time there were seven offers awaiting filling by the stock exchange specialist:

- Sell 200 shares at $18.50

- Sell 5,000 shares at $18.75

- Sell 30 shares at $19.00

- Sell 500 shares at the market (best available price)

- Sell 100 shares at the market

- Buy 2,000 shares at $17.00

- Buy 600 shares at the market

The specialist would look at this and settle the trades that were offered at the market price, which he would keep set at $18. The buyer wanting 600 shares would get them from the two people offering 100 and 500 shares. The other four offers would go unfilled until someone decided to adjust their offer up or down, or until a new offer came to the exchange floor.

Over the course of the last two months of 1997, the price of RGRDL steadily drifted lower because there was little or no good news about the company, and more sellers than buyers made offers each day.

For the fiscal year 1997, the company had revenues of $17,400,000 and expenses of $18,335,000. This left them with a net operating loss for the year of $995,000, or $0.995 for each share of the stock. Everyone who was interested in the stock (*following* the company) had to reach their own conclusions about whether the stock was a good buy or not.

---

[3] If you can believe that.

The Markets

It would be a terrible burden to have to find a seller each time you wanted to buy a stock (or a buyer each time you wanted to sell one). One million people in the United States may own shares of Ford when I want to buy some, but I don't know any of them, don't know where to find them, and don't want to go looking. I expect my broker to do that for me. That will work like this: All buy and sell orders go through brokers, and the brokers direct them to the appropriate specialists. So, the Ford orders all go to the desk where Ford is being handled on the New York Stock Exchange.

The Ford trading specialist sees all of the buy and sell orders and can match up the ones that have the best offering prices. For this service, both the brokers and the exchange specialist need to earn a living, so the individual investors pay a fee.

The functions of the market are (in simplest terms):

- to provide a common ground for brokers to match orders

- to provide orderly and fair pricing, and matching of offers

- to provide an orderly and regular pricing mechanism without excessive wild swings in prices

- to publicize the trading amounts and prices on a continuous basis so that all of us can see the current prices and what is being traded

The functions of the brokers are (in simplest terms):

- to provide individual investors access to the markets

- to provide individual investors current information on the conditions of trading

- to provide individual investors up-to-date, accurate reports on their trading accounts

- to advise individual investors who need help in deciding what to buy or sell

Both the markets and the brokers perform their roles with a high level of service and accuracy. The occasional dishonest or incompetent broker is the proverbial bad apple. These brokers are a great threat to their clients and their firms, but are, nonetheless, rare.

Preferred Stock

In August of 1998, Robert Reading decided to try to raise some more money. The banks offered him loans at 9.5 percent interest, which he declined. The current stock price was $17 per share, and he did not think that was a good price at which to offer further shares of ownership in his company. He thought the value of shares should and would be higher than $17. The other avenue for raising funds was a preferred stock offering.

Preferred stock is entirely different from the common stock that we discussed before. Reading offered 300,000 shares of preferred stock for sale at a price of $40. Each share carried these terms[4]:

Reading Riddles Corporation
One Share of Preferred Stock

This share of the preferred stock entitles the owner to a dividend payment of $3.30 per year, paid on the first of June of each year, beginning June 1, 1999.

In the event of default on this payment, no dividends may be paid to the common shareholders until such time as the preferred shareholders are brought up to full payment.

In the event of default on the payments to preferred shareholders, the dividends are guaranteed to the preferred shareholders by claim on the company's assets that may remain after all debts are paid.

Here are the differences between the common and preferred stocks:

Quality desired	Common	Preferred
Share of ownership of the firm	yes	no
Right to vote on directors	yes	no
Promised dividend payments	no	yes
Protection in case of bankruptcy	none	partial

---

[4] This avoids all pretense of legal correctness. It just shows the idea of preferred stock.

You should also remember that the sale of preferred stock is like any other business deal: Various conditions or terms may be added to make the deal more attractive to either party. The example above is just the simplest view of a preferred stock issue.

Compound Growth

If you own a stock that pays dividends, then you may do as you wish with the dividends. Some people like to say to their companies, "Keep the dividend payments and send me additional shares of stock"; or they tell their brokers to immediately reinvest all dividends in more stock.

Other people prefer to take the money and have a good time, but I have no good advice for them. Let's talk about reinvesting the dividends.

The Reading Riddles Company continued to grow and prosper after the first weak year. Beginning in the year 2000, they paid a dividend as shown in the following table.

Date of Payment	Dividend Per Share	Stock Price
4/20/2000	5¢	$18.50
4/20/2001	8¢	$21.00
4/20/2002	11¢	$23.50
4/20/2003	20¢	$25.50
4/20/2004	24¢	$28.88

If you owned 500 shares in April of 2000, you could receive $25 in dividends and buy 1.4 shares of new stock. Suppose you did that to increase your stock holdings and continued to reinvest the dividends each year. At the end of the period after April 20, 2004, you would own 514 shares worth $14,838, approximately $400 more stock value than you would have had without reinvesting. That is an example of compound growth, and for many individual investors it is a wise way to manage the dividends if, of course, the money is not needed immediately for other purposes.

The Market Is a Tool of a Crowd

If you ever buy stocks, then you will be hoping to make a profit on the deal. If not, don't buy stocks. How can you make a profit? One way is to buy low and sell high. Or at the least, sell high.

So you devise a plan to buy low and sell high. How can you be sure that you will always succeed? You cannot. You will not always succeed; don't kid yourself.

How can you be sure that you will sometimes succeed? You cannot. Some people consistently lose. If you find yourself losing money consistently—say on the first ten deals that you make—then quit. Some people are not temperamentally compatible with the financial markets. If you are one of these people, then stop trading stocks and just use mutual funds for your investing.

Then what is the plan? The plan is to win more than you lose. If you can do that, you will be a successful stock investor; if you cannot, then get out of the game. Try to achieve a success rate where at least half of your trades (buys and sells of a stock) are winners and that, on average, the winners gain substantially more than the losers lose.

Keep in mind that your success is always subject to the decisions and emotions of millions of other people. No matter how strong or incisive your analysis and decision making are, the decisions of others will control your ultimate rate of success. Why? Because they, as a mass, control the prices. You cannot.

If you buy into a little research and development firm in Silicon Valley for $14 per share because you think they have some possibility of earning $2 a share in a couple of years, that might be smart investing. If, two months later, the firm gets a lot of publicity about their new products and the price gets run up to $41 by a thousand other eager investors, then you have a chance for a large profit, 193 percent growth in two months. Part of that profit is due to your good decision to buy, but most of it is due to the mania of a mob of new investors that you don't even know. If you decide to hold the stock and it then falls to $25 a share over the next few months, then you might take a good profit, up 79 percent in five months, or cry over a lost opportunity, or just hold onto the stock as a continuing good investment.

Whichever the case, you should recognize that the good news and the bad is partially of your own making and largely of the crowd's making. The great mass of faceless and nameless investors out there will go their way with no regard for your success or failure. They will set prices on each stock accordingly as their moods reach a consensus. You may well try to anticipate some of their directions. You may assume that there is some element of rationality behind the fluctuations of some prices, but never fall into thinking that you have them all figured out or that your wise analysis will sweep the market in your preferred direction. Such a plan would be like trying to sweep back the waves, an assured plan for failure.

> **Lesson:** Don't be afraid of the markets. Just show them the respect they demand.

Reading Stock Tables

Most people who own stocks like to keep up with the prices of their holdings on a regular basis. The quick way to do that is by consulting a newspaper that will print the current price of a lot of stocks every day. If you check your local paper or the *Wall Street Journal*, you can find the previous day's closing prices on somewhere between a thousand and three thousand stocks. Those price quotations will include all of the most widely owned and most-traded stocks. The newspaper price listings require a little attention, and perhaps a magnifying glass to read, but they are fairly consistent and straightforward. Here are two examples that were published on the same day. The one on the left is from a local newspaper, and the one on the right is from the *Wall Street Journal*. These are reproduced the same size they were published by the papers.

The basic information is the name of the company and the price of the stock at the previous day's market closing. However, a lot more information than that is listed, and even the basic stuff is presented differently by the two papers. The *Journal* shows almost full names of companies and their stock symbols; the other paper shows only a rough abbreviation of the name. For example, Advanced Micro Devices is listed as *AMD* on the left and as *AdvMicro AMD* on the right. H. F. Ahmanson and Company is listed as *Ahmans* on the left and *Ahmanson AHM* on the right. The companies are listed in more or less alphabetical order, but that too is inconsistent, depending on how the papers abbreviate. In order to read the charts, you need to refer to the headings at the top of the column and the legend of special characters printed somewhere else on the page. The local paper shows, in order, the price-to-earnings ratio for each stock, the sales for the prior day (in hundreds—2680 actually means 268,000 shares of stock sold), the past year's high and low prices for the stock, the previous day's closing price, and the net change for the day in fractions. So, for AT&T you can read:

AT&T s 1.32 14 26030 42$^{7}/_{16}$ 30$^{3}/_{4}$ 40$^{1}/_{4}$ − $^{1}/_{8}$

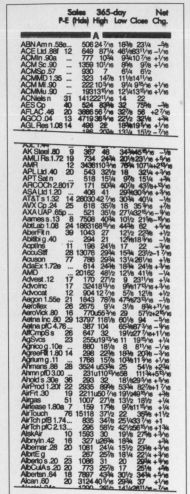

New York Stock Exchange Price Listings

Translated this says, "AT&T. Current annual dividend is $1.32. Current price-to-earnings ratio (P/E) is 14. Yesterday's sales were of 2,603,000 shares. The past year's high price was $42.4375. The past year's low price was $30.75. Yesterday's closing price was $40.25, which was down $0.125 from the day before."

The *Wall Street Journal* presents the story differently. Their legend at the top shows the past year's high and low, name of stock, symbol, dividend, yield percentage (the dividend divided by the price), P/E, yesterday's high, low, and closing prices, and yesterday's change in price. They add some notes and special symbols which I will cover below. For AT&T you can read their report as:

s 42⅝ 30¾ AT&T T 1.32 3.3 13 26030 40⁵⁄₁₆ 39¹³⁄₁₆ 40¼ – ⅛

Translated, this says, "AT&T stock had a prior year high of $42.625 and low of $30.75. The stock market symbol is T, the annual dividend is $1.32, which gives 3.3 percent annual yield based on today's price. The P/E is 13. The trading volume yesterday was 2,603,000, with a day's high of $40.3125 and low of $39.8125. Closing price was $40.25 for a $0.125 change from the prior day's close."

Don't believe everything you read. Those two reports are inconsistent, aren't they? The prior year highs and lows are different, but that may be okay; one of them is using fifty-two weeks and the other is using 365 days. Besides, the few cents difference in reporting old prices is not important to most of us. Somewhat more interesting is the difference in price-to-earnings ratios that they report. That difference is significant, and the values should be current. You can't check it unless you have more of AT&T's financial information available. We will have more to say on that question later in the book, but for now, the newspaper reports are pretty good and reliable, and the occasional small errors are not important. Just don't assume perfect accuracy in everything you see in print.

Now what about the special symbols? There are a lot of them and most of them are pretty obscure. But look at the ones in the *Wall Street Journal* list. See the little *s* to the left of AT&T? That means the company had a stock split or some kind of restructuring within the past year, so today's prices are not directly comparable with older prices. That is important information for people (like me) who look at a lot of old records. Some of the lines are in boldface type, meaning the price changed by 5 percent or more during the day's trading session. Some of the lines are underlined. Those stocks had unusually large trading volume for the day, compared to their usual trading volumes. Other stocks have a little "club" symbol next to the name, indicating stocks for which the *Wall Street Journal* will provide free financial reports and news releases on the company (telephone 1-800-654-2582). A great deal; try it some time!

Now we can go ahead with the main theme of the book: If you want to choose stocks to buy, how can you do it?

Recommended Further Reading

Downes, John, and Jordan E. Goodman, eds. *Dictionary of Finance and Investment Terms*. New York: Barron's Educational Series, 1991.

The Market Environment

O n Tuesday August 17, 1993, the stock price of IBM opened at $41.75. It closed the day at $40.75. Apparently, among the analysts and investors who were looking at IBM that day, the consensus was leaning towards selling because of lower prices or lower earnings, rather than buying because it was a bargain. For a moment during the day, IBM stock traded at $40⅝, the lowest price to be seen for a long time before or since. A year later the stock was worth $60, a year after that $100, and before the end of 1996 IBM traded at around $160. I hope that all the buyers on that fateful

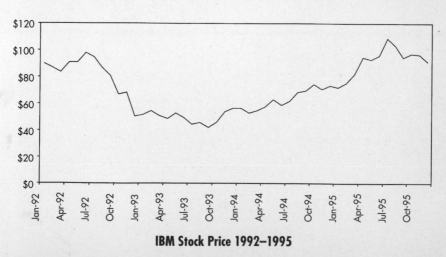

IBM Stock Price 1992–1995

day held on for a while. I hope that the sellers have reexamined their decision-making processes.

MagneTek, Inc. is a publicly traded company that manufactures and sells
electrical equipment. For most of 1991 and 1992, the stock price floated
between about $12 and $16, and that price appeared to be supported by
reasonably steady sales and earnings reports. In January of 1993, the consensus opinion, as expressed by market action, was that things were
improving for MagneTek. The price was rapidly bid up to $18, . . . $21,
. . . $ 24, and in February it reached a high of $25.50. Good news and bad
news, okay? The good news was that somebody had an opportunity to make
a serious profit on this stock. Nearly four million shares were traded in January
and again in March of '93. The bad news was that somebody was doing a
lot of weak analysis and decision making. The people who bought ten or
twelve million MagneTek shares in early '93 were paying too high a price.
Notice this doesn't say anything bad about the company. This says the stock
buyers were wrong at those prices. By October of 1993, the price had fallen
to $12, and in January 1996 it was $7. The long-term "buy and hold"
investors who got into MagneTek at the wrong time lost 60–70 percent of
their investment over the next three years. By the end of 1996, it was back
to about $11.

In both IBM and MagneTek we see well-known, respected companies
trading on the largest and best-regulated stock market in the world, the
New York Stock Exchange. All the financial reports of these companies and
their competitors were available for study to anyone who would ask. And

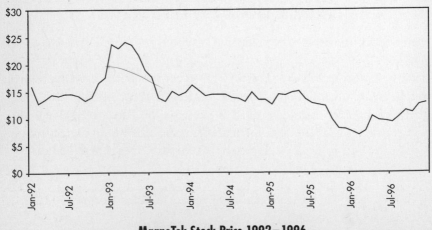

MagneTek Stock Price 1992–1996

yet, it is clear that a great many people made some bad decisions on what or when to buy or sell. It's a tricky business. Market prices are fixed by the opinions of investors, and those opinions are constantly subject to change.[1]

It is very likely that some experienced professional traders were on the wrong side of IBM and MagneTek in 1993. I, for one, was on the wrong side of trading IBM in 1994, just before it started it's rapid advance. How would you have felt about it if you had bought or sold either stock at the wrong time and lost 30, 40, or 50 percent of your money in that transaction? For me the result wasn't too bad, because a few months later I took the money that came out of the ill-timed sale of IBM and invested in another stock that turned out to be a better deal.

The point of all this is that if you are going to buy and sell stocks, then sometimes the market will go against you. Don't expect to be right all the time. Some experienced traders say you should only expect to be right about half the time, but by astute management of your trading positions you can restrict most of the losses to 10–20 percent and work the winners into something greater than that. If you can do that, then you will come out ahead in the long run. But keeping your head is not going to be easy. One factor that will help you keep your head is to have some method in your stock purchases and sales. You need to have something concrete to lean on. If you make a mistake due to a wild guess, it will be pretty difficult to rationalize that and figure out how to do better. But if you make a mistake in applying a well-thought-through method, then you can learn something from the experience and expect to do better the next time.

The Small Investor in the Markets

The financial markets are hard schools. Anyone can get in if they bring the price of admission, but the markets will chew you up and spit you right back out again if you fail to practice some work and discipline. Now you may think that millions of people participate in the stock market, and surely you are just as smart as most of them, so you ought to be able to do at least average. You are just as smart as most of them, but a great many of them are experienced professionals with tightly disciplined methods of

---

[1] It may happen that, on Monday, a lot of people are willing to buy and sell stock A at $45 per share, so the price gets fixed at $45; but on Tuesday, no one is willing to pay over $43, so the price falls to $43.

their own. Think of it like a poker game with four of your friends and neighbors and one professional gambler. Where do you think the money will flow?

Some people claim that the markets are not fair to individual small investors. I dispute that. My attitude is that as long as we are all free to participate or stay away, and we have ample opportunity to cash in and leave at any time, then the market is fair. In fact, the small investor even has some advantages relative to the professional money managers. It will be worthwhile for you to see some of the advantages and disadvantages of the individual investor.

Some disadvantages faced by individual investors in the stock market

Disadvantage 1: We don't watch the markets constantly, like the pros do. We have jobs and families and lives to live, so sometimes we will miss important news until after the market has already reacted to it. The news could be a big surprise in a company's earnings report, or something more profound, such as the report of manipulation of copper futures prices that came out on June 14, 1996. That news shook the prices of all the copper producers. This is one condition that encourages us to be "buy and hold" investors who look at the long-term prospects of companies, rather than trading based on rapidly changing conditions.

Disadvantage 2: We don't receive the lowest prices on commissions, as the larger traders and mutual funds may. That puts us at an immediate disadvantage in terms of opportunities for profitable trades.

Disadvantage 3: We don't hear early inside information that may be passed around among the Wall Street regulars before it hits the newspapers. The big-money guys who are in the brotherhood (or sisterhood) will occasionally get genuine hot tips that give chances for almost certain profits. We will not. Don't kid yourself. If your portfolio is under $2 million, then I would guess that you will never get the hot tip before a hundred professionals have heard it and taken the right action or passed on it.

Disadvantage 4: The pros usually work with companies or teams that can share a lot of financial expertise and experience. If a mutual fund manager is unable to decide on the merits of a given deal, she can probably get immediate support and advice from several other professionals who are experienced in that kind of stock. We are, to a great extent, left on our own. This, of course, is one of the reasons for joining investment clubs.[2] If you get in a club with fifteen other smart people, then you may have as good a decision-making process as the mighty Magellan Fund, maybe better.

Some advantages of the individual small investor

Advantage 1: You don't have your decisions reviewed or approved by a committee. Of course this works both ways, but at least if you decide one day that you have found a good deal, you can go ahead and buy (or sell) the stock right away, before the market runs away from you.

Advantage 2: You are not in a contest; the professional money managers are. The pros have to constantly worry about how their quarterly or even weekly performance is compared to their competitors. They sometimes even buy or sell stocks just to make their portfolios look good compared to the recent winners and losers. This may sometimes cause them to make poor trades just to make themselves look good in the eyes of people who are only comparing past market activity. You think that's dumb, right? You are right; it is dumb. But the mutual fund manager's main job is to attract new investors to buy into his or her fund. Sometimes that priority may get in the way of smart investing.

Advantage 3: You may set your own criteria for success. The professional money manager cannot. His boss and customers decide what is success or failure. The manager has to keep trying to guess what it will take to please them this quarter. This can sometimes get in the way of smart investing. Many fund managers pursue the goal of being near the top of their classes in a given quarter, even if it requires taking on more risk than they should for their advertised fund objectives.

Advantage 4: You may invest as little or as fully as you like. Sometimes you may decide to invest only 50 percent of your funds, sometimes 100 percent if you find enough good buys. Mutual fund managers are restricted by their charters to keeping a certain amount of funds invested in stocks, even when they might not see any attractive deals. They usually cannot be

---

[2] More on investment clubs in chapters 6 and 11.

100 percent invested because of the need to keep funds on hand to respond to possible calls for redemption of shares.

Advantage 5: You or I can buy and sell whatever we want, and usually complete the transaction within a few minutes, for a price that was very close to what we expected to get. But if a professional money manager wants to sell all of her stock in General Electric, it may require a week or longer to unload all of the stock without rattling the market into lower prices. We know that none of our trades will have any significant impact on market prices (well, maybe $\frac{1}{8}$ point), but the fund manager who holds 200,000 shares of GE knows that the price might fall just because the street hears that she is selling.

Markets

A stock market is a place or, in our times, an organization or computer network where shares are bought and sold (traded). Markets have existed a long time, but somewhere thousands of years back, men realized that the commercial stool needed three legs: production, consumption, and trading. It probably wasn't long after that some clever fellow said to himself, "If I could just buy low and sell high, this would be an easy way to make a living." He was right. However, the premise "If I could buy low and sell

"All those in favor of selling arcadian olives?"

high" turns out to be easier said than done. The search for the most efficient and effective ways to manage that problem has led to the formation of financial markets that specialize in gold, fine art, bonds, real estate, and common stocks. The markets generally serve the needs of two classes, and those support one another. One class is made up of the corporations or investors

The New York Stock Exchange

who need to participate in providing new capital to business. They buy and sell stocks and bonds for this purpose. The other class consists of those who only hope to make a profit from dealing in stocks and, perhaps, care little about the ultimate success or failure of the businesses.

In the United States, financial markets have existed in some form since roughly 1700. The earliest markets in the colonies were concerned with contracts for future deliveries of tobacco and wheat. But by 1790, there had developed in New York City some regular meetings of people who were specifically interested in buying and selling securities that included shares of ownership in companies. About the same time, some of them decided to specialize in brokerage work. They bought and sold on behalf of others. These stockbrokers began meeting under the buttonwood tree at 68 Wall Street, and out of that rose the New York Stock Exchange that exists on Wall Street today. The brokers agreed on their first organization and set of rules in 1817 and remained a largely self-regulated, or unregulated, business until the passage of the Securities Exchange Act of 1934. It would be far afield from my purpose to bring you much more of the history of the markets, but I strongly recommend two excellent books for further study: *The Stock Market* and *Once in Golconda*. Both are listed in the references at the end of the chapter. I urge you to study some of the history of the markets, as knowledge of it would undoubtedly make you a better investor.

The markets today handle very large volumes of buy and sell orders that come in through member brokerage firms who are representing the orders of their customers. In 1996, there were over sixty million separate trades on the New York Stock Exchange (NYSE). At the exchanges, such as the NYSE and the American Exchange (AMEX), there are market specialists who look at the incoming buy and sell orders and try to match them to satisfy each investor's needs as far as possible. The goals of the markets and the specialists are to provide the most efficient and reliable possible service to investors and protect the integrity of the market process.

Some of the services that the market provides, which you indirectly pay for through brokerage fees, include continuous pricing, fair matching of trades, specialists inventories, reporting trades as they occur, and reporting the daily history of trading and the market indices. Markets also oversee and attempt to control the practices of member firms to ensure that the members are following exchange rules and SEC[3] regulations. Each exchange

---

[3] The U.S. Securities and Exchange Commission.

handles the stock of any corporation that has satisfactorily completed the listing process and requirements and continues to satisfy these requirements. If you read some of the recommended further readings on market history, you should realize that the NYSE and all of the financial markets are like complex living organisms. They will continue to adapt to new conditions and public needs as time passes. The stock exchange of the year 2020 will probably be something that we would hardly recognize today.

Continuous pricing means that share prices move as gradually as possible given the current demands for buys and sells. Continuous pricing is managed by floor specialists who match up individual buy and sell orders that come to them from brokers. The effect of continuous pricing is to help us see a fair indicator of the prices at which we may expect to complete a buy or sell. If the price of GTE stock jumped around from 43 to 40 to 46 to 41 and so on in successive trades , then it would be very difficult to judge the price at which we might expect to sell our GTE stock. The floor specialist helps by keeping track of all trades and matching buy and sell orders to provide the best price available for each order, while keeping the price fluctuations minimal. Usually, depending on the orders coming in, the specialist will manage the price of an active stock like GTE so that over short periods of time the price does not vary a great deal. In times of market manias, when there is a mad rush to sell, the prices of succeeding trades may have to go down—42, 41½, 40½, 39¼, 39—until it finds a floor at which new buyers come in. However, the normal situation for a widely traded stock like GTE is that there will be a great many orders for both buy and sell coming to the specialist, and most of them will be close to the previous traded price, or simply market-price orders. The market price order allows the specialist to fill the order at the fairest price under current market conditions, almost always close to the last posted trade price. It is probably best for you to plan to do most of your stock trading with market orders. In other words, you must trust your broker and the exchange to provide the best service and fairest price available at that time. My experience with using market orders is that there are few surprises, and the ones that I encounter have more often been favorable than unfavorable to me. When I want to sell GM and ask for the current price, my broker might say bid 57, asked 57¼.[4] So I put in my order to sell two hundred at the market. What I expect is to

---

[4] Bid 57 means that the highest current offer to buy is $57 per share; asked 57¼ means the lowest current offer to sell shares is $57.25 per share.

The American Stock Exchange

get the trade completed at 57. That almost always works out okay, but once in a while, the price they report back to me may be 56⅞ or 57⅛. These are the kinds of results you may expect with highly liquid, actively traded

NASDAQ

stocks like GM. For some little-known and seldom-traded stocks, you may have to be more selective in naming your price or be prepared to accept larger surprises.

Continuous pricing is a great service to the individual small investor because it provides some predictability and assurance of fair pricing. Without it, very few individual investors would be willing to trust their brokers with market orders, and the exchanges' work would become vastly more complex and time-consuming. Liquidity and public confidence would suffer to an extent that the very nature of stock trading would be set back to the bad old days when it was the exclusive domain of brokers and stock manipulators.

The NASDAQ[5] is a market that has no physical stock-trading location. Instead, it exists as a computer network that links many brokers around the country. NASDAQ tracks and posts for general view the buying and selling bids available all day. When you offer to buy 100 shares of Dell Computer at 110, your broker should look at the system to see if there is an offer to sell at or below $110. If there is, she will confirm the trade for you at the lowest price for which 100 shares are available. If the match is

---

[5] National Association of Securities Dealers Automated Quotation System.

made, then both parties' brokers get confirmation of the deal through the system.[6] In the case of a market order where you are asking for the best price you can get at the time, then your broker should look at NASDAQ and find the best price for your trade among all the posted offers. In 1997 some new rules have been adopted by the National Association of Securities Dealers (NASD) that should give the individual investor better assurance of efficient and fair pricing through the NASDAQ system. The NASDAQ system handles stocks for thousands of companies that are not traded on the other stock exchanges, such as the New York or American Stock Exchanges. If you want to buy Microsoft stock, your broker will use NASDAQ. If you want to buy Chrysler, she will use the New York Stock Exchange.

Manias, Panics, and Crashes

You have probably noticed flocks of birds that gather closely together and then fly around to no apparent purpose, now diving, now rising, now east and now west. They stay in tight formation, all turning and swooping at the same moment as if some drill instructor were barking commands to them. Investors do much the same thing, and not just the small investors, but the most experienced and respected professional managers, too. When a crowd gets carried away with a rush in one direction it is dangerous. In a market we call that a mania.

In his book *A Short History of Financial Euphoria*, John Kenneth Galbraith wrote, "Recurrent speculative insanity and the associated financial deprivation and larger devastation are, I am persuaded, inherent in the system." Galbraith is a smart guy. He has written and studied more about the historical interpretations of current market conditions than any of us. It would be remiss of us, as both writer and reader, to begin this study without some consideration of risk. Let's begin with the risk that everyone wants to wish away: the market crash. A crash is a time when nearly all stock prices fall very rapidly. It is the product of a period of dumb investing, followed by a period of panic.

---

[6] In NASDAQ, this actually generates two trades: a sell to your broker and a buy from the other broker.

What are the conditions that lead to a crash?

Sometimes people get obsessed with an idea that something must be done. That kind of thinking can lead to a self-fulfilling prophecy, because people are more likely to accept and embrace an idea if they see many others accept it. Lemmings run to the cliffs, and investors hurry to buy or sell whatever the crowd is buying or selling. When the crowd urge grows to a certain level of enthusiasm, then the mass movement may become a mania. A good dictionary definition of mania is "excitement of psychotic proportions manifested by mental and physical hyperactivity, disorganization of behavior, and elevation of mood."[7] The alert and industrious small investor needs to be on the lookout for signs of mania in the stock market. That doesn't mean that they will be easy to spot. What are some signs of mania in the financial markets? They include popular belief that the markets, or one particular stock, can only go up. Manias are characterized by ever more people who think that they have to follow the crowd. They feel that their own limited knowledge of the investments and choices is not important, because "everyone is doing it." Especially among professional money managers, manias may be accompanied by a fear of "missing the boat." There may be great profits at stake, and whoever doesn't jump on the bandwagon quickly will miss out on the rewards, and perhaps thereby lose her job or professional reputation.

There have been many famous manias in various markets, probably none more famous nor more instructive than the tulip mania of the sixteenth century and the bull markets in American stocks of 1928–29 and 1995–97[8]. The tulip mania began with a reasonable and orderly demand for the beautiful flame tulips that were introduced in Holland around 1600. Most manias share that trait: They begin with reasonable and orderly markets where some dealers see new opportunities for profits. In this case, interest grew quickly, because the market was based on a commodity, the flame tulip, which was in short supply and could be reasonably considered to have some intrinsic value well above other tulips. People were making money, and the tulips were scarce. At some point—no one can define exactly

---

[7] *Webster's Third New International Dictionary.*

[8] For a fuller description of these and other manias, see *A Random Walk Down Wall Street* by Burton Malkiel, or *Manias, Panics, and Crashes* by Professor Kindleberger.

when (another characteristic of manias)—the crowd's attention became more attached to market speculation and the chances for fast profits than to the tulip business. Then the stories got out about the numbers of people who were making quick riches from tulips, and the surge to invest became a mob. Again, two characteristic flaws developed: First, people tended to buy tulips without reference to any intrinsic value, merely on the assumption (the speculation) of rapidly increasing prices; and second, the buyers began raising the money for purchase without regard to the soundness of their own personal finances. That last practice planted the seeds for panic when the price trend reversed and people felt obliged to sell in a hurry. Well, to make an interesting story short, some tulip prices went through the roof; individual tulip bulbs sold for more than the value of houses. Then as the number of potential buyers and their resources started to decrease, and more tulips became available, some people began to sell. Prices fell, and the previous buyers saw that they had to move quickly to protect their profits or the assets which they had mortgaged to borrow money to invest. Soon the fall in prices became an avalanche, and the rush to sell became a panic. Many people who thought they had great profits one day were left with large losses a few days later.

A similar thing happened in the American stock markets in the late 1920s,[9] and may be happening again today (early 1997). Average prices of stock in major American corporations increased 30 percent to 50 percent in 1921 through 1922, leveled off or fell a bit in 1923 and 1924, and then really started to take off in 1925 to 1928. The industrial stocks price average rose from about 100 at the end of 1924 to 200 at the end of 1927 and nearly 300 by the end of 1928. Then the same thing happened as in Amsterdam. Word got out that some people were making big money. This attracted speculators, many of whom didn't know anything about intrinsic value or reasonable returns from stocks. As the buying mania developed, more people started to invest (speculate) with borrowed money or other funds they could not stand to lose, setting the stage for the eventual panic because the speculators could not face up to the possibility of loss. When the panic came, it was a killer. Stocks lost 50 percent of value in the last quarter of 1929, lost more in 1930 and more again in 1931. From the peak in the

---

[9] For an excellent detailed history of the market mania and panic of the twenties and the aftermath, see *Once in Golconda*, John Brooks, Harper & Row (1969).

autumn of 1929 to the abyss in 1932, stocks lost almost 90 percent of their previous highest value.

"Very sad," you say. "But what has that to do with me? Am I not the new rational individual of the nineties? Do I not have computers and the Internet and personal communications devices?" Maybe, maybe. But the rest of the world is peopled with greedy and careless investors, and the value of all of your investments is directly dependent on what they do with theirs.

We can do no better than quote in part some of Galbraith's advice on manias and their consequences[10]:

> *Individuals and institutions are captured by the wondrous satisfaction that comes from accruing wealth. . . . The illusion is protected by the public impression that intelligence marches in close step with money. . . . So on to the moment of the inevitable mass disillusion and crash. . . .This last never comes gently.*
>
> *Inherent in this sequence are the elements by which in a comprehensive way it is misunderstood. The speculative episode, with increases provoking increase, is within the market itself. And so is the culminating crash.*
>
> *Let the following be one of the unfailing rules by which the individual investor, and, needless to say the pensions and institutional funds manager, are guided: there is the possibility, and even the likelihood, of self-approving and extravagantly error-prone behavior on the part of those closely associated with money.*

Observe what he says. The mania, panic, and crash are not just products of their unique times and places. No, no—the worse for all of us—they are rooted in the nature of markets and investing. The question is not if they will recur—the question is when.

So maybe you would like to see some of the telltale signs of the mania stage. This is not an exact science, and maybe there are 500 Ph.D.'s out there who would argue with us on these interpretations, but here are some things we might have seen in 1630 and 1929—and will see again some

---

[10] From *A Short History of Financial Euphoria.*

"I'm not sure these brokers are going to work out."

day. Buying manias are characterized by extreme rapid growth in market values. Prices appear to lose their connection to any prior standards of intrinsic value. You may see increased market participation by people who know little about the markets or the values of the things being traded; increased buying funded by borrowed money or other assets that the investor cannot stand to lose; euphoria, and the sense that everyone is going to get rich.

The stock market is not the whole economy, and it does not go its own way independently of the rest of the economy. There are some reasons to believe that other factors, such as federal monetary policy, created a situation in 1929 where no class of investing could thrive. Perhaps we shouldn't kick the speculators of 1929. Perhaps they were acting rationally. Perhaps, perhaps. What difference does it make? The prudent investor should always be aware that risk is just around the corner, and we cannot accurately foretell the appearance of and consequences of all the risks.

Shall I advise you to avoid the stock markets? No. My money is in there, and a lot of other cautious, conservative people have their money in, but be careful and be on the alert for the symptoms of buying manias. When you think a mania condition is starting to occur in the markets, then use extreme caution about selecting new stock purchases. Try to select those that may have a more defensive nature or for some reason ought to stand up under a bear market.[11] You might reasonably choose to simply stand aside from the markets and hold on to your cash for a while.

The Broker

If you are going to buy and sell individual stocks, it is very likely that you will need the services of a stockbroker. The selection of the broker will be one of the most critical decisions that you make.

Stockbrokers are, as a group, one of the most maligned professional classes in America. That reputation may or may not be deserved. It is not our province to pass judgment on the entire class. Your job is to find one who will work well and provide the services you need at a reasonable price. The stockbrokers, as a group, are pretty much like the rest of us. They are salespeople, to be sure, but the world needs salespeople. Think about where you would be if you had to go out and find someone to buy your stock whenever you wanted to sell. Stockbrokers tend to be fairly aggressive salespeople, but that is a necessary concomitant of the conditions imposed on them by the markets and their bosses. But still, my view is that if you draw 100 brokers at random from the population, then you could find among them a few who are exceptionally able and dedicated, a few who are stupid and lazy, and a lot who are all variations in between the best and the worst—just like the rest of us, whether doctors, writers, or anyone else. However, in the case of the brokers, you have to be demanding about which one you are going to use. If you get it wrong and hire an incompetent broker, it will probably be a year or two before you figure out the error, and another year before you get up your nerve to do something about it.[12] By that time, the broker may have done immense and irreparable damage to your financial portfolio. Therefore, get it right.

Easier said than done. The key to success is to take your time and do your homework. Begin by planning what service you expect to get from the broker. It's just like buying a car: Do you need two doors or four, big car or small, four cylinders or eight? Figure out what you need from the

---

[11] A *bear market* is a longterm decline of stock prices. More on defensive stances in chapter 9.

[12] This is a generalization based on conversations with many individual investors who have been through the experience.

broker. Here are some issues, based on a presumption that you will be investing in individual stocks and mutual funds:

1. Do I want the broker to handle just stocks, or also bonds
   and mutual funds? Which funds can this broker buy and
   sell?

2. Do I want to use the broker's research services for evaluating
   stocks and mutual funds, or should I do it on my own?

3. Do I want the broker to review and confirm my buying
   decisions, or just take orders?

4. Do I want to have a brokerage office close enough to visit on
   occasion, or can I handle everything by telephone or
   computer connections?

5. Do I want to buy mutual funds from several different
   investment companies?

Interview at least six or seven different brokers. Take notes. Insist on talking to brokers with several years experience. Don't let them rush you or
bully you. If your friends or relatives recommend a broker whom they have
used for four or five years, that recommendation should probably be taken
very seriously.

Discount or Full Service?

The world of investing changes rapidly. Whenever there is a lot of money
around, people will invent new ways to try to get their hands on your money
faster than you can keep track of their schemes. That applies to brokerage
services, too. As recently as 1975, all brokers charged the same standard
fees, but since then many new types of services and fee structures have been
offered. The first division was between the so-called "discount" and "full-
service" firms. The labels once meant that a discount broker would offer
lower prices for commission rates on trades, but would not offer individual
attention and counseling, or company-sponsored research reports. The full-
service firms would offer research and personal counseling, plus, possibly,
full financial planning with your brokerage account. In the last couple of
years, this situation has changed. Now, both groups want to attract more

customers, so both of them offer a mix of service levels at different costs. The full-service firms want to attract you on price, so they may offer some varieties of lower service options. The discount firms want to attract you on service, so they offer various intermediate service arrangements, but with higher fees attached. The whole business is intensely competitive and rapidly changing. It would be a mistake to rule out Merrill-Lynch just because they have been labeled "full service," and it would also be a mistake to rule out the firm Jack White just because they have been labeled a discount broker. Both of those firms have some different service options and price structures to consider beyond what they had a year ago. A good point of reference is *Smart Money* magazine. Each year in July, they present an article that evaluates about twenty different discount brokerage firms, and in November they present an article that evaluates about ten full-service firms.[13]

Recommended Further Reading

Brooks, John. *Once in Golconda*. Harper & Row, 1969.

Brimelow, Peter. *The Wall Street Gurus*. Alexandria, VA: Minerva Books, 1988.

Bernstein, Jacob. *Investor's Quotient*, 2d ed. New York: John Wiley & Sons, 1980.

Bishop, George W. *Charles H. Dow and the Dow Theory*. Appleton Century-Crofts, 1960.

Galbraith, John Kenneth. *A Short History of Financial Euphoria*. New York: Viking Penguin, 1993.

Kindleberger, Charles. *Manias, Panics, and Crashes*, rev. ed. New York: Basic Books, 1989.

Mackay, Charles. *Memoirs of Extraordinary Popular Delusions and Madness of the Crowd*. New York: Random House, 1995.

---

[13] It might be helpful to read chapter 4 in *The Small Investor*, by yours truly.

Watch out w'en youer gittin' all you want.
Fattenin' hogs ain't in luck.

—JOEL CHANDLER HARRIS, PLANTATION PROVERBS

The Signs of the Markets

A great many more people watch the markets and talk about stocks than ever do anything with them. A great many others make a good living by providing something for the first group to watch. The most popular indoor sport (maybe) has become discussing the trends and averages. You can hardly expect to be socially acceptable unless you are willing to discuss them, too.

More gossip and loose talk about the markets is printed and reported over the air every day than all the compact discs in the land could record. Among that popular wisdom there may be found both truth and trouble. Your task as the industrious and serious investor is to find some way to make the best of it.

Learn to protect yourself from bad information and to recognize and use good information. Easier said than done! It will become a matter of judgment and discrimination. Two famous culprits that are widely reported and misunderstood are the markets' trends and the averages. They are like oracles: They seldom tell you anything exact, but they always seem to point towards something interesting.

Trends

We have to talk about trends because everyone else does, but be careful. Trying to identify trends is risky business. Do not bet the ranch on what you think is a trend that will continue for any time into the future. Some risk-accepting investors plan their purchases and sales of stocks according to their views of market trends, especially relying on their ability to determine when trends will change. This practice is known as market timing. It is an extremely difficult and sophisticated business. Very few market timers consistently manage to make profits.[1]

The word on the street is "The trend is your friend." If so, perhaps we better get to know the trend. In fact, there are many trends, and they may all be either your friends or your enemies. Suppose the price of your Texaco stock has gone from 75 in May, to 79 in July, to 81 in September. That is a trend. It shows that over a period of time, many investors have been buying Texaco stock and expecting it to go higher. This trend, like other trends is likely to gain momentum just because the five-month history of the stock proves that a lot of people were buying. You may reasonably think[2] that there is a fair expectation that the trend will continue.

Notice, I did not *say* that you may conclude that the trend *will* continue. But there is a fair expectation. So, if you have done your research on Texaco, and if you think it looks like a buy at $81, then the trend gives one more supporting idea to believe it is a buy. If in addition to the first trend, you knew that the stock prices of all of the petroleum-producing companies were increasing throughout that summer, you will have another trend that supports the first conclusion. If in addition, the prices of most of the large industrial companies were increasing during that summer, then that is another trend to support the buying decision.

Trends are never hard and fast evidence that a stock price will go either up or down. No evidence will ever prove that the price must go one way, but trends can be used to lend some supporting argument either for or against a buying decision.

The granddaddy trend of them all is the trend of the average prices of the complete stock market. If you know that all stock prices, on average, have been trending down for the past four months, then many investors would say that the trend is trying to tell you something. Of course, the market could turn around and behave differently the next day, but many

---

[1] One highly respected market timer is Marty Zweig. If you must get into that subject, then read his excellent book *Winning on Wall Street*.

[2] In a strict statistical sense, you should not conclude anything about the trend continuing. I am using the words here in their common English sense, not teaching statistics.

investors believe that when a trend gets started in one direction and picks up enough support from believers to continue that way for a while, then there is a reasonable expectation that it will go on until some significant news turns it.

If you believe that you have identified a major trend in the stock market, and if you believe it will continue, then it would be risky to make a buy or sell decision based on finding one stock that will go the other way. That is the lesson of another popular old saw: "Don't fight the tape."

The overall market average, as indicated by the Dow Jones industrial average or the Standard & Poor's 500 index, is one factor that has strong correlation with an individual stock's price. When those averages are trending in one direction, they will tend to push the price of your stock the same way. If anyone could consistently forecast the direction of the trends in the major stock price averages, then that forecaster would be richer than Midas. No one can do that. Some people claim to be better at it than others, but nobody can do it consistently.

You should accept the fact that you and your broker and your friends cannot accurately and consistently forecast the trends in market prices. Do

"It's different this time!"

not invest heavily based on just your guess about the trends in prices. On the other hand, if you have identified a particular stock that you think you would like to sell and if you also think that it is likely that the overall trend of market prices will be down for the next few months, then that may be taken as one more thought to support your selling decision.

> **Warning:** A fair amount of statistical reasoning indicates that there are no trends in stock prices except for the ones we can measure in history. Some sophisticated and learned observers believe that no trends will do us any good tomorrow or next month. Be exceedingly cautious about risking your money on what you think has been identified as a trend. The meaning and usefulness of trends is subject to many strongly differing opinions.

Averages and Indices

Market averages or indices don't foretell the future. They just measure where we are each day. An index is a number that is reported to track changes in something else. One example is the consumer price index. It doesn't tell the price of anything, but it does indicate when prices are going up or down. Or the humidity index. It doesn't tell you how much humidity is in the air, but it does track when the air is relatively dryer or damper. A price index for stocks does the same kind of thing.

For those who like mathematical terminology, a stock index is usually a weighted average of some group of stock prices, normalized to give a value of 100 at some particular earlier date. But don't worry about the calculations. You never have to compute the index for yourself; other people, like Dow Jones & Co. or Standard & Poor's, will do it for you.

Think of the index as roughly tracking the total market value of a group of stocks. When the index is up 10 percent, you can believe that the total market value of that group is up about 10 percent also. If the Dow Jones industrial average or the S&P 500 index goes down 2 percent, then you may safely conclude that the total value of large company stocks on the NYSE has also gone down about 2 percent. Don't, however, treat it as an exact calculation; it's just an indicator.

Several different averages and indices are reported by various organizations. Few of them are computed as exact mathematical averages. Each one is devised to help you see something about the general movement of certain groups of stocks. We will look at a few of the most widely publicized, but there are many others.

The S&P 500 stock index is based on stocks of 500 large companies. It does not include all of the 500 largest, but most of them. Changes in the S&P 500 index can be expected to closely reflect the changes in total value of all investments in U.S. stock markets because those 500 companies represent about 80 percent of the total market value in American markets. The S&P 500 stock index and the Dow Jones industrial average are closely correlated. They generally go up or down about the same percentage amount at the same time. If you keep your investments in stocks of large and well-established American corporations, then you can use the Dow Jones Industrial Average or the S&P 500 index as an indicator of changes in the value of your total portfolio. If you invest in small company stocks, or only in utilities, then some other averages would be better for tracking your investments.

Market Capitalization

The market capitalization of any publicly traded company is the total price of all the stock issued and outstanding. It is found by multiplying the number of shares times the current price. For example, on January 14, 1997, Ruddick Corp.[3] had 46,461,290 shares outstanding, and the stock was trading at $14 per share. That gave them a market capitalization of about $650 million (46,461,290 x $14). That was how the market valued the entire corporation on that day.

In January 1995, Exxon Corp. had 1,242 million shares outstanding that were trading at $63. The market capitalization was $78 billion. That's a lot of money, but apparently not enough. In January 1997, they had the same number of shares that were priced at $106. The market valued Exxon at $131 billion.

Market capitalization is sometimes referred to as the price it would take to buy all the stock. That is a rough estimate. Market capitalization (or *cap*) is indeed the price of the stock at that time when you check the price and make your computation, but it is highly unlikely that anyone could buy all of the stock at that price. As soon as they started, or even if the market

---

[3] Harris Teeter grocery stores and American-Elfird Thread, symbol RDK on the NYSE.

heard about the idea, then people would start demanding higher prices for their stock and drive the market cap higher. However, market cap is a good way to get a handle on the size of a company and its weight in the markets.

Many investors prefer to buy and sell companies in a certain range of sizes. You will hear and read about small-cap, or mid-cap, or large-cap companies. Some mutual funds and individual traders make it their business to only work with companies in a certain range of sizes.

There are different opinions about where we draw the lines between small, mid, and large cap. Generally, you would probably be safe to assume that any market capitalization over $4 billion is considered large cap, and any market capitalization below $300 million would be considered small cap. Just be aware that some folks have different opinions on that.

Large-cap firms include all thirty companies used in the Dow Jones Industrial Average, which include (January, 1997 market caps):

Exxon	$131 billion
GE	$166 billion
GM	$45 billion
Alcoa	$8.5 billion
Westinghouse	$8.6 billion
Coca Cola	$71 billion

Large-cap firms also include most of the companies that are used to make up the S&P 500 stock index. For example:

Allstate	$28 billion
Tribune Company	$2.3 billion
Micron Technology	$6.5 billion
Computer Sciences	$4.4 billion

(Some people might draw the line at $5 billion and claim that Computer Sciences and Tribune Company are mid caps.)

Some mid-cap companies include:

Betz Laboratories	$1.7 billion
Western Resources	$2 billion (or maybe its a large cap)
Timken	$1.5 billion

And a few small caps:

Standard Commercial	$180 million
Cone Mills	$230 million
Handleman	$270 million
Huffy	$180 million
Johnson Worldwide	$110 million

These numbers change as the stock prices change, and as companies grow or decay. Microsoft was once a small cap, as was Wal-Mart.

Some of the Most Widely Watched Market Averages

Dow Jones Industrial Average	Based on 30 blue chip stocks with no utilities or transportation companies
Dow Jones Utilities Average	Based on 15 utility companies
Dow Jones Transportation Average	Based on 20 transportation companies
Dow Jones 65 Stock Average	Based on all of the above
S&P 500 Index	Based on 500 large-cap companies
S&P Mid-Cap 400 Index	Based on 400 companies with market capitalization between $300 million and $5 billion
S&P 600 Index	Based on 600 companies with their market capitalizations in the lower half of all stocks in the major American markets[4]
Wilshire 5000	A price index using most of the publicly traded American companies, it uses over 7,000 companies (use to be 5,000)
Russell 2000 Index	A price index that uses 2,000 small-cap companies

---

[4] The exact definition of the companies in the 600 is too involved to state here.

Why Indexing?

Indices are used in several ways. Even though you do not need to do any calculations with indices, you should be able to recognize how people use them in conversation or analysis. Here are the most popular uses of indices:

1. **To indicate general trends of stock prices:** The Dow Jones industrial average (DJIA) is widely publicized to indicate changes in stock markets. It is a fair indicator for the total market value of all stocks, and for the trends of prices of large company stocks, but it is not usually a good indicator for other special groups of stocks. The Dow Jones utilities average and the Dow Jones transportation average are better indicators for their groups, and the Russell 2000 is a better indicator for small-cap stocks. However, since the DJIA is so widely watched and reported, it has an immense impact on the attitudes and confidence of nearly all investors.

2. **To indicate the general trends of total market values** (total market capitalization): The DJIA and the S&P 500 indices are both good indicators of the direction of total market value. Other indicators would better reflect market value in their respective niches.

3. **To indicate changes in the value of an individual investor's portfolio of stocks:** This depends on having an index that matches well with the stocks that the individual owns. For example, I can be fairly confident that any time the S&P 500 goes up or down a certain percentage, then the value of my total investment portfolio will go up or down approximately the same amount. This is not an exact calculation, but it is a good approximation to help me understand week to week changes in my portfolio.

4. **To judge the investment skills and success of a portfolio manager:** Many people judge money managers by comparing their total return to the S&P 500 index. It is assumed that a first-level standard of success is for the manager to equal or exceed the growth rate of the S&P 500. In some cases that is a poor standard of measurement that may not make sense in terms

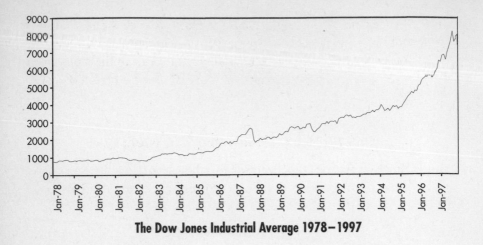

The Dow Jones Industrial Average 1978–1997

of the individual manager's investment style, but people use it anyway. Why? Because it is a convenient and widely available index that many people recognize and agree on.

Many individual investors also compare their own results to the S&P 500. That may be a mistake. Investing is not a contest. You should not be concerned about how anyone else or how any index is doing. Just keep your eyes on the prize, and watch how you are doing.

Another index used for comparing results of various stock investors is the rate of return from short-term Treasury bills. Those are bonds that have terms to maturity of ninety days or less. They are sometimes spoken of as

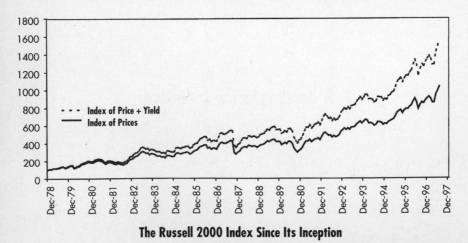

The Russell 2000 Index Since Its Inception

risk-free investments. We know that is not quite accurate[5], however, those Treasury bills are as close to risk free as you can get. It is a fair standard of judgment to say that any professional money manager in the stock markets should exceed the returns from Treasury bills over a period of a year or longer.

Confusion, Doubt, and Confusion

By this time you may be asking yourself two things. First, are there any signs or facts that I can count on to consistently give me reliable signals about which stocks to buy and sell?

No.

If picking stocks were that easy, then everyone would be trying to follow the same rules. Everyone would try to buy or sell the same stocks at the same time. Everyone would try to anticipate tomorrow's news and the new direction of the crowd. Eventually everyone would develop their own ideas about how to predict the direction of the reliable signals, and we would be back where we are now.

The market reveals itself in a collage of facts and opinions, some of which are clear at once, some less distinct, and some fading. Every investor will understand different parts of the scene according to his or her own education and experience. There will always be some elements of uncertainty in the outcomes.

The second question, for now, concerns the significance of the quote by Joel Chandler Harris at the beginning of the chapter. Are fattenin' pigs in luck or aren't they?

Not every reader focuses on and adjusts to the same words in the same way. It may be interesting to take a different perspective on the significance of the signs.

A Reading in the Long Run

The scene is set in investors' heaven. All the saints have been called to a great Roundtable in the Sky. On the arch above the entranceway is engraved in 135 languages the lesson for all time: Sell High. All the saints wear pins that say Sell High.

---

[5] There is no risk-free investing; anyone who tries to tell you there is, is not your friend.

In the back of the room sit 147,822 investors who lost money in the long run, though they had been cautious and deliberate about their investment decisions. They huddle and watch Louis Ruykeyser, who offers a knowing smile and a wink. The recognition is comforting to them. The other saints practice a polite deference towards the losers.

The reader, a small investor of a squirrely and nervous demeanor, approaches the lectern and waits for a sign of a top. The audience grows still. The reader gives a deep formal bow to Ben Graham, on behalf of all of us, and a less formal bow to Marty Zweig, on behalf of the worried. Marty is checking the time. The reader nods to Jim Rogers, who smiles and observes everything. The squirrely fellow scratches and begins reading:

The Long Run

> *When averages are fattenin'*
> *and all the signs are swell,*
> *the Intelligent Investor*
> *will be thinkin 'bout a sell.*

> *When ROA is 8%,*
> *and the T-Bond's 9.4,*
> *the Intelligent Investor*
> *may be strolling toward the door.*

> *The trends rush on like diesels,*
> *with P/E's out of hand,*
> *the Intelligent Investor*
> *has not built his house on sand.*

> *The ghost of Richard Whitney*
> *could not be with us today,*
> *for all our speculation,*
> *eventually,*
> *someone must pay.*

> *And even though they all believed,*
> *that this bull could not die,*
> *the losers' ghosts groan to advise,*
> *protect yourself. . . sell high!*

He pauses. The saints shuffle. He takes a drink of water, and finally recognizing the dilemma, puts down his notes and steps back from the lectern. Fifty-six percent of the saints applaud. Fourteen percent frown. The small investors chatter nervously among themselves, revealing their discomfort, and watch Louis Ruykeyser. Marty Zweig records the statistics and compares them with the prior two hundred roundtables. Jim Rodgers seems to have a few opinions of his own.

Recommended Further Reading

Blume, Marshall, Jeremy Siegel, and Dan Rottenberg. *Revolution on Wall St.* New York: Norton, 1993.

Metz, Tim. *Black Monday*. New York: Wm. Morrow & Co., 1988, out of print.

Goals

We see ads on television and in the papers frequently where some broker or investment company is encouraging people to have fun with their investing. Certainly the financial press and gurus make a regular habit of talking about "playing the market." Well, don't. If you play at it you are going to lose your money. Some people just invest in stocks with a little of their savings. The amount that they expect to win or lose is not going to have any appreciable impact on their lives, regardless of which way the market goes. These people are in just for the thrill of buying and selling stocks, the same way that some folks get a thrill out of gambling in Las Vegas. I wish them luck, but I cannot empathize with that approach. If you want to get some thrills out of your stock-market explorations, then good luck, but this book takes a drier approach. Our lessons and our work must keep us focused on what we are trying to accomplish. As you analyze stocks and evaluate your progress, keep your eyes on the prize.

What Are You Trying to Accomplish?

What do you need to accomplish through your stock market investments? For each reader the answer may be different, and for each the answer must be part of his or her personal investment strategy. The retired reader who only wants to manage and protect his retirement nest egg to provide a continuing stream of income should approach stock selection differently from the thirty-year-old professional who wants to work at building up her portfolio capital over the next twenty-five years. There are many reasonable answers to the question about your goals in the stock market, and many unreasonable answers. For the purpose of getting a handle on something we can work with, lets look at a simple way of considering our goals.

The PIG Principle

There are three things that any investor should want from a stock investment:

1. **P**rotection: We would like to buy stocks with some confidence that the original investment principal is not at great risk.

2. **I**ncome: We would like to buy stocks that are likely to produce a continuing yield, or cash return.

3. **G**rowth: We would like to buy stocks that are likely to appreciate in price per share, so that we can look forward to selling for a profit.

I call this the PIG principle.

You might think of your investment world as being a triangle, bounded by three points called *Protection*, *Income*, and *Growth*. Think of yourself as working within this triangle. The three kinds of reward are at the three vertices: protection, income, and growth. If you move closer to any one of them, you must also move a little further from one of the others. As you move closer to point P, you put more emphasis on protection, closer to point I, more emphasis on income, and closer to G means more emphasis on growth. You can go anywhere you like in the triangle, and at different times, or in different circumstances, as your needs change, you probably will move toward and away from each point.

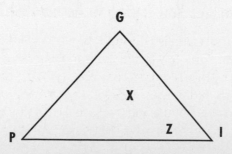

In this triangle, we can consider each position as representing an investor's blend of needs with regard to protection, income, and growth. Point X represents an investor whose decisions on stock purchases are driven 20 percent for protection, 40 percent for income, and 40 percent for growth. Point Z represents another investor who has 80 percent emphasis on income and 20 percent emphasis on protection. The percentages add up to 100 percent to show that this represents all of the investors' criteria for choosing stocks to buy.

For example, the point at the left labeled P is the position of a Mr. Conservative who is totally concerned with protecting his money without regard for income or growth. He should stay out of the financial markets. He might keep his money in a shoe box in the closet or, perhaps, in a bank savings account. He would stay away from stocks, bonds, and mutual funds. Is that smart money management? Probably not. The effects of inflation would erode the purchasing power of the money. Remember that the true worth of your money is not in the actual paper currency or the bank statement itself, but in what you can buy with the money.

Let's look at a couple of other relative points of investors' needs on the PIG triangle. Point G in the next figure represents Ms. Gotrocks, who is totally concerned with growth and never thinks about safety or income. She is either foolish, or she can tolerate the idea of losing all the money she has invested in stocks. This might be a reasonable view for some investors, but not many. For instance, if Ms. G. has $12 million in U.S. Treasury bonds, paying her an average of 6.4 percent a year, owns her own home, and has no troublesome debts, and then feels that she wants to put a speculative $500,000 into the stock market, for her position G in the triangle might work. She might decide to only buy stock in new, small, and speculative companies. Investing in those types of companies, there is some risk that she might lose all of the principal, and probably none of them will pay any yield for a long time. But if it suits her fancy, then okay.

A more normal case would be that of Norman and Susan W., who are struggling to face the real world every day. He is thirty-seven-years old; she is thirty-six, and they have two children, ages five and eight. They are sweating out the bills every month, but still manage to set aside $100 a month through his 401(k) at work. They have decided to risk part of that money in the stock market. We will leave unexamined for the moment whether that is a wise decision, but just accept that it is their decision. Then their place in the PIG triangle is something like the point labeled W, relatively closer to the needs of protection and growth, and not close to the objective of income. When they use their stock selection methods, they are looking most carefully at safety of the firm and stock, and chances for growth of the firm. They are not putting much emphasis on current income opportunities.

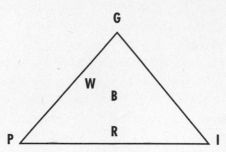

The point labeled B represents an investor who is equally concerned about protection, income, and growth. In stock selection, he or she would place about 33 percent of the decision criteria on each of the factors. Point R might represent a retired person, who just wants protection and income, about 45 percent emphasis on each of those two and 10 percent emphasis on growth.

Work out this exercise. Indicate whatever amount of money you might consider for stock investing now. What is your opinion about the relative importance of protection, income, and growth in your selection process? Put in some numbers to make the total emphasis add up to 100%:

This much money at risk
in the stock market: $ _____

Emphasis on protection   _____ %

Emphasis on income   _____ %

Emphasis on growth   _____ %

Make a note to return to this page after you have finished reading the book. Consider then what your emphasis for each factor might be. It probably will have changed from today. Return to this exercise again after you have been practicing stock investing for two years. Try the numbers again. I'll bet there will have been another significant shift in your thinking. The PIG balance that you use may change for different times and needs. For instance, if you own several high-yield stocks, then you may decide to lessen the emphasis on yield for the next stock selection.

You may think of other factors to consider, such as diversification, socially responsible investing, or pride of ownership. There are many good reasons why one of those might be more or less important to you at different times, but if you consider protection, income, and growth for each stock purchase (or sale) decision, and if you do enough work to form an intelligent judgment based on them, then you should be able to make reasonable investment decisions that fit your needs.

The Special Role of Income

There is some controversy over the role of income (dividend yield) in different stock selection methodologies. Some advisors and brokers say that income doesn't count anymore. Certainly in 1997, there were a lot of people buying thousands of stocks who were behaving as if income did not count anymore. Let's pause for a bit and consider the special role of income. The dividend of a stock is a payment, taken out of the annual earnings of the company, that the directors decide to send each shareholder. The total income you receive from your stock investment will be the number of shares times the dividend paid for each share. The dividend yield is the dividend per share divided by the share price.

Let me make my own personal bias clear. Income is important. Anyone who evaluates stocks for possible investment without considering the income factor is foolish and will come to a bad end. That does not mean that you have to buy stocks with high dividend payments, nor that income is the most important of the PIGs (protection, income, growth). What it does mean is that income will always have an influence on other investors' evaluation of stocks, and income will always have some influence on the safety and growth potential of a stock. So it seems clear that it would be foolish to ignore income. At any rate, the dividend yield to be expected from a stock is usually one of the easiest factors to estimate, so it would seem shiftless not to do so. The safety or continuation of the dividend is perhaps more difficult to judge for some stocks.

Let's look at a simple example to illustrate how income figures into the picture: For our example, we'll use the (mythical) Alpha-Beta Publishing Company, a company with 18,900,000 shares of stock publicly traded. Its symbol on the stock exchange is ABPCO. ABPCO has sales of $97 million, and the stock has a price in the markets of $6 per share. After paying salaries, costs of goods sold, leases, capital costs, interest on their long-term debt, taxes, and setting something aside for depreciation of property, plant, and equipment, they have a $4.6 million profit. This profit could be used in several ways. To keep things simple, let's say there were just three ways to use the profits:

1. Pay off some of the long term debt

2. Keep the money in retained earnings to fund new business

3. Pay some cash dividends to the stock holders

The important thing to notice first is that *each of those choices acts to increase value for the shareholders*. If the debt is too large, the directors might use $1 million to pay off some of the debt earlier than required by their loan agreements. That would act to the favor of the shareholders by increasing the value of the firm by $1 million and reducing the next year's interest payment. Or the directors might decide that there was a very promising new book project available that would cost $1.3 million, and they want to set aside part of this year's earnings to help fund that project next year. Again, this acts in the interest of shareholders because it increases the capital reserves of the company and provides for more profitable activities next year. Or the directors may decide to reserve $2.3 million in retained earnings and pay out $2.3 million to shareholders, both of which act in favor of the shareholders' interest. If they adopted the last decision, then each shareholder would receive 12¢ in dividend payment for each share ($2.3 million dividend ÷ 19.8 million shares). Based on the $6 share price, that gives a 2 percent yield.

The directors of the company must decide what to do with the profits. Some companies have a history and tradition of paying out a cash dividend. Some even like to raise the dividend every year. In November 1991, when I bought Ford at $27.50, the company and the stock had been in the dumps for a while, and nobody had any confidence in the American automobile industry. I don't think that any professional commentator had anything good to say about Ford at the time. But I looked at the dividend history. It seemed to me that the company and their directors were committed to a strong dividend payout. Some evidence suggested they would try to get the dividend back up to $3, where it had been before the recent troubles. I liked their cars and thought they would find some way to muddle through. Then, if the dividend did get back to $3, that would be one heck-of-a-good yield on my investment, and it would take all the risk out of the principal investment. Well, guess what? They lost money and cut the dividend again in 1992, but since then, the profits and the dividend have steadily advanced to a point well over the yield level I was looking for (yield adjusted for a stock split in 1994).

Some companies and some directors have a commitment to putting money back into the hands of the shareholders. Some don't. It can make sense either way. In 1993, Cree Research went public with their first stock offering to raise money for research and product development. For the next four years, they hardly made a penny, but they did develop products and markets, which is exactly what the investors wanted them to do. It would have been silly for Cree to start paying dividends. They needed all the cash they could get to build a viable company. The expected payoff to the shareholders was a pie-in-the-sky to come in the form of increased share value and price. Guess what? In December 1994, you could have put $10,000 into Cree stock, and within a year, you could have sold it for almost $100,000. They still haven't paid any dividend. Dividends are usually good, but a stock without dividends may be good, too, if the company has something better to do with the money. It depends on each company's situation.

For years, many investors have looked at electric utilities as good choices for safe investing. There are a number of reasons why, but certainly one reason is the steady income stream that most of them produce. Look at a few examples over a period of years. From 1980 to 1995, CIPSCO (Central Illinois Public Service) paid dividends that rose from $1.39 to $2.03 per share per year and only decreased once, by 3¢, during that period. Central & S.W. Corporation paid dividends that rose from 75¢ to $1.72 per share per year, and never decreased any year. DPL (Dayton Power and Light) paid dividends that rose from 77¢ to $1.24 per share per year and never decreased[1] in any year. Some cautious and conservative small investors who

---

[1] *Never decreased* means except to compensate for stock splits. The actual payment to a buy and hold investor was never decreased.

invested $5,000 in DPL stock in 1985 and held it through 1996 have collected approximately $5,210 in dividend yield, and now own 425 shares of stock worth $10,200. If they reinvested all the dividends in new stock as they went along, they never had any extra cash to spend, but at the end of 1996, they held approximately 915 shares worth $22,000. No, that is not a misprint.[2] Welcome to the amazing world of compound earnings!

So here is the news: Dividends *are* important, but there are many good reasons why the directors of different companies may want to treat them differently. You might make good money with stocks that carry a strong dividend yield. You also might make good money with stocks that carry no dividend yield.

So why do some people say that dividends are not important? Let me try to explain the logic behind it. In 1995, 1996, and 1997, the major U.S. stock markets and price averages went on a tear. Many mutual funds returned 15 to 30 percent each year, and many individual investors did just as well. The expectations of investors changed. Many people forgot about protection and income and just invested in search of growth. People began to think about finding companies that had the potential to make dramatic gains in sales and earnings, which led to dramatic gains in share price. They wanted to find stocks like Cree Research that went from $3 to $30 in a year. Many money managers and individual investors fell into the habit of trying to pick stocks for quick stock price growth. Those rapid-growth stocks typically are not going to be your utilities or other large, long-established companies. If the price of the stock is to increase rapidly, then something must happen that few people expected. New products, new markets, or new manufacturing methods must be created that cause unexpected growth of either revenues or margins. Those things, in turn, are fueled by retained earnings.

Earnings paid out in dividends do not contribute anything to growth of the company or new products. Companies that retain their earnings are likely to develop more new opportunities and new revenues. At any rate, the retained earnings contribute just as much to the shareholder's net valuation as the earnings that are paid out as dividends. Based on that logic, some analysts say you should not worry about dividends.

The opposing point of view holds that dividends are important. Strong dividends affect the thinking of many investors and make a stock more

---

[2] If you have to see the calculations, write to me, and I will send a copy.

*"I want to pick up a few shares of Barnes & Noble—
has anybody published a book yet?"*

attractive. A history of sustained strong dividend payments makes a stock appear safer. Any firm that demonstrates both the will and the capacity to pay out a consistently high[3] annual dividend over a long period of time is unlikely to ever fall too much in stock price. If you bought a stock at $16 that paid a steady $1 per share (6 percent) annual yield, you would have the security of knowing it should not drop too far in share price. Even if the price fell to $12, you would still have the comfort of the income from dividends. With $1 dividend, the stock would be paying about 8 percent yield at that price. By similar reasoning, any dependable dividend payments for a stock tend to give some indication of safety in the investment. Good income automatically tends to provide protection in a stock purchase. So the investor gets two benefits for the choice of one.

So do you choose stocks for dividend payments or not? Both sides of the discussion have merit. In the interest of diversification, it is probably good to try both approaches in your stock selection. Buy some high-yielding stocks, but don't expect a great deal of rapid price appreciation from them. Buy some low-yielding stocks, but take a very hard look at the safety and stability associated with the companies. If the directors do not pay out the earnings as dividends for shareholders, then what are they doing

---

[3] A "high dividend" is in the eyes of the beholder; let's assume that high means somewhere close to the yield on five year Treasury notes, maybe 4 to 6 percent per year.

with the earnings? If you are not buying income, make sure you know what you are buying.

Total Return

Let us return to the matter of protection, income, and growth. Protection is difficult to quantify and must be dealt with under the general heading of risk analysis in a later section. However, income and growth can be directly measured and reported in dollar value or rate of increase. Many investors lump them together and say they are looking for profit, wherever it may be found; that is, if they earn a dollar from income or they earn the dollar from growth, one is as good as another[4]. If they have a stock or a combination of stocks that sometimes produces more income and sometimes produces more growth, that may be a good way to invest. The total return from an investment is the combination of income and growth or loss that is produced. The rate of total return is the percentage of total return expressed on an annualized[5] basis.

Let's look at some examples to illustrate total return and the rate of total return:[6]

1. In December 1992, a clever fellow bought Chrysler stock for $32 per share. He kept it until June of 1995 and sold for $48. During that time, he collected $1.90 in dividends per share. The total return was $17.90 ($16 in growth of the stock plus $1.90 in yield). That gives 56 percent (17.90 ÷ 32) total return over thirty months. The annualized rate of total return was 19.4 percent, as 19.4 percent per year applied over 2½ years would yield 56 percent.

2. In April of 1995, a savvy lady bought Adaptec stock (symbol ADPT on the NYSE) for $34 per share. She sold it in November 1995 for $47, but received no dividends. The total return was $13 per share just in price appreciation. The

---

[4] If the income is taxable, that's another issue; let's say you earn a dollar after taxes.
[5] *Annualized basis* means a growth rate per year that would give the same total return.
[6] In these examples, allow me to ignore taxes and brokerage fees.

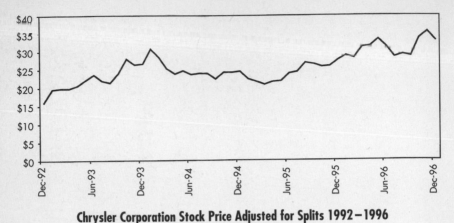

Chrysler Corporation Stock Price Adjusted for Splits 1992–1996

percentage total return was 38 percent (13÷34 = 0.38) in seven months. The annualized rate of return was 74 percent (74 percent over a year = 38 percent over seven months).

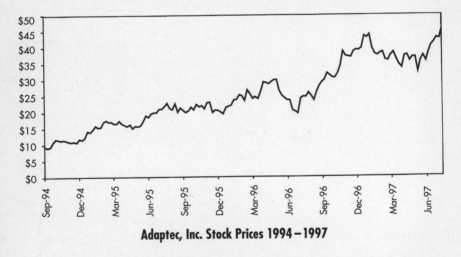

Adaptec, Inc. Stock Prices 1994–1997

3. Mr. Rogers had a portfolio of stocks that over two years produced 36 percent growth in share values plus an additional 5 percent in income from dividends. His total return over the two years was 41 percent. His annualized rate of return was 18.8 percent, since 18.8 percent annual return would produce 41 percent gain over two years.

From here on in this book, and in most financial publications, *total return* means the gains from share price growth plus the gains from dividends (plus any other gains if there are any others). The *rate of return* means the annualized (and compound) percentage rate of growth of the investment.

The No-Brainers

This is a book about stock selection methods, but it will be worthwhile to pause and consider for a moment the non-method methods, the no-brainers, the fads. In 1991 and 1992, almost any company in the biotechnology area was considered to be a buy. Many investors, led by their brokers and advisors, thought that bio-babble was the wave of the future and anything in that area was certain to make money. Many of those companies didn't make money and had no products, but they had great expectations. Some of their stocks were reasonable investments for people who could evaluate the risks associated with their markets and their competition. But how few of us can do that? How few of us can in any way guess at the profit potential for a new drug that has not gone into the FDA approval process? How few of us can guess at the potential for a competitor to bring out a better product? Some investors bought Biogen at over $40 a share in 1991 and had a rough ride for the next four years. Some investors bought Amgen for $70 (or higher) in 1992. It did not get above $80 until the middle of 1995. And no dividends were being paid. Some of those unhappy investors were the victims of happy talk and the popular mania to buy bio. Many of them bought into a no-brainer on the advice of a broker or friend. That is not smart investment practice.

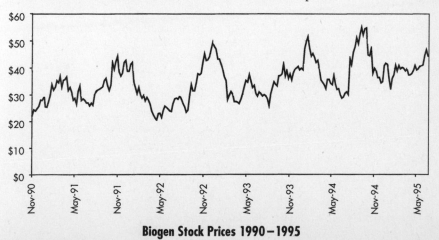

Biogen Stock Prices 1990–1995

A similar mania in the early seventies comes down to us in legend as the Nifty-Fifty fad. The story of the time was that certain famous blue-chip firms were always going to grow and be successful. Any investor could expect to buy the stocks at any time, at any price, and just sit back and count the profits. These stocks would always become more profitable and appreciate in price. Some of the firms in the Nifty Fifty were American Express, Disney, Westinghouse, and Xerox. Now you should notice an important lesson here: Those were all successful, profitable, well-managed firms that have survived and grown until today. However, that does not mean that their stocks were good buys at inflated prices. Well, the prices of the Nifty Fifty were bid up and up again, out of proportion to their intrinsic value, until the bear market of 1973–74. During that bear market, the Dow Jones Industrial Average lost nearly 50 percent of its value. However, American Express lost 73 percent, Disney lost 86 percent, Westinghouse lost 85 percent, and Xerox lost 71 percent.

Other fads have developed before and since the Nifty Fifty. A lot of people rushed into buying Internet stocks in 1996 and many lost money at it. The lesson in this is that the money is not just lying around on Wall Street waiting for us to rake it up. You have to do some work. Part of that work is research and analysis and decision making. Any time a broker or friend tells you that this one is automatic, a can't miss opportunity, then step back and ask yourself why that deal is coming to you.[7] If *you* heard about the chance, then you can be sure a thousand professional investors heard about it first. Why haven't they already bid the price up to a fair value? Why is it still available to you at a low cost? If you are told that a stock will always go up, no matter when you buy or at what price, then step back and read some market history. It doesn't work that way, folks. It's not that easy. If you want to make money through investing in individual stocks, plan to do some work and dedicate some time to it.

The "no-brainers" are indeed no-brainers. Don't buy them unless you have done a lot of careful research. Maybe even after your research don't buy them, because fads are unhealthy. A fad in the stock market is like a plague in the streets. It may hurt you even when you are trying to be careful.

That brings us to one of the reasons why this book was written. Not everyone wants to, or is able to, do the same research and analysis. Depending on your experience, education, and the mixture of risk and reward that you

---

[7] If your broker tells you that, then get a new broker.

are looking for, different methods and sources may work better for you than for other investors. Throughout this book, we will consider how much work it takes to do certain types of stock analysis and what education or experience may be needed. The objective is not to find the one true method for everyone, but rather to find something that works for you.

No Guarantees

The stock markets are risky places to send your money, regardless of how much effort you put into your research. There will always be the chance that you may lose part or all of your money, or that you fail to do as well as a bank certificate of deposit (CD). Before starting to study methods and individual stock investing, you must face up to the possibility of loss. If you don't want to deal with it, then *do not put your money into buying individual stocks*. It would be safer and smarter for you to invest through mutual funds that buy stocks, bonds, or both. It might be better for you to buy bank CDs, use the money to pay on the mortgage, or take a vacation.

*"Petro, if this thing doesn't make money,
I'm gonna feel really bad for you."*

Graduate School This Ain't

This book presents a lot of ideas of varying degrees of complexity and sophistication. It does not contain everything you could ever possibly need to know about the stock markets. Some books that deserve your consideration are listed in the references at the end of each chapter. They have some ideas that overlap parts of this book, but may also require more experience and sophistication and judgment. For example, Vic Sperandeo's books have many good ideas, but he assumes that the reader can combine and evaluate a lot of factors that might only be accessible to experienced or professional investors. However, he does have some well-stated and basic counsel too:

> *If every trade and every position you hold fills you with fear and doubt, then quit trading. Chronic fear and doubt will take a toll on you physically, emotionally, and financially.*

Good advice.

Philip Fisher's book is excellent, never mind that it's thirty-five years old. He places a lot of emphasis on finding companies with earnings growth. His advice is clear and strong:

> *This example brings into clear relief what the common stock investor must do if he is to purchase shares to his greatest advantage. He must examine factually and analytically the prevailing financial sentiment about both the industry and the specific company of which he is considering buying shares. He should be extra careful when buying into companies and industries that are the current darlings of the financial community . . . that he is not paying a fancy price for something which is the investment fad of the moment.*

The Graham and Dodd book is one of the all-time classics, and you must look at it some time. My only reservation is that it requires extensive research and analysis that may be beyond the means of most of us. You can't argue with their methods, but the question is whether they are practical for all of us. Some of the ideas in this book have been derived and refined from the teachings of Graham and Dodd. Anyone who hopes to use or teach securities analysis is indebted to their pioneering work.

Recommended Further Reading

Fisher, Philip. *Common Stocks and Uncommon Profits*, rev. ed. Woodside, CA: Pacific Publ. Group, 1989.

Fosback, Norman G. *Stock Market Logic*. Chicago: Dearborn Financial Press, reprinted April 1995.

Graham, Benjamin and David Dodd. *Security Analysis*. New York: McGraw-Hill, 1996.

Nichols, Donald R. *The Income Investor*. Chicago: Dearborn Financial, 1990.

Sperandeo, Victor. *Trader Vic: Methods of a Wall Street Master*. New York: John Wiley and Sons, 1991.

If there were dreams to sell,

What would you buy?

—THOMAS LOVELL BEDDOES, "SAILOR'S SONG"

Managing Your Investments

There is more to this business than just selecting individual stocks to buy. You have to manage a portfolio (a collection of stocks), which entails managing costs of trading, methods of trading, and risk allocation across the portfolio. It requires fitting stock selection and the legwork that goes along with it into your personal time horizon. In this chapter we are going to look at some ideas that apply more to the overall investment strategy than to just selecting individual stocks.

Dividend Reinvestment Plans

Sometimes you can buy and sell stocks without using a broker—for example, when you go directly to the company that issued the stock and set up an account with them. This is a way to save money. Hundreds of companies with publicly traded stock do this, including Merck, McDonald's, and NationsBank. Usually, when one has an account like this, the dividends will be reinvested in new stock and added onto the account, rather than being paid out in cash. For that reason, the accounts are widely referred to as *dividend reinvestment plans*, and given the acronym DRIPs. Some of the companies require that you already have some stock (maybe just one share) that you have purchased through a broker, and some do not.

DRIPs are good things, generally. Some people think that the only sensible way to invest is through a DRIP. Other people don't like them. The greatest advantage of using a DRIP is the reduction of your costs, but you have to be careful about this because each company, if they offer a DRIP at all, will write an agreement to specify costs and other conditions as they see fit. Some of those agreements turn out to be appealing for the individual small investor, and some do not. You have to read the agreement. Do not sign up for a DRIP or send in any money until after you have determined how that particular company manages the accounts and what they charge.

There are two primary advantages of DRIPs. The first is the elimination of brokerage fees. No broker is involved. The second is that DRIPs usually do serve the investor who wants to invest just a small monthly amount. If you used a broker to buy two or three shares a month, the sales commissions would ruin the profit potential in the account, but in a DRIP you can normally expect to buy a few shares at a time for a reasonable fee. However, you have to check what fees the company might impose for handling your account. Some accounts are free, while others have significant charges. For example, Merck charges a fee of $5 plus a penny per share when you buy stocks for your DRIP. That makes it impractical to buy one or two shares at a time; the $5 fee would eat into your capital. But if you are going to buy twenty shares at a time, that is a far better deal than going to a broker. McDonald's has added so many fees to their DRIP that it is simply not an attractive option for the individual who wants to invest $50 or $100 a month. Read the full description of the DRIP. You can obtain it free by calling the company. The description will explain the fees and whatever other rules they have for reinvesting.

But there are at least three distinct disadvantages that come with DRIPs. The significance of these is something you have to decide for yourself. You might think that these three alleged disadvantages are of no consequence.

The first disadvantage is that you have separate accounts for all of your investments. If you use ten DRIPs with different companies, they will all send out separate statements, perhaps once a month, or once a quarter, or once every six months. If you want to know how your total portfolio is going you will have to check all ten separately, probably look up some of them in the paper, figure out how many shares of each you own just then, do your own arithmetic, and work out your own total investment report. That may take an hour or so of searching, calculating, and combining, and you might want to do that once a month. Not a big deal, but a minor nuisance.

Second, if you want to sell a stock and buy another using DRIPs, the process might very well take two to four weeks. If you had a broker to call and give the orders to, you could accomplish the same thing in a few minutes. With the DRIPs you would have to send them a letter for the sale of one stock, wait, probably two to five weeks for them to process the order and get a check to you, set up the new account, write a new check, mail that in, and wait perhaps a week or two for the transaction to be completed. For most of us that delay is not a big deal. You are probably equally likely to gain or lose a few dollars due to the wait, but it is an annoyance.

The third disadvantage is the smaller number of stocks you would have available to work with. Sure, there may be 700 to 800 companies with DRIPs, but if you worked through a broker, you would have your choice from over 8,000 companies. The DRIP companies include some of the largest and soundest of the blue-chip stocks. They do not include very many new, small, and relatively unknown firms. Which ones do you want to have available for your investing?

In summary, DRIPs are good things, generally. But you should look at them individually to see what you are getting into, the costs, and what you may be passing up. The rest of this book will hardly mention the subject of DRIPs, but since we are talking about your choices for buying stocks, I thought I should mention them. Your local library probably has a guide to companies that offer DRIPs, with telephone numbers to contact the companies and get their prospectuses. You might also just call any company that you find interesting and ask if they have a DRIP.

Your Time Horizon

You have probably heard stories about people who made great profits in the stock market in a few days, a few weeks, or some other short time period. Let me tell you about those stories. Many of them are exaggerated beyond all credibility, a few of them are true. But that's all right. Don't worry about them. You are not in a contest. Probably no one except your spouse will ever pass judgment on your investing results. That is one of the advantages of the small investor. It would be very pleasant to make a pile of money in three months, but it's not going to happen, so relax and plan towards a more realistic time horizon. What time horizon? There's a tough question.

Your time horizon, or investment horizon, is the time you have to work the money until you need to spend it. For individual investments, the time horizon is the furthest time over which we can reasonably forecast something about that stock, or the length of time we plan to hold it.

The time horizon that you use in evaluating individual stocks and in managing your total investment portfolio is an individual concern. What is right for you may not be right for someone else. Your investment plan may call for using the money in five years or not taking anything out of the investments for the next twenty years. Only you and, perhaps, your significant other can decide about that. However, we can be more particular and more specific in terms of evaluating individual investments. Let's take a hard look at three time-related issues that will inform your investment practice:

1. In selecting individual stocks you need to decide for yourself whether you will consider taking profits when they are available.

2. You need to decide how long you might want to hold a particular investment and how frequently to reevaluate it.

3. You need to determine how far out into the future you might possibly forecast the fortunes of the company in which you invest.

Let's talk about the first two questions; about fast profits and about the famous buy-and-hold philosophy. There is no disgrace in taking a profit. Some people make money that way. But there is a famous and widely advertised philosophy known as *buy and hold*. The buy-and-hold strategy is based on a couple of reasonable ideas and is probably the right strategy for many people. We won't try to knock it down, but let's examine what it means and whether it is always right for you. You should take a critical look at every investment practice you hear about and especially, as with buy and hold, any idea that is so widely touted as good for everyone.

Buy and Hold

The basic ideas of buy and hold are these: First, for small investors, the commissions and fees that go along with buying or selling can be substantial. Second, your investment horizon is probably five to twenty years, and you might want to find investments that will stand up over that long term.

Look at sales fees. Small investors often pay between 1 percent and 2 percent of the principal amount on any stock trade, first for the buy and again for the sell. That means that each small investor has a significant hurdle to pass just to cover brokerage fees on each stock investment.

Suppose you had bought 100 Texaco shares in January of 1994 at $63, and sold for $66 in April of 1995. Those are realistic numbers, and I assume that you were tired of holding the stock as it did nothing all through 1994, so you decided to take the small profit on the sale. If the commissions on the buy and again on the sale were $75, then here is where you stood on Texaco:

Income from sale	$6,600
Dividends collected	$ 40
– Cost of stock	$6,300
– Commissions	$ 150
= Net profit over 16 months	$ 190

A decent mutual fund invested in government bonds might have returned 10 percent in the same time, that's over $600 dollars profit. Even a money-market account would have paid 4–5 percent for a profit of between $250 and $300, with very low risk. To focus on our main issue in this example, the gross profit on the stock was $340 (100 x 3 + 40), however the commissions eroded that decent return into a poor return ($340 – $150 = $190).

The lesson here is that if an individual investor makes a lot of short-term trades, paying 1 or 2 percent on each transaction, then the fees eat away a lot of potential profit. It is difficult to be successful that way; therefore, buy and hold makes sense.

The second argument in favor of buy and hold is based on a reasonable and realistic appraisal of what you are doing in the market. You are not

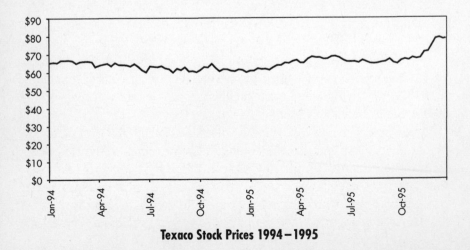

Texaco Stock Prices 1994–1995

trying to get rich quick. One of my favorite quotes on that subject was from Charles Dow, who founded the *Wall Street Journal* and the Dow Jones Industrial Average. Dow said (in rough paraphrase) that he had known a lot of people who tried to get rich quick, and most of them ended up losing money; but he also had known a lot of investors who simply tried to earn a consistent fair return on their money, and some of them ended up getting rich. The moral of his lesson is that most of us are not going to get rich quick in the stock market. Most of us are going to do average, and you may create trouble for yourself by not admitting that. Therefore, plan and manage your investments to take advantage of long-term trends in solid, profitable companies. Don't do a lot of trading in companies for which you think you have found some rare analysis and opportunity that will lead to a quick run-up in price. You would usually be wrong if you think you have outwitted the 20,000 professional analysts in New York. The stock price will usually not be primed for a hot run-up, and the commissions on the frequent transactions will eat away a lot of your profits. Therefore buy and hold makes sense.

There is no reason to argue with the logic behind the buy-and-hold philosophy. It is unassailable. However, there is no reason to just stick your head in the sand either. Buy and hold is fine, as long as it works. Buy and hold works for many investors most of the time, but buy and hold *does not mean* buy and forget about it.

My approach to buy and hold is to try to make it work. Every time I buy a stock, or even study a stock, I look for a long-term investment. Every stock or bond or fund that I buy I expect to hold for two to four years. I will not buy any financial asset unless I think it appears to be a solid and profitable investment for the next several years. But after buying the stock, bond, or fund, we should keep our eyes open. Business conditions change, market conditions change, interest rates change. It would be foolish to assume that a company is a good investment in 1998 just because it looked good in 1996. After having bought the stock, it is possible that you find some good reason to sell it six months or a year later.

For example, I bought IBM in 1992, while it was falling, at 85¼. I thought it would be a good long-term investment. Almost immediately, the price ran up to $100, and I said "Hey, look at this. Aren't I smart?" Almost immediately it started falling rapidly. So there I sat with what was supposed to be a long-term investment, with a chance to grab some quick profits, and the price falling rapidly. What to do? I put in a stop loss sell order at

93 and got sold out at 92⅞. After sales commissions and one dividend payment, that turned into about an 11 percent gain in three months. Good enough for me!

Where would the buy-and-hold philosophy have sent me on that IBM investment? It would have had me watching the price fall to near $40, and taking three years to get back to the price at which I had purchased it. No, thanks; I'll take my profit. You probably know that in 1995 and 1996, IBM was one hot potato. The price climbed to near $160, so there was a good opportunity to make a profit in the stock, but I didn't want to sit through all the misery waiting on it.

So here is Gard's modified buy-and-hold philosophy:

> Buy and hold is fine, as long as it works, and as long as you have confidence in the stock. However, keep your eye on the stock. Every now and again, reevaluate the deal. Is it still a good hold at the current price level? Is there any news on the company, their markets, or their competitors that would significantly alter your appraisal from when you bought it? Are you uncomfortable with the stock? Are you losing sleep over it? Do you have a chance to claim a strong profit, or is it time to cut your losses? Make your decisions for today based on the information that is available today, not the old news.

Think about it. Buy and hold does not mean buy it and forget about it. The most important lessons may only come in the school of hard knocks, after a couple of years. If you find yourself repeatedly holding losers for a long time, without their becoming profitable, then you are doing something wrong, and buy-and-hold thinking is hurting you. If you find yourself running up large trading fees that are eating away too much of your profits, then consider trying more buy-and-hold investing. If you find yourself frequently passing up chances at good profits when a stock runs up quickly, then consider watching your investments more closely and consider grabbing a profit once in a while.

More on the Time Horizon

Our third question from early in this chapter concerned how far ahead you can see. This is a tough issue. The question is what time frame can you

"I'm telling you—Rome won't be built in a day!"

reasonably use when trying to evaluate a stock? Assume that we are looking for good long-term investments: no market timing and no get rich quick schemes. If you expect to hold the stock for a year, then you want to have some idea about the prospects for longer than a year because, when you are ready to sell, the other investors will be forecasting out a year beyond that date. The most important issue is to estimate earnings as far out as possible. We will return to that in a moment, but first look at other timing issues.

If the company you are studying is a brand new Internet technology company with a popular new product, then can you estimate the likelihood that a competitor will come out with a better and cheaper product next month? Probably not. However, if the company and their product has captured 65 percent of the market before the competition gets in, then can they stand up against a strong competitor? Probably so. If you are analyzing Chrysler and their sales for this year decline in the face of new products from General Motors, then do you believe that Chrysler will be able to withstand the assault and reclaim part of the lost markets within a couple of years? These are the different kinds of questions to keep in mind.

You have to apply different time frames to different kinds of companies. Look at Netscape, Chrysler, and GTE. Netscape is a relatively new small company producing products for the highly volatile and rapidly changing Internet services market. It would be difficult to forecast anything about their sales or earnings for more than a year ahead without allowing for a very wide margin of error and uncertainty. Chrysler, of course, has been through the valley of death and has come back strong. So we see two things: A very large and long-established industrial corporation has staying power and can recover from near death, and even the blue-chip firms are subject to some dangers in their markets. GTE is a rock. They have been highly successful, growing, and prosperous for many years and, by the nature of their markets, are unlikely to suffer any disastrous problems for the foreseeable future. In terms of analysis and predictions for those three firms, we could estimate different levels of confidence in our predictions and time frames of confidence.

Company	Time Limit of Predictability	Confidence Level
Netscape	6 months to 1 year	very uncertain
Chrysler	1 year to 2 years	variable
GTE	1 year to 3 year	fairly strong

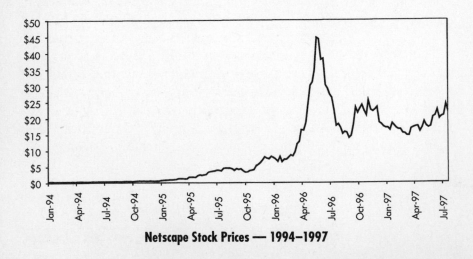

Netscape Stock Prices — 1994–1997

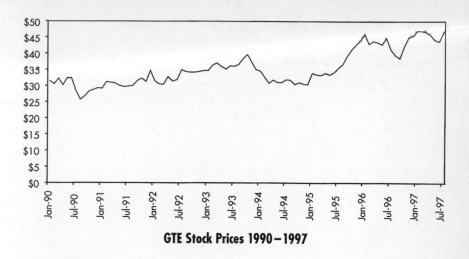

GTE Stock Prices 1990–1997

You or your broker or investment advisor may disagree with the above suggestions, but it doesn't matter. The key issue is that you have to approach different companies differently with regard to earnings estimates, and there is a relatively short time limit beyond which no earnings estimates have much validity. I will suggest as a point of debate that few earnings estimates have any validity beyond two years, and virtually none are valid beyond three years. That is not to say that the analysts and estimators are weak, but it is difficult business. Even the best and brightest will have difficulty forecasting earnings more than a year out. For point of illustration let's refer to the best and the brightest. Some of the most reliable sources[1] of stock investment information that you could ever hope to see are the *Value Line, Zacks Analyst Watch, First Call Consensus Guide*, and *Standard & Poor's Earnings Guide*. I have the greatest respect for those folks, but, at their expense, let's illustrate the difficulty of estimating earnings. The chart below shows a few companies, the dates of the estimates, the end of the forecasted period, and the actual result for the forecasted period. This does not show which of the sources produced which estimate because it doesn't matter. They are all very good sources, and this just illustrates the difficulty of the practice. Values listed are all earnings per share (total earnings ÷ number of shares).

---

[1] See chapter 15 for much more information about the sources and references.

Company	End of Fiscal Year	Date of Estimate	Estimated Earnings ($)	Actual Earnings ($)
Dayton Hudson	Jan '96	Dec '95	4.76	1.29
Great Lakes Chemical	Dec '95	Dec '95	4.50	4.52
Cree Research	June '96	Dec '95	0.31	0.04
Standard Commercial	Mar '96	Dec '95	0.85	1.10 loss
Chrysler	Dec '93	Dec '92	3.00	6.77
Chrysler	Dec '94	Mar '93	5.20	10.11
Delta Airlines	June '94	Mar '93	1.10	3.73 loss
Dixie Yarns	Dec '96	Apr '96	0.15	0.27
Duke Power	Dec '96	Apr '96	3.33	3.37
Mattell	Dec '96	Apr '96	1.48	1.44

Lesson: It is difficult to foretell the future of a company or a stock, even if you do a lot of careful analysis. And the further out you try to forecast, the more difficult it will be. So even if you are a buy-and-hold investor, or if you just want to keep a stable portfolio without excessive trading commissions, it still pays to review everything occasionally.

Risk Management

Most individual investors will work to find some combination of total return and protection. As we shall see later, safety can be influenced by the factors that contribute to total return. Just for initial examples, higher dividends are usually thought to contribute to safety, as are higher earnings. The whole question of protection, or risk management and risk avoidance, is complex and subject to differing opinions. You may read and hear many ideas and opinions about risk that will be partially contradictory, incomplete, and sometimes quite obscure. However, since market risk is dependent on the opinions and ideas of other investors, try to understand some of the common conceptions and misconceptions about it. Remember that it is never wise to try to prove the market wrong. Never set your fortune up against the combined wisdom of all the other investors. Even if you're right, you will lose in that game.[2] Many experienced successful investors preach that "the trend is your friend."

So let us return to protection of your money—that is to say, risk avoidance and risk management.

Do not seek risk-free investments. There are no such animals, at least not in the stock market. Every time you let the money out of your hands, there is a chance that you will never see it again. Rather, seek investments that have the kinds of risk and degree of risk that you may be able to live with. You should not invest in certain stocks unless you are willing to face the possible loss of all of your money—for example, new Internet software developers. You could invest in other stocks and feel quite confident that, over the next two or three years, it is practically unthinkable that you could lose more than 25 percent of your money—for example, the local telephone operating companies.

For openers, we need to figure out what risk is. Unfortunately, academics and economists have seized the initiative and tried to tell us what risk is. Their views and theories have become widely accepted and discussed. It is necessary that we understand them, so that we may understand the ideas of other financial analysts and commentators.

The rest of this section is debatable and subject to conflicting evidence. We can't avoid that, but I will try to give you enough information to help you decide how you want to manage your money. It will help preserve your peace of mind if you remember again that investing is not a contest. You do not have to prove that others are right or wrong. All you have to do is find some approach to risk management that works for you.

First there is the question "What is risk?" I prefer a simple English definition such as you may find in a dictionary. However, we will begin with the economists' view. They say that you can only manage the risk that you bring into your own investments by choice, by selecting certain stocks to buy. You have a choice of, in effect, buying the market and accepting average market risk. For instance, you could buy a mutual fund that tracks the S&P 500 stock average, so another stock must be measured in terms of how it performs relative to this passive investment that merely tracks average market action. Now beyond that, they say that risk is measured by how

---

[2] You can, however, sometimes profit by taking advantage of the combined foolishness of other groups of investors, but that is the subject of contrarian investing for chapter 14.

volatile the stock price is. Volatility means how much the price moves up and down relative to the market average. The opinion here is that investors are not so much afraid of price changes, but, rather, afraid of price changes that are excessive relative to the changes in the market averages. For the moment, we will assume that the value of the S&P 500 index represents the general trend of stock prices. This view of risk in terms of price volatility relative to the index leads us to compare percentage changes of a given stock price to percentage changes of the index.

For instance, if you own stock KXKX, which is priced at $30 while the S&P 500 average is around 700, you might consider these kinds of action:

1. If your stock lost $15 dollars (that's down 50 percent) *while the market was steady*, then this appears to be a dangerous stock, with high volatility and high risk.

2. If your stock lost $10 *while the market was also losing 230 points* (both down about 33 percent), then it appears that your stock was keeping pace with the market. It does not appear to be unduly risky relative to the overall market action.

3. If your stock held fixed in price *while the market average was up 70 points* (market up 10 percent), then it appears that your stock was risky for not going along in a general market advance. In other words, by selecting KXKX you have lost the opportunity to move along with a general market advance.

There is a statistical method used to measure this kind of risk. We call it the measurement of volatility, and give it a name ß (the Greek letter *beta*). Here's how it works: If the stock generally moves up or down the same way and the same percentage amount as the market average, it is said to have ß = 1. If it generally moves up or down twice as fast, but in the same direction as the average, it is said to have ß = 2. If it generally moves up or down the proportional amount, but in the opposite direction as the market averages, then we say ß = −1. There are statistical and algebraic methods for calculating beta for any stock over any period of time. Don't worry about those. Beta is widely calculated and shown in various publications we will talk about later. Just think to yourself, that if the historical patterns persist, then for any stock for which you know ß, you can think to yourself that the percentage change in your stock price should be approximately ß times the percentage change in the market average[3].

The lesson in all that fog is this: If you want stocks that have average volatility, look for ß close to 1—these stocks should not change in price too much differently from the overall market averages. If you want more volatile stocks that are likely to change in price faster than the market averages, look for higher ß. If you want less volatile stocks that change in price more slowly than the averages, look for smaller fractions values of ß like ½ or ¼. Look for stocks with negative values of ß if you want stocks that are likely to move opposite to the overall market averages[4].

Here are some pictures: At first you see a chart of the market index over twelve months, then a stock with ß = 1, which is considered to have average volatility, average risk, and to be just as safe or risky as the market index. The next stock has ß = ½. It is half as volatile as the market index. The third stock has ß = 2. It has high volatility, but moves in the same general direction as the market index. The fourth stock has ß = -1. It moves opposite to the broad market index. In practice, it is quite rare to find stocks with beta either greater than 2 or negative. The values of beta for all stocks are distributed around an average of one.

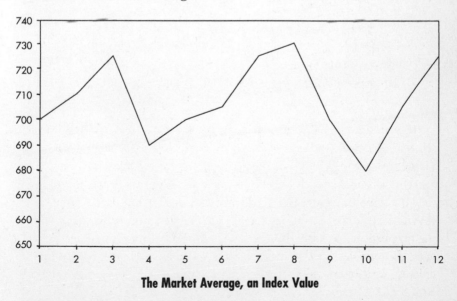

The Market Average, an Index Value

---

[3] Meaning, on average, over a long time period.
[4] This is rare.

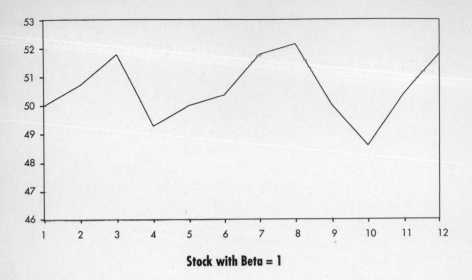

Stock with Beta = 1

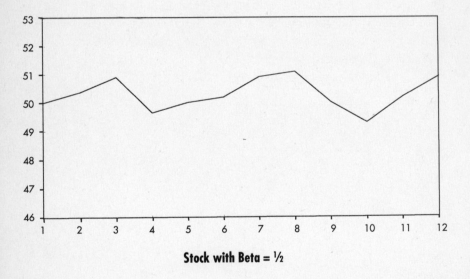

Stock with Beta = ½

Any of these stocks might be good investments for some people and not for others. The value of beta can be used to adjust how much risk/volatility you are bringing into your portfolio. There are some academic theories to the effect that the only constructive thing that you, the individual investor, can do to manage risk is to manage the average value of beta for your overall investment portfolio. Other respectable theories

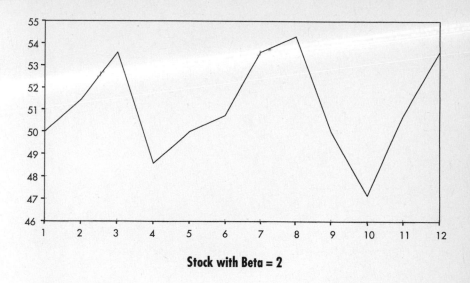

Stock with Beta = 2

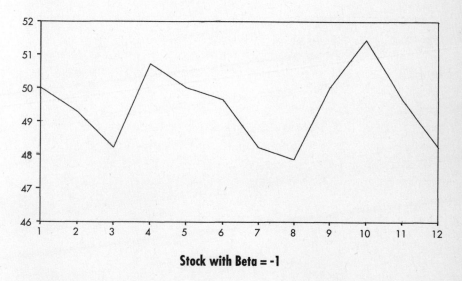

Stock with Beta = -1

deny that.[5] Beta is useful if you own ten different stocks and you want to know what kind of volatility to expect in your overall portfolio. You can

---

[5] One of the most interesting discussions of risk is in a paper by Professor R. A. Haugen of U.C. Irvine, "The Effects of Intrigue, Liquidity, Imprecision, and Bias on the Cross-Section of Expected Stock Returns," *The Journal of Portfolio Management*, summer 1996.

average beta for the ten stocks (get the values from the *Value Line*, or another reference), and that should give you some idea of your overall portfolio volatility. Whether it actually measures risk is another question. I happen to think it does not, but if you are concerned about volatility, it is a useful indicator.

To use a specific example, in chapter 3 we talked about Biogen stock over the period from 1990 to 1995. The price fluctuated a great deal. Biogen has a ß = 1.5. That is an example of a highly volatile stock.

The chart on page 52 shows the price of Texaco over a few years. It is far less volatile than Biogen. Texaco has a ß = 0.65, which is uncommonly low.

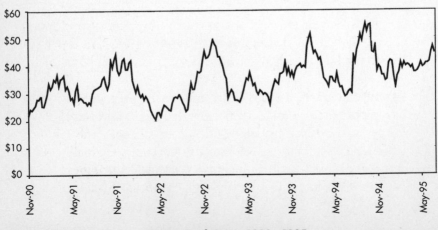

Biogen Stock Prices 1990–1995

All right, so much for beta. If you want to measure volatility, then focus on beta. If not, then don't. Now, however, suppose we have a different view of risk. Let me suggest a somewhat simpler and yet still useful view of the subject of risk.

If you are not an economist, then you should not trouble yourself with a broad general and theoretical approach to measuring risk. Rather, try this: For each stock, consider the factors that appear to offer some promise, hope, and reward—that is, some total return in the stock. Consider everything about the company, their products, and whatever else makes the stock attractive. Then, after you have worked yourself into giddy ecstasy over the promise and the reward in each investment, take a cold shower and consider as carefully as you can everything that might go wrong with all of the positive factors you identified.

For example, if you think their new products are excellent, what evidence do you have that the general public will like them? If, in fact, the new product line falls flat, then what happens to company revenues and earnings for the next year or two? Does the company have a high debt position but manageable current interest payments? Then what happens if overall interest rates shoot up 3 percent over the next year? If the company is dependent on a new technical product for measuring blood oxygen levels that they sell for $35,000 a copy, is there much likelihood that someone else is working on a substitute for half the price? If the company is part of the current Wall Street fad of a group of stocks that "everyone must buy, because they must go up," then what happens if the herd's opinion changes one day while you are at the beach?

Types of Risk

To make things a bit neater, we can assign some organization and system to identifying these risks. There are several distinct classes of risks that you may want to think about when you are analyzing any stock.

1. **The market risk:** You cannot escape from market risk unless you get out of the market. Remember, "a rising tide raises all the boats." However, the falling tide lowers all boats. The single strongest influence on the prices of your individual stocks is the price trend of the markets in total. When the markets are falling, you must expect your stocks to fall;

when the markets are rising, you may expect your stocks to rise. If you want to estimate how much your stocks might rise or fall relative to the broad market averages, this is one place where beta makes sense. If you think that overall market prices are too high and subject to a great risk of a bear market, then any stock you buy is also subject to that same risk.

2. **The risk of the competition:** Any stock you buy represents a company with products or services to sell in some market. There are other people out there who would love to take that market, and the customers and profits along with it. Before you buy the stock, make sure that you have looked at the competition; if Ford looks great, than maybe Chrysler looks better.

3. **The risks in the economy:** Any company is at some times, in various ways, exposed to the risks of inflation or recession. They can't sell those refrigerators or cars if the people don't have jobs. If the product is new refrigerators, then sales will turn sour in a recession. If the product is telephone service, then sales will not fall too much.

4. **The risks from government interference:** As we all know, there is no end to the inventiveness of the people in Washington. Even if they create reasonable rules, the costs of compliance and the risks of misunderstanding create major hazards for every business in the land. I suppose you heard about air bags? and OSHA?

5. **Monetary risk:** If you buy stocks from a foreign country, there are many new risks to face. But even if the stock is great and the company is strong, changes in currency exchange rates may take away all your profits. If you buy stock in an Italian company, and the stock returns 10 percent in lira, but the lira loses 10 percent in dollar value, then you have no profit. If you buy stock in a company that is dependent on foreign sales, then a strong dollar will hurt their sales and earnings.

6. **The risk of your own weak analysis:** If you are going to buy
   stocks based on your own analysis and judgment, then you
   must keep in mind that it is complicated business. Any time
   you do the job quickly, or you think this one looks easy, then
   you are very likely overlooking something that might go
   wrong. Even when you do a lot of careful and exhaustive
   research, be humble. It's not easy. Something may go wrong.
   Diversify.

Recommended Further Reading

Lowenstein, Louis. *What's Wrong With Wall Street*. Reading, MA: Addison
   Wesley, 1988.

Engel, Louis, and Brendan Boyd. *How to Buy Stocks*, 8th ed. New York:
   Little, Brown and Co., 1994.

Sperandeo, Victor. *Trader Vic: Methods of a Wall Street Master*. New York:
   John Wiley and Sons, 1991.

The Annual Report

Builders and Planners

A man wanted to build a new house. He was in a hurry. He went to his banker and told her he needed a loan of $75,000 to work on the house. She said they would be happy to establish a loan for him, but first she needed to collect some information about how the loan would be used.

"First, tell me where the new house will be built."

"I don't know."

"Then, how have you estimated the costs, the type of foundation, and planned to meet the building and zoning requirements?"

"I haven't."

"Well, I'm afraid that we need to see some of that essential information before we can analyze the loan request."

"But I don't have time for that."

"Surely you will need to take care of those requirements before you can start construction."

"No, I don't have time for that."

"But you have to know about the land and topography and soil and zoning requirements before you can make a blueprint."

"No, I don't have time for that. I just want to start building. I'm a builder, not a planner."

Sorry to say, he never received his loan and never built his house.

A similar situation exists for us. We keep our eyes on the prize, the goal, the reason for reading this book, which is to evaluate stocks and make smart decisions about whether to buy or sell. However, we must go through some preliminaries, just as when you needed to learn algebra, and the prerequisite was to know how to add, subtract, multiply, and divide. When you wanted to speak French, you had to study vocabulary and the rules of grammar first. Well, the same thing applies in financial analysis. As Aristotle said, "Well begun is half done."

This chapter and the next two may be a bit demanding, or perhaps dry,[1] but they are nonetheless important. You may want to do your own financial analysis, or you may decide to rely on references that include evaluations and recommendations. In either case, you will have to know words that people use in financial analysis.[2] As I have said before, many different methods are widely practiced by various analysts or writers; it would be good for you if you were able to read and understand their work and decide for yourself which parts of it make sense for your needs.

I will introduce some terms that may seem obvious and simple to you, such as price, earnings, and yield. When those terms come up in this chapter, read the section anyway. It will be quick and painless, and will ensure that you will understand the terms in the same sense as I use them in the rest of the book. Other terms, such as cash flow or price/earnings ratio, might not be familiar to you. Understanding them will demand a little more time and attention, but try to follow along; these terms are part of the language and tools of investing.

To make this as straightforward as possible, I will follow a pattern as we go through the separate terms. I will:

- explain why and when a concept should be useful to you

- define the term in its technical sense and in common English, and explain whether different writers or analysts might use the term differently

---

[1] Let us not say boring.

[2] I urge you to buy a copy of *The Dictionary of Finance and Investment Terms*, published by Barron's Educational Series. Keep it near at hand. There will be many terms that I will not cover, and a few that you might not recall easily. The dictionary is excellent.

- illustrate any required calculation or explain where you can find the data

- show some simplified calculations for a company that has been made up for the purpose of illustration

- show some samples and the interpretation of the data for real companies that are being actively traded in the markets

- discuss the problems and confusion that sometimes occur when using each concept or calculation

All of the concepts and calculations will be used later when we talk about specific selection methods. They will be explained further as the need arises.

The Fiscal Year

The fiscal year adopted by each publicly traded corporation is a time period of one-year duration that they choose to mark the beginning and end of their financial reporting periods. Some companies choose January 1 to December 31, and others choose periods like April 1 to March 31. The fiscal year must also be broken down into quarters for additional interim reporting during the year. General Motors' fiscal year runs January 1 to December 31; Honda's runs April 1 to March 31. The fiscal year is identified with a calendar year according to the usage of the company. For example, GM's fiscal year 1997 ran from January 1, 1997, to December 31, 1997. For Honda, fiscal year 1997 ran from April 1, 1997, to March 31, 1998.

Financial Reports

Every publicly traded company is required by the Securities and Exchange Commission (SEC) to publish regular financial reports. The reports may contain a lot of opinions and predictions from the officers of the company, or not. The reports may be written in such a way as to make them easy to read and useful for an investor, or they may be complicated and difficult. If you are studying a publicly traded company, you should look at the annual and quarterly reports that they send to shareholders and/or the annual and quarterly reports that they send to the SEC. Those reports to the SEC are called Form 10K or Form 10Q for annual or quarterly reports respectively. We will review some of the standard parts of the annual reports, using an example company that was made up solely for illustration. The financial reports will always contain the prior year's figures for reference.

The Alpha Beta Publishing Company in these examples is purely fictitious and has no relationship to any company or business that has ever existed. The annual report will always contain at least three parts: the earnings report, the cash-flow report, and the balance sheet. Each of these is explained in the next few pages.

Annual Report to Shareholders

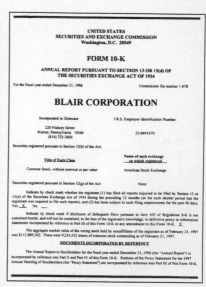

10-K Report to SEC

Earnings Report

The earnings report, also called the income statement, shows how the company made and spent money (the items in parentheses reduce earnings):

Alpha Beta Publishing Company

Fiscal Year 1997

Statement of Income:

(dollars in thousands,[3] except for per-share data)

	1997	1996
Net sales	$97,000	$94,500
– Cost of goods sold	(87,500)	(84,400)
Gross profit	9,500	10,100
– Selling and general expenses	(3,600)	(3,700)
Operating profit	5,900	6,400
Other income		
+ Investment income	246	237
+ Sale of music division[4]	758	0
Net income	6,904	6,637
Other expenses		
– Interest on debt	(198)	(200)
– Income taxes	(2,100)	(2,050)
Net earnings	4,606	4,387
Average # of common stock shares outstanding during the year	18,900,000	18,700,000
Net earnings per common share	$0.24	$0.23

[3] To say "dollars in thousands" means that you will multiply each reported number by 1,000 to obtain the true value. For example, the gross profit above actually represents $9,500,000.

[4] This sale of the music division shows what we call an extraordinary item—it produced revenue in 1997, but does not look like part of normal ongoing business activity.

The final figure on the Alpha Beta earnings report is the earnings figure that analysts are always trying to forecast, which, as we saw in chapter 3, is no easy task.

Cash Flow

The next part that you may always expect to see in the annual reports is the statement of cash flow. The statement of cash flow explains how the company handles cash and cash equivalent[5] accounts. This statement will show the impact on operations and finances due to changes in accounts receivable, accounts payable, short-term or long-term debt, inventory, and depreciation.

Cash flow is the money that a company can generate to run the business during each fiscal year. After the goods are sold and the bills and operating expenses are paid, then money is left to do things that the directors want to do—for example, reduce long-term debt or pay dividends. As such, the cash flow is widely regarded as a broad indicator of the overall financial health of the company. If the cash-flow statement in the annual report is not terribly complex, then you may want to look at it there. Otherwise, good sources are the *Value Line* report on the company, or whatever reports your stockbroker's research division might create.

To illustrate the idea of cash flow and why it is different from profit, let's look at a very simple little company, Nancy's Needles. In 1997, Nancy had sales of $214,000, and the cost of goods sold was $122,000. That left her a gross profit of $92,000. She also paid $17,000 in expenses for the mortgage on her shop, electricity, and part-time help. That left $75,000. She also planned that in six years she would have to buy a new store. She figured that her old store was losing value at a rate of $15,000 per year, and she needed to set aside $15,000 towards eventual replacement. That was depreciation on the store. Then she had $60,000 left that looked like clear profits, and the business paid $20,000 in taxes, leaving $40,000 in earnings for the year.

---

[5] A *cash equivalent* account is an account of the company that might soon be converted into cash at a set and fixed value, such as holdings of short-term bonds.

Her earnings statement looked like this:

Revenues	$214,000
– Cost of goods sold	(122,000)
= Gross profit	92,000
– Operational expenses	(17,000)
– Depreciation	(15,000)
= Net profit	60,000
– Income taxes	(20,000)
= Earnings	40,000

But her cash flow is different from her earnings. She set aside that $15,000 for a future expense, but in fact she still has that money in the bank and can do as she pleases with it. Her cash flow is $40,000 + $15,000 = $55,000. Some analysts say that cash flow presents a better view of the company than just the earnings statement.

A company may or may not be healthy, regardless of whether it is generating profits. For example, suppose that the Broad Line Bus Company[6] has a fleet of fifty buses that are between five and ten years old, but are being operated at a small profit. If the cash flow is $200,000 per year and the expected cost of new buses is $80,000 each, then it is unlikely that the company could ever generate enough new cash to pay for replacement buses. If they wanted to borrow $2 million to buy twenty-five new buses, then the expected interest and principal on the loan would be over $200,000 per year, so they could not finance it out of operating profits. This company is not generating enough cash flow to save funds to maintain ongoing business operations. As the current fleet of buses dies out, then so will the company. In this case, the cash-flow statement shows a substantial weakness of the company.

To analyze cash flow directly from the annual report may be complicated, but it is certainly worthwhile to look at the cash flow statement and see what you can make of it. Think about what the company may need for new operations and what they have in terms of cash on hand. If the annual report is too messy to allow you to read the cash flow statement, then check the *Value Line* report on the company. If cash flow is a problem, they should tell you. As another interesting exercise, ask your stockbroker to tell you

---

[6] Broad Line Bus has no connection to any real company.

his opinion of the cash flow condition of any company that he recommends for purchase. See if he knows what is going on.

Here is how the Alpha Beta Publishing Company might represent their cash flow. They start with the net earnings from the income statement.

Alpha Beta Publishing
Fiscal Year 1997
Cash Flow Statement

	1997	1996
Net earnings (thousands)	$4,606	$4,387
Adjustments to operating income		
+ Provision for depreciation[7]	405	410
− Flooding at Gerwain plant	(99)	0
Adjusted operating income	4,912	4,797
Adjustments to receivable and payable accounts		
Change in the payables account	(146)	96
Change in receivables account	51	88
Net cash flow from operating activities	4,817	4,981
Uses and other sources of cash		
Sale of stock[8]	1,000	0
Reduction of long term debt	(500)	0
Dividends paid	(2,835)	(2,115)
Net change in cash and cash equivalents	2,482	2,866
Cash and equivalents at beginning of year	37,486	34,620
Cash and equivalents at end of year	39,968	37,486

---

[7] The treatment of depreciation in a cash-flow statement is an accounting issue that I will not try to explain here, but it usually adds to cash flow.
[8] 200,000 shares were sold for $5 each.

As a first taste of financial analysis, we can learn a few things from this company's income and cash-flow statements. The shares sold for $5 when the new stock was sold. At the end of the year, the stock was selling for $6, which you could read in the *Wall Street Journal*. The cash and equivalents[9] are worth $39,968,000, which gives $2.11 for each outstanding share: $39,968,000 ÷ 18,900,000 shares = $2.11 per share.

This illustration shows two unusual things. First, it partially explains the $246,000 in income from investments in the earnings statement. That income must have been interest earned from the almost $40 million of near cash assets they hold. It looks like they held part of that money in a money market account or very short-term bonds. That looks like rather careless cash management. Anybody could put $40 million to work and earn 5 percent a year, which would be $2 million. Why is Alpha Beta earning so much less?

Second, the cash position indicates that the stockholder, in a sense, only has $3.89 per share exposed to any great risk in this stock. That is, $2.11 per share is safeguarded by the cash equivalent assets of the firm, so the rest ($6 − $2.11 = $3.89) is the risk portion of the investment. (Also note that this conclusion is arguable. Some analysts might take a different point of view, and that is why we have stock markets.)

You can also compute from what we have seen so far that the dividend on the stock is 15¢ per share and the yield percentage on the stock is 2.5 percent:

- dividends paid divided by the number of shares = $2,835,000 ÷ 18,900,000 = 15¢ per share

- dividend divided by the share price = 15¢ ÷ $6 = 2.5 percent yield rate

If you don't like doing those calculations, there are many publications that will show them for you. Later, I will describe many of those publications to help you decide where to look.

The Balance Sheet

The third and last standard ingredient of every financial report is a balance sheet. The balance sheet shows what the company has, and how it

---

[9] The equivalents are items that might be easily converted to cash.

is allocated among different uses, how much is currently financed by debt, and how much the company actually owns free and clear.

The balance sheet should show three things about a company: assets, debt, and shareholders' equity. The information on a balance sheet is much like a homeowner's equity position. If Sam owns a house valued at $138,000 but he carries a mortgage balance of $77,000, then his balance sheet shows:

Asset	Debt	Owner's Equity
$138,000	$77,000	$61,000

It works the same way for a business. The assets are everything the company owns, with a dollar value attached. Each asset is assigned to some particular account which describes the assets and use, such as inventory, buildings, freight cars, or accounts receivable.

The debt consists of short-term and long-term borrowings and payable accounts.

The shareholders' equity is simply everything left after you subtract the debt from the assets. The shareholders' equity may include something called preferred shareholders equity, which refers to the value of the preferred stock. It behaves more like a debt for the company, like bonds, but is usually classed with the equity. It is usually not perfectly clear how the company assigns a value to preferred equity. We generally just accept that there is some logic in it. If the balance sheet shows any preferred equity, then you should investigate just how they assigned the value to it, and what it means.

Here is the balance sheet for our Alpha Beta Publishing Company:

Balance Sheet As of December 31, 1997

Assets (in millions of dollars)

Real estate	$20.82
Equipment	9.74
Accounts receivable	6.61
Cash and near cash	29.38
Inventory	3.02
Goodwill	1.00
Supplies	<u>1.15</u>
Total assets	$71.72

Liabilities

Long-term debt	$2.48
Debt due within a year	0.33
Accounts payable	<u>2.77</u>
Total liabilities	$5.58
Equity (assets – liabilities)	$66.14
Preferred shareholders' equity	$ 2.50
Common shareholders' equity	$63.64

If you were considering this stock for part of your investments, then you would want to dig into the financial statements and see what you could find. Sometimes you will find something and sometimes you won't. For Alpha Beta Publishing, I will show you some things that some analysts or investors might find of interest in this report. Don't worry if this seems difficult to follow. It is just to illustrate the kinds of work that some stock pickers get into. In the next few chapters we will get into more specific details about how you can go searching for valuable information on your own.

We can learn a lot from this balance sheet and the other parts of the ABPCO financial reports. Part of it is good news and part is not very good. The good news: The total debt is small (2.48 + 0.33 = 2.81) compared to the equity. The debt-to-equity ratio equals 2.81 million ÷ 66.14 million, or 4.2 percent. Most analysts would regard that as a pretty low debt figure, which is good.

More good news: The company has an annual net income that is roughly twenty times the current required annual debt payment. If this company wanted to borrow money, they could certainly make a very strong case to the bank that they would be a safe borrower. They probably should not want to borrow money, since they are sitting on so much cash. But if they did want to start a new line of business, or perhaps buy out another company, they could probably raise the money.

Even more good news: The total inventory on hand is $3.02 million, and that is good when compared to the annual sales of $97 million from the earnings statement. They appear to sell out their inventory thirty-two times a year, which is outstanding for most lines of business. If you were studying this stock, you would want to compare that with the inventory turnover of their competitors. This appears to be very good, a sign of good management and healthy markets.

The bad news (maybe): The company has too much idle cash; the total assets equal $71.72 million, but the cash reserve is $29.38 million. The rest of the assets, $42.34 million, represents what is actually working and operating the business. The cash (short-term investments) is earning $246,000 in the year, less than 1 percent of the cash total. That appears to be very weak cash management; why aren't they doing something more productive with that money? The assets other than cash, the $42.34 million, are earning the rest of the total income, almost $6 million (after taking out the sale of the music division). That means the $42.34 million of active, working assets brings in about $6 million of operating income, which is 14 percent of $42.34 million. It seems as if the management ought to put the cash to work and try to produce another 14 percent in income. If the $29.38 million of cash (and short-term investments) were put to work earning 14 percent through business operations, revenues would increase by $4.1 million.

This is, of course, speculation, because we don't know what they would do with the cash, but the earnings statement leads us to estimate that an extra $4 million of operating profits might come down to the bottom line as perhaps $3 million of net earnings (an estimate). That would translate into an extra 16¢ a share in earnings for the shareholders to make a total of 40¢ a share of earnings.

Since the stock currently trades at $6, which is twenty-five times the current earnings, we might assume that in case of higher earnings, it would also trade at twenty-five times the earnings, which would put the stock price at $10 (25 x 40¢).

Therefore (subject to some estimations and assumptions we made), by putting the cash to work effectively, the management might cause the stock value to grow from $6 to $10. Why aren't they doing it? This question should be raised in the annual shareholders' meeting. If the management has a plan to put that cash to work, then fine. If they don't, then you vote the bums out.

All of the above discussion of bad news has been conjecture and estimates. For example, if they put the cash to work, you don't know if it would generate another $3 million in earnings. We are just estimating based on what the current assets are earning. However, this is the kind of thing that financial analysts do. They usually cannot guarantee their analysis and conjectures based on the balance sheets, but they should be able to present a reasonable argument. This is a little taste of financial analysis. Some people, like me, think it's fun and interesting. Some don't. The real world is more complex than what I just showed, because the financial reports of real-world companies will be more complex than the example we used. We will refer back to the financial data for Alpha Beta Publishing throughout the rest of the book.

You can get copies of financial reports by calling or writing to the companies. To get telephone numbers, ask for help in your local library, or check in the *Value Line*. You can also get copies from the SEC, or download them through the SEC Web site, keyword Edgar. Some publications, such as the *Value Line*, will show condensed and simplified tables of the financial information covering the past few years, so you do not have to read the actual reports unless you want to go further in looking for details.

For example, look at the reports of the three companies described below. You may want to call the companies and request copies of their reports. Space precludes reproducing them here, but the corporations are happy to send you copies.

The National Presto Corporation (symbol NPK on the New York Stock Exchange, tel: 715-839-2121) produces a report that is about as short and basic as the law allows. Presto runs a fairly simple and straightforward business. They produce and sell household appliances, such as coffeemakers or irons. One family controls the business because they control most of the voting power of the stock, so they don't have to worry about explaining much beyond the legally required information (and they don't).

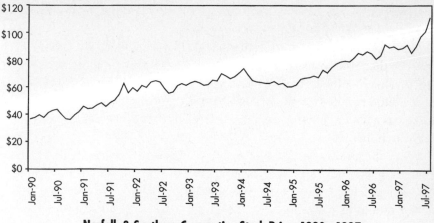

Norfolk & Southern Corporation Stock Prices 1990–1997

Another example can be obtained from Norfolk and Southern (Railroad) Corporation (symbol NSC on the NYSE, tel: 804-629-2680). They are one of the largest, most successful, and best managed railroads in the country. They also publish what I regard as one of the very best annual financial reports. It contains a great deal of useful and well-organized information, and a minimum of baloney. The notes are few, and well organized for the reader's use. Take a look at it.

The third example is Ford Motor (symbol F on the NYSE, tel: 800-555-5259). Ford's reports have to be far more complex because their business is more complex. They have operations worldwide, dealing in many different nations' currencies, and they run a financing unit that produces a substantial profit. They also own a rental-car business. The financial reports have to reflect all of those factors, so they are naturally more involved and challenging to read.

Here I sit with a Ford annual report in hand, trying to decide what to do with it. Let's see. The first twenty pages are advertising and malarkey and pictures of the directors, but all very high-class stuff: nice paper, nice photography, nice color. Then it has a forty-two–page financial section. The financial section contains a one-page summary of operating highlights, a basic bottom-line view of the business; that's helpful. Then come eight pages of management's view of the financial condition and results of operations. That's important because it tells you something about how they intend to manage the business and whether they recognize any problems. This is followed by the blessing of their independent auditor.

Next, they have one page each for the income statement, the cash-flow statement, the balance sheet, and an analysis of equity. The analysis of equity shows some of the division of ownership between common stock and their class B stock, and also the capital in excess of the common stock, and the retained earnings, with an adjustment for foreign currency–translation effects. All of this is followed by twenty pages of notes to the financial statements explaining things that are not sufficiently clear in the main financial reports, a necessary consequence of the size and complexity of Ford's business. If you plan to read and analyze financial reports, then you must plan to read and analyze the notes, too. Much explanation and new material may be squirreled away among the notes, and some of it might cause a drastic reconsideration of the numbers in the earnings statement or cash-flow statement.

There have been cases (not the three companies above) of companies whose management have wanted to mislead the shareholders or investment analysts about the nature of their results. When managers want to mislead, one way is to present what appears as a favorable picture in the financial statements and then explain in the notes that a lot of the values have hidden factors or adjustments that make them mean something different. This may be enough to satisfy the auditors that the total package conforms with generally accepted accounting principles, yet still throw a fog over the interpretation of the reports.

> **Lesson to remember:** If you intend to read financial reports, then you must read the notes, too.

At the end of the Ford report, they have a one-page summary that breaks down the annual results among four quarters and among the automotive and financial services businesses. Next they give a ten-year summary of auto sales in a dozen geographic markets, followed by a ten-year summary of financial results. Those last two items are useful, especially for a large, well-established firm like Ford; the trends are important in understanding where the business might go.

"Go over that part about cash flow again—this is all Greek to me."

What About Financial Reports?

This is a challenging question. Some expert investors say that if you want to invest in stocks, then you have to read financial reports and do your own research (due diligence). Others say that there are good investment methods that should work for you that don't require any financial research. Part of the purpose of this book is to help you decide how you will handle that problem. Certainly, one of the reasons why we love mutual funds is to avoid having to do that kind of work.

But suppose you choose to buy your own individual stocks. Then what? Let's assume for the moment that we have focused on one particular company, call it the Hot Dog Company. If Hot Dog is a large, well-known, and long-established company, then it is very likely that a lot of professional analysts study and analyze them regularly. In that case, it is unlikely that you will discover any opportunities or problems in their financial reports that haven't already been seen, analyzed, and widely reported by the professionals.

It is a certainty that any important facts in their reports have already been reflected in changing stock prices before you even have a chance to read the reports. In such a case, don't worry about reading the financial reports, but do read the published opinions in newspapers, magazines, the *Value Line*, Standard & Poor's research, Zacks, or your stockbroker's published research and opinions. Your decision as to whether to buy or sell such a well-known stock can probably be based on all of that public analysis and on other factors, such as the company's markets, competitors, trends in their sales and earnings, and trends in the stock price. That is not to say that you will necessarily make the right decision (there is no risk-free investing!), but it does mean that your independent study of the financial statements is unlikely to reward you with any new information that would significantly improve your decision. That applies to large and widely watched corporations like Ford, GE, Microsoft, or other members of the S&P 500 index.

On the other hand, let's say that Hot Dog is a relatively smaller and less well-known company. Only one (if any) professional analyst regularly follows their financial reporting. Real-life examples would include the real estate investment company Highwoods Properties during their first year in business, or Standard Commercial Corporation during 1994 and 1995 (when the investment world lost interest in them), or Cree Research during the first two years after they went public. Those are all stocks where I have made significant profits by buying companies that were not widely followed by the pros. In cases like these, it is certainly worthwhile to study the financial reports. There is a fair chance that you may uncover some fact or analysis that sheds new light on the value of the company. At any rate, the general presentation and logic in the financial reports should tell you a lot about the acumen and intentions of the people who run the company, and that should affect your decision. Don't buy stock in companies where you don't trust the management, no matter how good the financial numbers may look.

But the financial reports don't tell the whole story, no matter how carefully you may look and think. The financial reports don't tell you much about their market segment, their competition, interest rates, the national trend on employment, or their products. So even if you study the financial reports, there will be many other factors that affect your decision to buy or sell the stock.

And what about companies that don't fit either category described above? Should you study the financial reports of those companies? That has to be a judgment call. It partially depends on how much other information you find, how much confidence you have in that other information, how much time and effort you want to put into research, and how you feel about your own ability to understand the financial reports. It should never do any harm to look at the financial reports, and it is easy to get copies, but you have to balance the time and work of the research against the benefits. It's a personal thing.

Stock Splits

If you had a ten dollar bill and exchanged it for two fives, you would be even. You would have more pieces of paper, at a smaller value for each, but the total value would be unchanged. That is all a stock split does.

Directors of companies usually like to encourage broader ownership of the stock and more liquidity[10]. Greater liquidity helps all of the share owners because it makes a stock easier to buy and sell whenever you want to. There are a couple of ways greater liquidity can be realized, and both are achieved by stock splits. One goal is to simply create more shares of stock without diluting the ownership of current shareholders. The other goal is to reduce the stock price when it gets too high, without hurting the investment value of current shareholders. Again, think about getting two fives for a ten. Sometimes the two fives are more convenient.

Suppose the Zebra Corporation had two million shares publicly traded at a price of $51. That is a relatively small number of shares for a publicly traded company, and the price may be a little high to attract a lot of individual investors. The directors could fix that by creating a two-for-one stock split. They would announce that, on a certain date, each shareholder would receive an extra share for each one they owned, and the price would be cut in half. That would leave four million shares in circulation at a price of $25.50. Each prior shareholder would then have double the number of shares, but still have the same percent ownership of the company and the same total value.

The two-for-one split (like when you get two fives for a ten) is the most common stock split, but occasionally the directors get a different idea. They might use a three-for-two split, or a three-for-one split. In each case,

---

[10] *Liquidity* refers to the amount of trading in a given stock or other security. It also refers to how quickly and easily the owner could exchange the security for cash.

they increase the number of shares in circulation but do not change the investment value of current shareholders. In a three-for-two split, each prior shareholder would receive three new shares for each two shares previously held, and the price per share would fall by one third. If you held 200 shares priced at $90 before a three-for-two split, then after the split you would have 300 shares priced at $60.

Stock splits do not directly change the value of anyone's holdings. They only change the number of shares and the price of the shares.

See if you can get it right (answers in footnotes)[11]:

> *In the summer of 1995, Bombardier Inc. stock was selling for $34. They made a two-for-one stock split. What was the value of the shares after the split? Before the split, Martha owned 200 shares at $34. After the split, what did she own? How much profit or loss did she incur on the stock split?*

Split-Adjusted Prices

During 1995, when Chrysler's price changed from $54 to $34, was that a loss? No, it was not. It was a gain because there had been a two-for-one split during 1995. In order to compare prices, you have to make an adjustment. The January 1 price of $34 for one share of Chrysler stock was for one old share, but in December of '95, that was equivalent to two new shares, so the value had grown from one share at $54 to two shares at $34, i.e., from $54 to $68. The value of the Chrysler shareholders' stock grew by 26 percent during the period.

In this book and other references, you will frequently see data shown as *split-adjusted price*. That means that either the starting or ending price has been adjusted to make them comparable in order to show the true gain or loss after a split. In the following example, the split-adjusted price for January 1998 has been adjusted to be comparable with the January 1997 price:

---

[11] After the split she owned 400 shares at $17; she did not incur any profit or loss on the split.

January 1997 Price	February 1997 Split	January 1998 Price	January 1998 Adjusted Price
$30	two for one	$20	$40 (a 33 percent gain)
$150	two for one	$60	$120 (a 20 percent loss)
$80	three for two	$50	$75 (a 6 percent loss)

When you see data reported with a note that says *split-adjusted price*, that just means that either the beginning or ending price on the data you see is not the actual price of trading on that day, but an adjusted price meant to compensate for a split so you can fairly compare values.

To illustrate the idea of the stock price and the price adjustment, here is a chart of the stock price of a company. It was selling at $41 per share in January 1995 and went up to over $60 in May. The directors made a two-for-one stock split effective on May 30, 1995. The actual reported trading value of their shares was $41 on January 3 and $37 on October 3, but that price is misleading because of the split. The comparable, split-adjusted price of a share in January was $20.50.

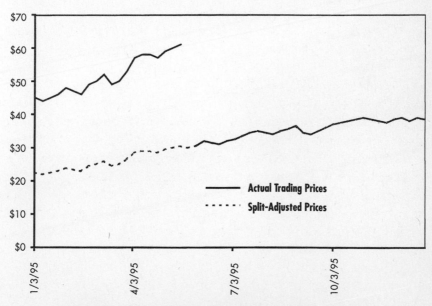

Split-Adjusted Prices After Two-for-One Split on May 30, 1995

Look beneath the surface; let not the several
quality of a thing, nor its worth escape thee.

—Marcus Aurelius Antoninus, *Meditations*

What Is a Stock Worth?

Almost every stock is appealing to somebody. Practically every day each listed stock has buyers, so there must be some features that make people take an interest. However, many of the potential investors will reject a stock because the price does not look good to them. The financial data that you find in a company's annual report or the *Value Line* will help you decide two things:

1. Are you interested in owning the stock?

2. What price would you be willing to pay for it?

Our goal here is to see how to estimate a fair price to pay for a stock. Either a diamond or a lump of coal may sometimes be found at too high or too low a price. You need to learn to decide what is a good price for each stock you study.

Price

Now we will separate the ideas of evaluating the company and evaluating the stock. The financial statements tell us the most about the health of the company, but whether the stock is a good buy is an altogether different question.

The simplest and most immediately obvious approach to evaluating a stock is to look at its price. However, even this can become a point of debate. The price of a stock is set by the markets and varies every day. A fair price for any given stock at a certain time is whatever a willing buyer and a willing seller can agree on for a trade. However, a fair price is not necessarily a smart price for you to accept for a buy or sell. You always have the right and the opportunity to stand aside from the market and say, "If $43 is the best price I can get to sell my IBM stock today, then I think I'll just pass." You may see in the next day's market report that 350,000 shares of IBM traded at prices between $42 and $43.75 that day, but that still does not mean that $43 was a smart price for you to accept to sell yours.

In August 1993, a lot of people bought Long Island Lighting stock at $29 a share. They paid the fair price when they bought. By the end of 1994 it was down to $16 per share.

In the summer of 1994, a lot of people paid between $16 and $18 a share to buy the stock of Steel Technologies, Inc. They paid the fair price at the time. At the end of 1994, it was selling at around $12 a share. At the end of 1995 it was selling at around $10 a share.

In January 1995, over fifteen million shares of Cirrus Logic, Inc. stock were bought and sold at prices close to $24 per share. In September they were trading close to $100 to $110 per share, and the company split the stock two for one. So each original share then gave two shares priced at about $50 to $60. At the end of 1995, those shares (after the stock split) were trading at around $20.

Along the way, Jack sold 100 shares to Susan in January at $24, Susan sold the 100 shares to Katherine in June at $50. Katherine held past September, so she got the two-for-one split. In October she held 200 shares priced at $58; she offered to sell them in October at $60, but got no buyers willing to pay that price. She held them until early November and sold the 200 shares to Jim at $38. At the end of the year, Jim still held the 200 shares and the stock market reports said they were selling at $20.

So how are we doing?

- Susan bought 100 for $2,400 and sold them for $5,000.

- Katherine bought 100 for $5,000 and sold 200 for $7,600.

- Jim bought 200 for $7,600 and held them till the end of the year, when they were valued at $4,000.

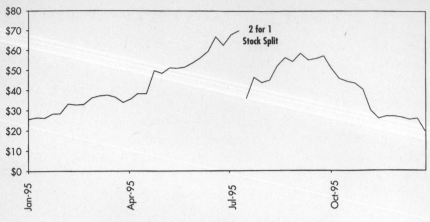

Actual Trading Prices of Cirrus Logic Stock in 1995

Each one of our four traders got fair prices for their buys and sells. Jack took his $2,400, but missed out on a chance at a big profit. Susan made a great profit, but missed a chance for more. Katherine made a good profit, but missed a chance for more. Jim lost money, in terms of portfolio value, but still holds the stock.

Notice that this doesn't say anything about what the stock was worth. With a stock price that bounces around that much, it is obviously tough to get any professional consensus on what the stock is worth, but we do know what the fair prices were each day. Those were the prices at which willing buyers and sellers completed deals.

> **Lesson:** The fair price for a stock may be an entirely different thing from what the stock is worth. The fair price is determined in the marketplace every day. It is whatever a buyer and a seller agree to. The true worth (value) of the stock is a subject for much analysis and possible disagreement.

Net Worth and the Question of True Value

The net worth of a company is the amount by which the assets exceed the liabilities. If the balance sheet showed

Total Assets	$4,325,000
minus Total Liabilities	$2,125,000
= Owners' Equity	$2,200,000

then the net worth of the firm, by the accounting point of view, would be the owners' equity, $2,200,000.

Maybe this company could be bought for $2,200,000 if the buyer would also take over the debt of $2,125,000. If the owners thought that the company was worth more, then you could not buy it for just the net worth. If the owners were particularly in a hurry to sell and had not found another willing buyer, then it might sell for less than the net worth. If the buyer felt that the assets list included a lot of overvalued, obsolete goods, then the buyer might bid substantially less than the net worth.

However, net worth does represent one view of the intrinsic value of the company. Net worth may be considered a reasonable estimate of the "true value" of the firm because the financial statements have to follow generally accepted accounting principles. Both the chief financial officer and the independent auditor have good reason to try to ensure that they are accurate. On the other hand, net worth is a frail representative of true value of the firm in some cases. Consider a small, new biotechnology firm with assets of $17.9 million and liabilities of $13.4 million. Then the net worth, in the accountant's sense, is $4.5 million (17.9 – 13.4). However, suppose that this firm has a new drug in development which they believe may bring them a new patent. Perhaps they will sell the patent to Bristol-Meyers for $30 million. Aha! Now we see the true value of the firm is well over the equity figure. On the other hand, suppose they have just been sued in a class action that claims that one of their drugs caused skin discoloration in ninety-four children. Now you may think that the true value of the firm is zero.

Lesson: The net worth of the firm is a well-defined and simple concept that can be easily determined from the balance sheet. It may or may not give a good measure of the value of the firm. Remember that the balance sheet only reflects those facts that the accountants have been told to measure.

Another view of the worth of a company is based on the individual investor's situation. What we expect to get back from an investment in the shares of a company is said by many to be the current value of the long-term future earnings of the company. Remember that, given decent management and decisions by the board of directors, all of the earnings of the corporation would go to increased value for the shareholders.

Example: Ford Motor Corporation's annual report for 1995 showed that, at the end of 1995, the net worth (from the balance sheet) was $24,547,000,000. For ease of use, let us say $24.5 billion. At the same time, the market cap of Ford was close to $30 billion. If you actually wanted to buy the company, it probably would have taken a good deal more than that to buy up all the shares. So it is not clear exactly what the true value of Ford was on December 31, 1995, as the net worth and the market cap gave us two different rough estimates.

The equity per share of Ford common stock was about $25, which is the total equity divided by the number of common shares. About the same time, the Standard & Poor's April 1996 *earnings guide* reported that Ford had a net tangible book value of $15.53 per share. This net tangible book value is the number they compute after taking the equity and subtracting some items that are in the assets or capitalization reports but are of uncertain real value. That includes, for instance, something called *goodwill*[1], which shows up in the assets listing but is of debatable worth to the corporation. In the case of Ford, it would be worth a lot, because it would include the value of the name *Ford*.

Example: The Southern Company's annual report for 1995 showed a net worth of $10.1 billion from the balance sheet. At the same time, their stock was valued at $25 per share for 667 million shares. So the market cap was about $16.7 billion. Evidently, stock market investors, on balance, thought the future earnings of the company were worth more than what

---

[1] *Goodwill* is hard to nail down. For some companies the goodwill figure simply represents some excess valuation over the hard assets that has been built up over the life of the firm. That may include the value of the regular clients list. It is always made up of intangible assets. In some cases, the goodwill may include the value of a name that might be sold with the corporation. If you bought the Pepsi corporation, you would pay a lot for the value of their name, which is counted among the goodwill assets.

the accountants showed on the balance sheet.[2] The earnings per share for the Southern Company from 1991 to 1995 were $1.24, $1.51, $1.57, $1.52, $1.66. The stock was priced so that investors thought that a continuation of that trend (whatever trend they saw) was worth a current valuation of $25 per share.

Net worth is essentially a backward-looking concept. It summarizes the total values the company has established over its history, but says little or nothing about where the products and sales may be going next. As such, it is more widely used by value-oriented investors, who want current facts, and less used by growth investors, who are inclined to speculate more about new developments.

> **Lesson:** The net worth of a firm is easy to find. This may be considered a rough guide to the true value of a firm. However, each case must be considered separately to see whether the net worth is reliable. Most analysts prefer to talk about the worth or value of a firm in terms of per-share values, because it becomes easy to compare to stock price.

Book Value Related to Net Worth and True Value

Many analysts and publications look on book value as a measure of the true intrinsic worth of a corporation. If the company has no preferred stock, then book value is equal to the net worth (assets – liabilities).

If a company has preferred stock, then the preferred stock must be considered as additional liabilities. That is, if you wanted to know what the common stockholders actually own, then you would have to start with assets, subtract the liabilities and also subtract the cost of paying off all the preferred shareholders to find what the common shareholders own.

As an example, let's look again at the Alpha Beta Publishing Company. From our earlier discussion we saw from the financial reports that they had total assets of $71.72 million (and liabilities of $5.58 million), but that

---

[2] It is very important to remember that it is not the accountants' job to value the stock or to help predict future pricing of the stock. Their job is to report the financial status of the company, and any changes in that status, as accurately as they can using generally accepted accounting principles. Never blame the accountants for your success or failure as an investor.

included $1 million of goodwill. They had 18,900,000 common shares outstanding at a current price of $6, and they had $2.5 million of preferred shareholders' equity. So we may calculate several different measures of the value of the company.

For ABPCO we can start with:

Assets	$71.72 million
– liabilities	–$5.58 million
= Net worth	= $66.14 million

Then see different ways to measure the "value" of ABPCO:

Stockholder's equity =	$66.14 million
Net worth =	$66.14 million

The net worth of the common shareholders' part is $63.64 million because we subtract the preferred stock value ($2.5 million), but we get a more conservative estimate of the book value if we subtract out the goodwill asset of $1 million:

Book value (conservative) =	$62.64 million
Market cap =	$113.4 million (that is $6 x 18.9 million shares)

To look at value on a per-share basis we could calculate:

Net worth per share = ($66.14 million ÷ 18.9 million)	$3.50
Common stock net worth per share = ($63.64 million ÷ 18.9 million)	$3.37
Book value per share = ($63.64 million ÷ 18.9 million)	$3.37
Conservative book value per share ($62.64 million ÷ 18.9 million)	$3.31
True value of the stock	whatever you think it is
Future value of the stock	whatever you predict
Fair price of the stock	whatever a willing buyer and a willing seller can agree on to make a trade

Lesson: It is not always perfectly clear what people mean when they talk about the value of a company or its stock. Different investors and analysts have differing opinions as to which of the preceding views is more useful, and views may also vary from one industry to another.

Some investors may set the value of a company higher or lower for reasons of their own. For example, some may choose to never invest in cigarette companies, banks, or companies that profit from nuclear power. That is entirely a personal decision. If you have personal reasons for avoiding or preferring some business factors (that is, reasons that do not show up in the financial analysis), then you might want to pursue the topic of socially responsible investing. That is far afield from my purpose in this book, but you can find many mutual funds that will help you with such conscientious investing.

Value Investing

Value investing is the practice of finding and buying stocks for which the market price is less than the true value of the firm. Which true value? That is open to debate, but many investors will use indicators such as the net worth or the book value per share. Other indicators of value include the current earnings and the projected future earnings. We will look at many other indicators of value later. It is possible to present compelling arguments that certain combinations of measurements almost guarantee getting a good indication of the value of a stock. One fine book that has a clearly stated argument in favor of value investing, along with clear rules to follow for a method of value investing, is *The Intelligent Investor* by Ben Graham.

Ratios

Analysts usually try to measure and describe the past, present, and future of a company. The success or failure of each investment must be worked out in the future, but they hope that the past and present, as shown in the financial statements, will help to forecast the future. Many of the indicators that can be measured are computed by taking ratios. Examples of useful ratios that we will learn to use include

- profit per each dollar of assets

- profit per each share of common stock

- debt per each dollar of equity

The first two ratios are measurements of the past year's business operations. The last one is a measure of the current financial strength of the company and the business philosophy of the managers.

Suppose you are looking at two companies and know that one stock is
priced at $18 and the other at $52. Does that tell you which is the better
deal? No, it does not. Many other factors have to be considered. Suppose
you are looking at a quart of milk and a pair of shoes. The milk is $1.10
for the quart, and the shoes are $97.50. Does that tell you which is a bet-
ter product or a better buy? No, it does not. You need to compare comparable things—apples to apples, not milk to shoes.

The same consideration holds true in investing. In order to help in comparing comparable things and comparing the value of stocks, we express

"So, what do you think?"

many measurements in ratios. Frequently the ratios show measurement per common share. We have already made some comparisons in looking at net worth, equity, and book value. The most used measurement of all is the stock price, which is always quoted in price per common share.

Suppose you were interested in buying Procter & Gamble and asked your broker for the price. She comes back at you with:

"The Procter & Gamble Company is selling today for $95.9 billion."

"Uh, no. I just wanted a few shares."

"In that case, you can divide the price by the number of shares outstanding."

"Uh, no, I thought you might do that for me."

"Yes sir, the number of shares outstanding is 1.35 billion, so the price per share is $110. Let me help you into 200 of those."

You see, in some cases you expect or require your broker and the newspapers to give you the data in per-share values.

Price-to-Earnings Ratio

If you were evaluating two similar businesses by looking at their estimated earnings in 1998, you might find the Zebra Company estimated to earn $20 million and the Giraffe Company to earn $18 million. That does not tell you which of the two stocks is the better buy. Suppose you know that the price of Zebra stock is $5 per share and the price of Giraffe stock is $8. That still doesn't tell you which is a better buy because it does not show what you get for each dollar invested or for each share purchased. What you need is the earnings per share of the company. Suppose, now, that I tell you that Zebra has twelve million shares of common stock and Giraffe has sixty-five million. Then you could compute something:

Zebra earns $20 million to be shared among twelve million shares. That means each share earns $20 million ÷ 12 million, which is $1.67.

Giraffe earns $18 million to be shared among sixty-five million shares. That means each share earns $18 million ÷ 65 million, which is $0.28.

For the Zebra Company stock, you would pay $5 to get your $1.67 of each share's earnings. For the Giraffe Company stock, you would pay $8 to get your 28¢ of per-share earnings.

Is it better to pay $5 for a Zebra share to earn $1.67, or to pay $8 for a Giraffe share to earn 28¢? Obviously, Zebra looks better.

> **Lesson:** The first point of evaluating earnings is to compare how much you pay per share of stock to how much each share will earn. The way we compare those two things is to use a price/earnings ratio.

The price-to-earnings (P/E) ratio is the price per share of stock divided by the earnings per share (EPS). For Zebra, the P/E ratio is $5/$1.67 = 3; for Giraffe, the P/E ratio is $8/$0.28 = 29. For Zebra, the price is 3 times earnings; for Giraffe, the price is 29 times earnings.

Another way to look at this is to ask how much you would have to pay to obtain stock to earn $1. The P/E ratio tells how much. For Zebra stock, you would pay $3 to earn each $1. For Giraffe stock you would pay $29 to obtain enough stock to earn $1. The P/E ratio is the number of dollars you would have to invest to earn $1:

- If the P/E = 10, then for each $1 of earnings, you pay $10 for stock.

- If the P/E = 6, then for each $1 of earnings, you pay $6 for stock.

- If the P/E = 32, then for each $1 of earnings, you pay $32 for stock.

Here is another way to use the P/E ratio. Suppose that you had $2,000 to invest in either Zebra stock or Giraffe stock. If you bought Zebra, then your stock would earn 2,000 ÷ 3 = $667 per year; if you bought Giraffe stock, your stock would earn $2,000 ÷ 28 = $71 per year. Again this makes it appear that the Zebra stock is a more attractive buy than the Giraffe stock.

These calculations using the price/earnings ratio do not by any means tell the whole story of the stock purchase question, but they do tell one important part of the story that should be considered by all investors. There probably would be some good reason why Giraffe sells for twenty-eight times earnings and Zebra sells for three times earnings. This means that the

*"If I can just compute these ratios . . .
then we're gonna make some money!"*

market in general puts a higher valuation on Giraffe[3]. An astute investor
would find out why. But all investors (except pure technicians[4]) look at and
consider the price/earnings ratio as part of their decision-making process.

Now suppose you were analyzing the earnings of two companies, say
Apple Computer and Dell Computer in April 1996. In their 1995 fiscal years,
Apple earned $413 million and Dell earned $260 million. Apple had 124
million shares and Dell had 95 million. In April 1996, Apple's share price
was $25 and Dell shares sold for $41.

The earnings per share (EPS):

Apple EPS = $413 million ÷ 124 million shares = $3.33

Dell EPS = $260 million ÷ 95 million shares = $2.74

The price-to-earnings ratios:

Apple P/E = $25 ÷ $3.33 = 7.5

Dell P/E = $41 ÷ $2.74 = 15

---

[3] That might occur if Giraffe had a new product line that looked very impressive or if Zebra had suffered some bad publicity recently.

[4] The author confesses that he has never met or heard of a pure technician.

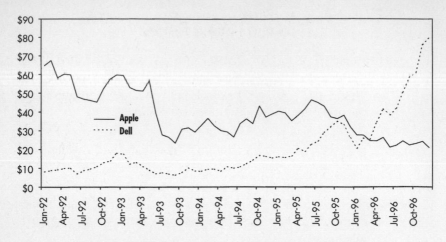

Stock Prices of Apple Computer & Dell Computer 1992–1996

In terms of the P/E ratio, you now see two things. First, Apple would have provided $1 of earnings at half the cost of Dell. Strictly in terms of earnings power, Apple looked like a better buy. However, this also tells you that the market in general valued Dell much higher. The market was willing to pay higher to get a dollar of Dell's earnings. This implied that other investors, on average, either thought that Dell would grow faster to produce higher earnings, or else they thought Apple carried higher risks of not maintaining their earnings.

In January 1997, Apple was selling at $18 per share and losing a lot of money on operations, while Dell was selling at $60 per share and making more than ever before.

> The market tells you a lot about other investors' opinions, and you should pay attention.

> **Lesson on P/E ratio:** The P/E ratio is one significant piece of information to look at in evaluating a stock. It does not tell the whole story.

Yield and Payout Ratios

The yield of a stock is the ratio of dividends paid (annually) divided by the stock price. The yield changes whenever the directors change the dividend payment, or the market changes the stock price. The payout ratio is the dividend per share divided by the earnings per share.

Example: In their fiscal year 1992, the FPL Group, Inc. (then Florida Power and Light) reported earnings of $2.65 per share and dividends of $2.43 per share. The stock price at the end of the year was near $37. The yield was the dividend divided by the stock price, 2.43 ÷ 37 = 7 percent. At the time that was regarded as a pretty good yield. This stock was attractive to most of those investors for whom income was an important need. The dividend had been steadily increasing for over ten years, and appeared to be safe because the company was increasing earnings fast enough to continue to increase the dividend. One significant factor of evaluation for those investors who wanted to buy FPL for the dividend was the safety of the dividend, which could be considered by looking at how much of the earnings had to go to pay dividend. In the case of Florida Power and Light, the dividend ($2.43) was 92 percent of the earnings ($2.65). That is a lot to pay out, but if earnings are steady and predictable, and if the company has a long tradition of paying high yield, then it is probably okay.

The next year the earnings and yield of FPL went up: the 1993 EPS equaled $2.75, and the dividend equaled $2.47. The dividend was then 90 percent of the earnings. However, in 1994 the directors of FPL made a decision that they had better things to do with the earnings. They made a decision to keep more of the earnings to generate and support new business. In 1994 and 1995, the earnings and yield were

1994: EPS = $2.91, dividend = $1.88

1995: EPS = $3.16, dividend = $1.76

The payout (dividends-to-earnings) ratio fell to 65 percent and then to 56 percent. So for FPL in 1995, it was $1.76 ÷ $3.16 = 56 percent. The payout ratio tells you two things. First, it reflects the attitude and wisdom of the directors in deciding how they should take care of the earnings; how much they should keep within their own control for new business or emergencies and how much they should pay to the shareholders. Second, it indicates something about the safety and predictability of the dividend.

If a company is paying out nearly 100 percent, or even more than 100 percent, of the earnings in dividend, then any surprises or problems in new earnings may leave them unable to continue the dividend level. That would be a problem for investors who need and depend on the dividend for their living expenses.

In the case of FPL, many of their shareholders were bitterly disappointed and hurt by the decision to lower the dividend payout. The price of the stock fell sharply at the time, but has recovered and gone on to new highs since then. Many shareholders were doubly hurt because they not only lost their dividend, but they also probably sold the stock at the wrong time to move into another higher-yield stock, and thus had to sell at the low price.

In evaluating a stock for purchase, regardless of whether dividend is important to you, you should realize that it is important to many. Look at the history of the dividend yield over ten years or more and also look at the history of the dividend payout ratio to estimate whether they can maintain it. Remember that the individual investor who needs dividend is at the mercy of the directors who set the dividend policy. You do, however, get to vote for those directors, so try to elect directors who support your needs.

If you find a company—for example, SCANA Corp. of Columbia, SC— that has consistently paid out a dividend and consistently raised it every year for many years, then it is reasonable to presume that the directors intend to continue that practice. The only question would be whether the earnings will hold up sufficiently to protect the amount of the dividend pay-out. In the case of SCANA, you would see (you could find this in the *Value Line*) that the payout ratio usually stays around 75–80 percent, and the earnings are steadily growing, so the dividend should be safe for a while.

One anomaly of payout deserves attention. On occasion, you may find a company where the payout ratio is greater than 100 percent for a year or two. That means that the directors have decided to pay out all of the earnings and also take some from previous years' retained earnings to pay the dividend in the current year. They may do that to cover up for one year's poor earnings when they want to maintain their long-term record of protecting the dividend. That may be a smart thing to do on rare occasions, but it obviously cannot go on long. The corporation cannot consistently pay out more than they earn. If you see a company with a payout greater than its earnings, then take that as a warning sign. If it happens twice, then it is a substantial red flag. However, just for balance, you may note that

*"Don't tell me it's down! I know what that stock is worth.
Don't tell me that!"*

Chrysler, Ford, and General Motors all paid out more than they earned in 1990 and 1991, and they all returned to substantial profits in the next four years. In fact, 1991 was the prime time to buy all three. Somebody said you want to buy when there is blood in the streets. Maybe so. You also want to keep your head down and your eyes open.

Recommended Further Reading

Graham, Ben. *The Intelligent Investor*, 4th rev. ed. New York: HarperCollins, 1986.

The Easiest View of
Financial Analysis

Financial analysis is the science, or art, or magic, of taking the figures
reported in the financial reports and making sense out of them. We have
already seen a little of that. You can take the earnings and dividend amounts
and compute a payout ratio, then try to figure out what that means for a
decision on buying the stock. A great many other such calculations are useful. We will look at some of the most important basic ideas in this chapter.

Price-to-Cash-Flow Ratio

An illustration of cash flow: Arcadian Wine was a company that grew
grapes and sold wine. In 477 B.C. they sold wine for 39,000 drachmas,
and paid 33,000 to workers and middlemen. They set aside 2,000 drachmas for next spring's gift to the Temple of Apollo, and paid taxes of 1,000
drachmas. Here is what they reported to the tax collector, and what they
had in the bank:

	Reported to Tax Collector	Cash on Hand
Revenue	39,000 DR	
minus expenses	33,000 DR	
minus Apollo fund	2,000 DR	——-> 2,000 DR
Equals income	4,000 DR	
minus taxes	1,000 DR	
Equals earnings	3,000 DR	——-> 3,000 DR
	net cash flow =	5,000 DR

The point is that they have the 5,000 DR in the bank. They promised it to Apollo, but they have the money and could use it for any purpose if they got in a bind. So the cash flow is a better indicator of their financial strength than the earnings reported.

In current business reporting, instead of a gift to Apollo, corporations might set aside money (before taxes) for depreciation. That money goes into a fund to replace current buildings or equipment, but it's still cash on hand that they could use. Cash flow is good for a company. Higher cash flow means the management has more choices to pursue new lines of business or reduce long-term debt, or reward the shareholders. Positive net cash flow for the year goes directly to increase the company's reserves and financial strength. Negative net cash flow has the opposite effect. Some analysts consider cash flow as the best indication of the overall strength of a company.

More cash flow at a lower price is good for a stock buyer. The price-to-cash-flow ratio is used to measure how much the stock buyer pays to earn a given dollar of cash flow. Higher cash flow gives management more flexibility to control the company's situation. With more cash flow, they might accumulate cash, reduce the debt, pay higher dividends, or plan to start new lines of business. If you can buy a stock with higher cash flow for a low stock price, then that points to a good deal for the buyer. It is a *value* indicator.

The price-to-cash-flow ratio equals the price per share divided by cash flow per share (use the annual cash flow). It directly measures how much you would pay to get a dollar of cash flow from this company. Lower values of price-to-cash-flow ratio are better than higher values. A lower value indicates that the stock buyer pays less to get a dollar of cash flow.

Examples using price and cash flow values: If you could buy a stock for $22 per share that had $2.90 per share in cash flow, then the price-to-cash-flow ratio would be 22 ÷ 2.90 = 7.6, a respectable and decent value for this ratio. But if the same stock were priced at $28, then the price-to-cash-flow ratio would be 28 ÷ 2.90 = 9.7; it would then be a somewhat less attractive deal with regard to cash flow (it might still be a good buy for other reasons). If another stock were priced at $22 also, but had cash flow of $3.70, then its price-to-cash-flow ratio would be 22 ÷ 3.70 = 5.9, which is a very appealing number for that ratio. However, if another stock also priced at $22 had a lower cash flow, say $1.50, then its ratio would be 22 ÷ 1.50 = 14.7 which would be unattractive.

For Alpha Beta Publishing Company, in our earlier example (see p. 75) we found the net cash flow from operating activities to be $4,817,000 for 1997. In this example, the company had sold $1 million of new stock, but we should not include that in cash-flow analysis because that was an isolated one-time event. We are interested in the normal, ongoing business operation, so we use the cash flow from ordinary business operations. For the same reason we will subtract the proceeds from sale of the music division from the cash flow. That amount had been included in the earnings and income analysis, but it is obviously a one-time special event, not part of regular operations. That $758,000 (from the income statement) is subtracted from the cash flow, leaving $4,059,000. The cash flow per share for 1997 equals $4,059,000 ÷ 18,900,000 shares = $0.215. If we look at the stock in January 1998, when the price per share was $6; the price-to-cash-flow ratio equals $6 ÷ $0.215 = 28.

One way to read that is to say that to buy $1 of cash flow, you have to invest $28 in stock purchase. That should be compared with other publishing companies. If we check the fifteen publishing companies listed in the *Value Line*, we find that their price-to-cash-flow ratios vary from a low of 5 to a high of 19 for the thirteen companies that are profitable. This shows that Alpha Beta does not do as good a job of generating cash flow as most of their competitors. This is still indirectly related to that problem of the high level of idle cash that they have. If the cash were earning as much as 6 percent instead of only 1 percent, then the cash flow would improve by $1.75 million per year, and the price-to-cash-flow ratio would change to 20, which would be better.

Price-to-Sales Ratio

The price-to-sales ratio measures how much the stock buyer pays for each dollar of sales. It is calculated as the stock price per share divided by the sales per share. Sales per share can be calculated by taking total sales (or revenue) and dividing by the number of common shares.

Example: For Alpha Beta Publishing, the annual sales were $97 million and there were 18,900,000 shares. The sales per share would be $97 million ÷ 18,900,000 = $5.13. The price-to-sales ratio would be $6 ÷ $5.13 = 1.2.

A low price-to-sales ratio is a good indicator of value in the stock, but should be compared across companies in similar business, or within industry groups.

The following table shows some companies' price-to-sales ratios, and price-to-earnings ratios, at end of 1995, and the change in stock price over the next year (price measured at end of 1996):

Financial Ratios for the End of 1995

Company	Price $	Sales per Share	Price/Sales Ratio $	EPS $	P/E Ratio	Percent Price Change[1]
Apple Comp.	32	90	0.4	3.33	9.6	– 28%
Dell Comp.	32	57	0.6	2.74	11.7	+250%
Duke Power	47	23	2.0	3.25	14.5	0
Potomac Electric	26	16	1.6	1.70	15.3	– 4%
General Motors	51	225	0.2	7.20	7.1	+ 10%
Chrysler	54	177	0.3	5.30	10.2	+ 26%

Price-to-sales ratios vary widely among industries. Look at the two computer companies, Apple and Dell. Apple had the better (lower) price/sales ratio and the better (lower) price/earnings ratio, yet over the next year, Dell was a better investment. Both of those companies' ratios would have been regarded as attractive in December 1995. In the automobile industry, GM had a more appealing price/sales ratio and a more appealing

---

[1] Adjusted for splits in Chrysler and Dell.

price/earnings ratio than Chrysler, but Chrysler turned out to be the better investment. Again, with those two, both ratios would have been regarded as attractive by most investors. In the electric utilities industry, comparing Duke Power and Potomac Electric, these ratios are not so useful as value indicators. The total return in utilities will be much more a function of their yield and safety.[2]

> **Lesson:** A low price-to-sales ratio is one indicator of a possible attractive price for a stock, and a low price-to-earnings ratio is also. These ratios taken alone do not provide a sufficient basis for deciding to buy a stock.[3]

Return on Investment

For the individual stock investor there are several ways to measure the return that the investment provides. We saw one earlier, the rate of total return obtained from the dividend and stock price change over a year. Other ways of measuring return address the question of how well the management is using the assets of the company. You can examine that by measuring earnings as a percentage of total assets, one measurement of the managers' skill at their jobs. You can also measure the earnings as a percentage of the stockholders' equity, a measure of what the managers are doing for the stockholders. Another way of measuring return is to look at return on capital.

In discussing these different measures of return on investment (ROI), we will frequently need to refer to the usual average values within various groups. I will be using approximate values over the past five to ten years taken from the *Value Line*'s industry summaries that they show for ninety-nine different industry groups. Those summaries are included in their regular monthly reports, and about five to ten of them are updated in each monthly issue. You can also find those values in the *S&P Industry Reports* and annual surveys of business by magazines such as *Forbes* or *Business Week*. Most of those sources can be found in a local library.

---

[2] This will change over the next five years as deregulation sets into the industry.
[3] There is, however, some statistical evidence that for buyers of large amounts of stocks, such as 50 or 100 different stocks, the ratios may be taken as adequate selection indicators by themselves. See O'Shaughnessy's book, *What Works on Wall Street*.

Return on Assets

The return on assets (ROA) is the annual earnings divided by the total assets. This should be interpreted relative to the rate shown by other companies in the same industry. ROA varies widely among different industries. For instance, the major automotive manufacturers may have a return near 10 to 15 percent in good years. The utilities have return on assets consistently near 7 to 8 percent. Banks will typically have return on assets close to 1 percent. If you want the current assets of the firm you can look in the *Standard & Poor's Stock Guide*, probably in your library. The *Value Line* does not list the total assets, and it is difficult to compute it from what they do list.

For Alpha Beta Publishing, the return on assets equals earnings divided by assets or $4,606,000 ÷ $71,720,000 = 6 percent. For other publishing companies, it is typically close to 15 percent. Once again, Alpha Beta is not looking good.

Return on Equity

The return on equity (ROE) measures how much the earnings give in relation to the total amount of ownership capital the shareholders have in the firm. This figure is found by dividing the earnings for a year by the shareholders' equity. Just use the common shareholders' equity. To get the common shareholders' equity, take the equity from the balance sheet and subtract the preferred shareholders' equity. You can find good reference values for the return on equity from several sources, but you have to be careful how you read them. Some sources report the percent earned on total shareholders' equity, which includes preferred stockholders' equity, and some report the percent earned on common equity.

> *Shareholders' equity = total assets − total liabilities*[4]
>
> *Common equity = shareholders' equity − preferred shareholder's equity*

Different sources that you read may use either of these equity values to calculate the return on equity. For some companies it won't matter a great

---

[4] The *Value Line* uses the term *net worth* instead of shareholders' equity.

deal which equity value you use because the common shareholders' equity may be practically all of the total shareholders' equity.

When you look for reference information using the return on equity, you may go to the *Value Line, Standard & Poor's Industry Reports*, the *Business Week* annual and quarterly reports on corporate profits, or *Forbes' Annual Report on American Industry*. All of these sources contain a wealth of information for the stock buyer. Just be sure that you are comparing apples to apples. Compare values that all used total equity, or else all used common equity. Try not to mix those numbers. Also compare values within an industry group. It would not be useful to compare the rates of return of Coca-Cola and The Southern Company (at least not until after the power companies are totally deregulated). The return on equity, like so many other figures, only becomes useful when you use it to compare numbers within an industry group. For the chemical industry, it should usually be 16 to 18 percent. For the drugstore industry, it should typically be 13 to 15 percent. For the household products industry (Clorox, Kimberly-Clark, Oneida), it should typically be 23 percent to 26 percent.

For the publishing industry, it is usually 18 to 22 percent. For Alpha Beta Publishing Company, the return on total equity equals $4,606,000 ÷ $66,140,000, or 7.0 percent, and the return on common equity equals $4,606,000 ÷ $63,640,000, or 7.2 percent.

The two values are close enough together so that either would be good enough for your decision-making process. For example, we see here that Alpha Beta is not up to par among its industry group. Also, it is not a very strong figure for return in any sense, since you can get almost as much from Treasury bonds and have a far lower risk than investing in stock.

To give you a few examples of how stock prices may move with return on equity, here are some results reported in 1994, 1995, and 1996.

	1994	1995	1996
Black & Decker			
Return on equity (%)	11	13	15
End-of-year stock price ($)	24	36	32
End-of-year P/E ratio	18	19	20
Potomac Electric			
Return on equity (%)	11	11	11
End-of-year stock price ($)	19	25	25
End-of-year P/E ratio	11	15	15

	1994	1995	1996
Proctor & Gamble			
Return on equity (%)	25	25	25
End-of-year stock price ($)	61	83	110
End-of-year P/E ratio	20	22	23

Many other factors are at work here, and you cannot infer much from the numbers above, but generally speaking, a higher return on equity supports a higher price/earnings ratio.

Potomac Electric pays a high yield. Many investors look upon it as an income investment, not growth oriented. Therefore, the stock price is strongly affected by prevailing long-term interest rates. The dividend is very predictable, and investors will adjust share price bids so that the yield stays close to the yield on long-term Treasury bonds. Because it has been a regulated utility, investors assumed that the management could not do much to get the return on equity much different than 11 percent. That may be changing. The utilities industry is a place for some brave entrepreneurs and smart investors to make some money over the next ten years (or lose some).

Black & Decker is strongly affected by opinions about their new products each year, and the results of those products should be reflected in that year's financial results (fiscal year ends 12/31).

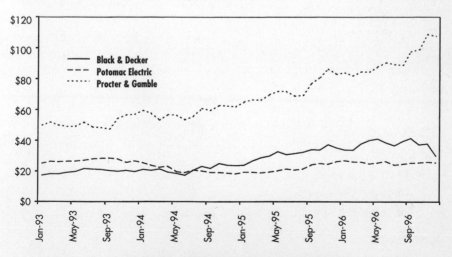

**Stock Prices of Black & Decker, Potomac Electric,
and Procter & Gamble 1993–1996**

Proctor & Gamble is widely regarded as a "growth stock." People believe that the earnings will continue to grow faster than most other businesses, and that deserves a higher P/E ratio.

Rate of Growth

Rate of growth has a strong effect on the price and P/E ratio of every stock. If revenues and earnings stay the same, or nearly the same, for years on end, then many investors will assume the value of the stock should stay the same, too. However, if the company has a history of continually growing earnings, then people will assume that the stock price will continue to grow, and they will bid it higher. This is most clearly represented in the P/E ratio. If investors are willing to pay ten times the earnings for a stock with no growth, then they may be willing to pay fifteen times the earnings for a stock with slow, steady growth, and twenty-two times the earnings for a stock with sustained high growth. Here are some examples.

Potomac Electric is not considered to be a growth stock.

	1992	1993	1994	1995	1996
Earnings per share ($)	1.66	1.95	1.79	1.70	1.80
End-of-year stock price ($)	24	26	19	25	25
End-of-year P/E ratio	14	13	11	15	14

Campbell Soup has shown good, steady, but not spectacular growth.

	1992	1993	1994	1995	1996
Earnings per share ($)	1.95	2.21	2.51	2.80	1.88
End-of-year stock price ($)	43	40	45	50	50
End-of-year P/E ratio	22	18	18	18	27

Coca-Cola is growth in a bottle. Besides, Warren Buffet likes the company, and a billion Chinese can't wait to get their Cokes; this may be a no-brainer.

	1992	1993	1994	1995	1996
Earnings per share ($)	1.43	1.68	1.98	2.36	2.80
End-of-year stock price ($)	41	42	50	78	108[5]
End-of-year P/E ratio	29	25	25	33	39

Stock Prices of Potomac Electric, Coca-Cola, and Campbell 1992–1997

Whatever price/earnings ratio the markets allow a stock is usually called its multiple. Multiples change over time as investors grow more optimistic or more cautious. Multiples are usually fairly consistent with companies in similar businesses, except if one of them is not doing well. If we look at Ford, Chrysler, and GM for 1986 through 1994, we see these average price/earnings ratios:

	1986	1987	1988	1989	1990	1991	1992	1993	1994
Chrysler	4	6	5	18			15	7	5
Ford	4	5	4	5	21			11	6
GM	9	8	6	7				21	8

[5] Split-adjusted values. There was a stock split in 1996.

The blank spaces show when the earnings were negative. When the company loses money, then the P/E ratio doesn't mean anything.

This table shows that in 1986 the market valued Ford and Chrysler earnings less than GM's. In 1989 it valued Chrysler's higher. All of these price/earnings ratios were founded on prices determined in the market by investors trying to look a year or two ahead at each company's prospects.

Stock Prices Over Ten Years

Calculating the Rate of Growth

Many investors are influenced by a company's prior year's rate of growth in sales and earnings. Many analysts make assumptions about continued rates of growth of sales and earnings. As we have seen, it is difficult to forecast those values reliably. You can calculate prior years' growth rates exactly from the reported earnings statements, but future forecasts based on assumed growth rates are fragile. It is risky business to make a buy/sell decision about a stock based on forecasted growth rates. You should use the growth rate calculations as supporting evidence of the possible fair value for a stock, along with everything else you can learn about the company.

Here are some examples of growth-rate calculations. The first example is fictitious, to make the numbers nice and easy. Let us say that the company is the Riotous Managed Care Corporation, and their annual reports for the past five years have shown:

	1993	1994	1995	1996	1997
Revenue (million $)	187	215	250	290	332
Earnings per share ($)	0.12	0.15	0.19	0.23	0.30
End-of-year share price($)	1.20	1.75	2.40	3.95	5.11

That is an annual growth of approximately 15 percent in revenues and approximately 25 percent in earnings, consistent over the five years.

Let us assume that at the end of 1997, you are considering whether you should buy this stock. Assume also that you have already studied everything else you can learn about the company, and you are convinced that they are sound and will continue to grow and strengthen their business. The question before us now is what price makes the stock a good buy.

The P/E ratios over the five years have been 10, 13, 13, 17, 17, and the share price has climbed steadily. Some analysts use a rule of thumb that if the percentage of sustained growth rate of earnings is greater than the P/E ratio, then the price is good to buy the stock. In this case, the percentage of sustained growth rate of earnings is about 25 percent. According to that rule of thumb, the $5.11 price is attractive for these shares because the current P/E ratio is less than 25.

This rests on an assumption that the growth rate of earnings will continue as it has in the past. In order to calculate from past growth rates, you must make some assumptions about growth continuation, and that is where a high degree of judgment and risk come into the picture. However, in this case, let's say that you are willing to make that bet. Then you might reasonably expect, over the next three years, to see that the earnings and share price go like this:

Earnings increase by 25 percent each year:

	1998	1999	2000
Earnings per share ($)	0.38	0.48	0.59
P/E ratio	17	17	17
Share price ($)	6.46	8.08	10.09

This table assumes that other investors will continue to like this stock enough to maintain a P/E ratio of 17. But that is what you expect from a growth stock. The share price will be the P/E ratio times the earnings per share.

You might even want to assume that the P/E ratio will continue to climb since the stock is getting a lot of attention, and the P/E ratio has climbed for the last few years. Suppose that you look at a case where the P/E increases each year.

Earnings increase 25 percent and the P/E ratio is forced up by the market:

	1998	**1999**	**2000**
Earnings per share ($)	0.38	0.48	0.59
P/E ratio	17	20	25
Share price ($)	6.46	9.60	14.75

This looks like very dramatic growth and profit in the share price. Surely you want to buy this stock. Put all your money into it. Mortgage the ranch and sell the car. It's a no-brainer!

It will be easy to whip yourself into a frenzy. Remember that all of these numbers are dependent on assumptions (guesses) that the growth rates will continue. Also remember that trying to predict future earnings is tricky and unsteady business.

Current Assets, Current Liabilities, and the Current Ratio

Some of a firm's assets are intended to be used sooner and some later. Some are available for immediate use, and some are not. If the company has $300,000 cash in the bank, that could be used for any immediate purpose. If the company has $3 billion worth of coal inside a mountain, that may not be usable for any purpose for a few years.

Current assets are those assets that are either cash or near cash. *Near cash* means assets that may reasonably be expected to be converted to cash soon. Near cash would include the accounts receivable, assuming they are normally paid in full within a year. Another current asset is inventory for sale, since it is normally expected to be sold soon. Whatever is listed in the balance sheet as current assets is normally assumed to be converted to cash within a year or might be converted to cash soon if the company needed the cash.

The current assets are usually in a state of change as goods are built and sold, payments are collected, and money is spent on expenses.

Current liabilities are those liabilities that must be paid within a year. That principally includes accounts payable, current interest on debt, income tax, accrued wages, and debt that is due in the year. It may also include special items, such as legal settlements.

The company will usually pay the current liabilities out of the current assets. Most of those payments will eventually come out of the cash account. Analysts always look to see whether the current assets are sufficient. The common way to do this is to look at another ratio, the current ratio. The *current ratio* is defined as the current assets divided by current liabilities. If this number is much higher than one, then the current accounts are safe; the company should not have any trouble paying bills within the coming year. If the current ratio is near one, then the current payments may be safe, but will require close attention and management. A current ratio near one may be an indicator that the managers have had a problem in cash flow that has gone unchecked for the past few years.

Example for Alpha Beta Publishing Co. (from Their Balance Sheet)

	($ millions)
Accounts receivable	6.61
+ Cash	29.38
+ Inventory	3.02
Total current assets =	$39.01
Notes due within a year	0.33
Accounts payable	2.77
Total current liabilities =	$3.10

The current ratio for Alpha Beta is 39.01 ÷ 3.10 = 12.58, an unusually high and safe number for the current ratio.

In the real world, let's look at Ruddick Corporation. They own the Harris Teeter grocery stores in the southeast United States, and American and Efird Thread Company. Looking in their 1996 annual report for current assets and current liabilities, one sees current assets of $298 million

| Consolidated Balance Sheets
Ruddick Corporation and Subsidiaries
September 29, 1996, and October 1, 1995

(Dollars in thousands)	1996	1995
Assets		
Current Assets		
Cash and Cash Equivalents	$ 21,033	$ 18,959
Accounts Receivable, Less Allowance For Doubtful		
Accounts: 1996 – $1,398; 1995 – $1,727	70,809	57,906
Inventories	183,649	177,395
Other Current Assets	22,569	32,131
Net Assets of Discontinued Operations	413	13,063
Total Current Assets	298,473	299,454
Property		
Land and Buildings	109,999	96,143
Machinery and Equipment	462,102	400,708
Leasehold Improvements	113,850	92,833
Assets Under Capital Leases	1,920	1,920
Total, at Cost	687,871	591,604
Accumulated Depreciation and Amortization	277,304	252,077
Property, Net	410,567	339,527
Investments and Other Assets		
Investments	29,841	28,729
Other Assets	62,821	47,608
Total Assets	$801,702	$715,318
Liabilities and Shareholders' Equity		
Current Liabilities		
Notes Payable	$ 7,118	$ 5,852
Current Portion of Long-term Debt	5,247	9,192
Dividends Payable	3,252	6,491
Accounts Payable	134,780	143,537
Federal and State Income Taxes	1,945	(253)
Accrued Compensation	34,677	28,911
Accrued Interest	20,530	13,623
Other Accrued Liabilities	25,790	18,360
Total Current Liabilities	233,339	225,713
Non-Current Liabilities		
Long-term Debt	159,188	119,760
Deferred Income Taxes	43,598	34,527
Other Liabilities	18,721	19,082
Commitments and Contingencies		
Shareholders' Equity		
Common Stock — Shares Outstanding:		
1996 – 46,461,290; 1995 – 46,373,666	55,599	54,816
Retained Earnings	293,654	262,921
Cumulative Translation Adjustments	(2,397)	(1,501)
Shareholders' Equity	346,856	316,236
Total Liabilities and Shareholders' Equity	$801,702	$715,318

The accompanying notes to consolidated financial statements are an integral part of these balance sheets.

and current liabilities of $233 million. Their current ratio is 298 ÷ 233 = 1.3, which is okay, but not great. Looking in the *Value Line* industry summary , most grocery stores show a current ratio between 1 and 1.7. Several of them show current ratios less than 1. Ruddick seemed to be satisfactory in this regard, but not too exciting.

If the current ratio is less than one, then current accounts are in trouble. Management will risk a nonpayment or potentially bankrupt condition within a year unless they do something to remedy the current accounts. Remedying the situation may be easy or difficult, depending on the debt position of the company and their continuing lines of credit, but a current ratio less than one is at all times a sign of trouble, and perhaps several years of trouble. At times, a company may be forced to sell (liquidate) inventory, always risky and nasty business. If they have to sell off inventory in a hurry to pay current debt requirements, then they may, in fact, end up getting less than a dollar for each dollar's worth of inventory they had in the assets list. Things don't always bring face value at a fire sale.

In case of a distress sale of inventory, then the total assets of the firm would be reduced, the shareholders' equity would be reduced, and that would almost always reflect unfavorably on the credit worthiness of the firm. If you don't want to calculate the current assets total and the current liabilities total from the balance sheet, then the *Value Line* will do it for you. When you do compute the current ratio of the firm, compare it to others in the same industry. That will give you the best indicator of what is normal and healthy for that industry.

Examples working with the current ratio (based on data reported in the *Value Line*): In the spring of 1996, the *Value Line* had fifteen companies reported in their section on the semiconductor industry group. Fourteen of the group had current ratios between 1.4 and 3. The fifteenth had a current ratio of 5.5. A ratio between 1.8 and 2.7 appears quite normal for the industry, and the ratio of 5.5 for Linear Technology Corporation (symbol LLTC on NASDAQ) was unusual. Let's look at three of those companies: Linear Technology, Micron Technology (symbol MU on the NYSE) and Analog Devices (symbol ADI on the NYSE).

Company	Current ratio
LLTC	5.5
ADI	2.1
MU	1.4

What shall we conclude about the current ratios? All three companies appear to be safe in regard to current payments for liabilities, because all three have current ratios above one, and near or above their sector average. The current ratio by itself indicates that these companies are satisfactory in the current liabilities management. It does not indicate that any one of them is necessarily a stock to buy. If you are a cautious investor, you might want to look a little closer into Micron Technology's cash-flow statement to make sure that 1.4 coverage on current liabilities was safe, but there is no big red flag waving here.

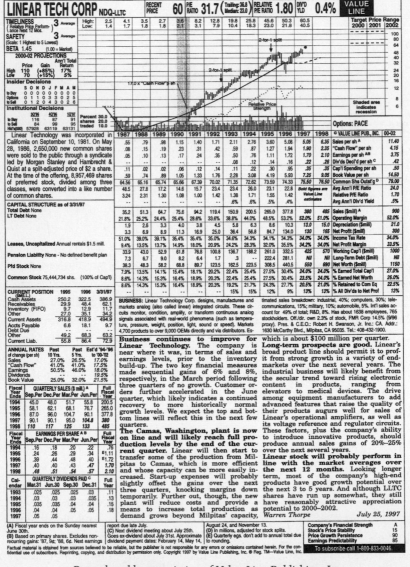

Reproduced by permission of Value Line Publishing, Inc.

But the current ratio is not the only factor to consider. If you like to buy larger companies, then MU looks better than the other two companies. It has total assets over $2,500 million, while both of the others are below $600 million. If you like to buy a lower P/E ratio, then again MU wins because its P/E ratio is about 11, while the others are much higher. If you like to buy companies with low long-term debt, then LLTC is better. It has no long-term debt, but the others have low debt. If you like to buy companies that pay a high yield, then none of these companies are satisfactory. All three pay dividends below 1 percent of their prices.

> **Lesson:** A high value of the current ratio, say over two, may indicate one aspect of safety for a company. Looking at any one ratio never tells you enough to decide that the stock is a good buy; however, it might tell you enough to decide that the stock is risky. It might indicate that you have some more research to do on a stock, or that you can find other safer candidates.

Long-Term Debt

Long-term debt is like a mortgage and is a fact of life for most corporations, just as for most homeowners. If they plan to buy long-lived assets, such as new buildings or land, they usually finance that through long-lived debt. Then the payments can be spread out over the productive life of the asset, and the liability for payment is more predictable and regular than new short-term debt financing. So most companies have debt that may last for ten or twenty years.

As an example, let's look at a homeowner. Eddie owns a home that has a fair market value of $140,000. The amount remaining to pay on his mortgage is $88,000. Then Eddie's equity is the difference, $140,000 − $88,000 = $52,000. His debt-to-equity ratio is 88,000 ÷ 52,000 = 169 percent.

The idea and the calculations work just about the same for corporations. One concern of the investor is the amount of long-term debt for a company and how it compares with the owners' equity. *Leverage* is a term used to indicate how much borrowing is used to finance the company. The leverage of a company is the ratio of long-term debt to the shareholders' equity.

There are two important, but differing views of leverage in stock selection. First, higher leverage may be dangerous because it means higher debt that the company is obliged to repay. The company also has to pay the continuing interest every year. If they had trouble with lower sales one or two years, then the higher debt might be a problem. On the other hand,[6] higher leverage means the management has borrowed money to build up the business. If the management is sharp and the business is sound, then the extra assets from the borrowed money should pay back more than they cost. Leverage is an important tool of all business managers. It is like a chain saw; it may be dangerous, but it may also help to get the job done.

Some sources will report the debt ratio as the long-term debt divided by the total capital. The important point for you in using such sources is to be consistent and to know that higher debt ratios indicate some higher risk.

Examples: The *Value Line* reports debt ratio as long-term debt divided by total capital. By total capital they mean the long-term debt plus the preferred and common shareholders' equity. The *S&P Stock Guide* shows the long-term debt but not the debt ratio. The *S&P Industry Reports* show the debt-to-equity ratio.

For an example, say that a company showed

- long-term debt = $47 million

- common shareholders' equity = $65 million

- preferred shareholders' equity = $3 million

Then *S&P Industry Reports* would show a debt-to-equity ratio of 47÷68 = 69 percent, while the *Value Line* would show a debt ratio of 47÷115 = 41 percent (because they compute the total capital as 47 + 65 + 3 = 115). Either of these numbers may be useful to you, but they are not directly comparable. You want to stick with one way or the other when looking at debt ratios.

Suppose there is no, or little, long-term debt. This situation is safer because the company doesn't have the ongoing repayment problem hanging over their heads for many years. It might also be some evidence of timidity or lack of imagination by the management. If the management and the business are any good, they should be able to earn more than the long-term cost of borrowing. If they did borrow some $100 million or so and expand

---

[6] In financial analysis, there is always "On the other hand. . . ." Every sword is two-edged.

the business, they should expect to earn more than enough to repay the loan and show a profit. Why don't they do it? Sometimes it may be because the company generates so much cash flow that they don't need long-term debt (for example LLTC, which we looked at earlier in this chapter).

Certain industries—for example, the electric utilities—usually maintain large leverage. Their capital expenses tend to be very large (power plants, power lines into new neighborhoods), and the state regulatory agencies keep them from earning too much anyway, so they might as well raise money by borrowing. Other industries, such as semiconductors, typically keep lower leverage because they tend to have strong cash flow to finance their new projects.

If the leverage (or debt ratio) is low, that is an indicator of safety and may mean the management should be more aggressive, but it also means they probably will have good credit to borrow more when they need to. If the debt is high (40 percent or more of capital, 67 percent of shareholders' equity), that raises a question about safety and will be a long-term drain on the cash flow as the company makes repayments.

In any case, the leverage for any one firm should be compared with others in the same line of business to compare the strategies and aggressiveness of management. Here are some examples of the debt ratios for companies in a few different industries. These numbers are reported from the ratio of long-term debt to total capitalization.

The first three are from the home appliance industry, the next three from the steel industry, and the last three from the furniture industry (1996 values).

Company	Shareholders' equity ($ millions)	Long-Term Debt ($ millions)	Debt Ratio %
Black & Decker	1500	1550	51
Maytag	710	460	39
Whirlpool	1880	980	34
Lukens, Inc.	300	220	42
Nucor Corp.	1380	110	7
Worthington Ind.	640	300	32
Ethan Allen	190	130	41
Ladd	130	100	44
Bassett	300	0	0

This shows us that Bassett and Nucor appear to be relatively safe from the viewpoint of debt management.

That does not mean that you should rush out and buy the stock, but if you prefer safe companies, those two might deserve further consideration.

Consolidated Balance Sheet

Bassett Furniture Industries, Incorporated and Subsidiaries

Assets

	November 30,	
	1996	1995
CURRENT ASSETS		
Cash and cash equivalents	$ 57,285,005	$ 51,331,119
Trade accounts receivable, less allowances for doubtful accounts (1996- $1,355,000; 1995 - $1,470,000)	65,416,910	68,591,514
Inventories	67,082,490	81,226,607
Prepaid expenses	1,492,506	1,757,658
Prepaid income taxes	844,737	-0-
Deferred income taxes	2,597,000	2,008,000
	194,718,648	204,914,898
PROPERTY, PLANT AND EQUIPMENT		
Buildings	74,596,633	73,478,686
Machinery and equipment	139,556,776	133,933,234
	214,153,409	207,411,920
Less allowances for depreciation	162,149,761	158,665,871
	52,003,648	48,746,049
Land	4,375,016	4,378,297
	56,378,664	53,124,346
OTHER ASSETS		
Investment in securities	29,625,435	39,055,319
Investment in affiliated companies	45,820,750	40,398,574
Other	8,621,947	9,227,317
	84,068,132	88,681,210
	$335,165,444	$346,720,454

Liabilities and Stockholders' Equity

CURRENT LIABILITIES		
Accounts payable	$ 20,541,014	$ 23,425,858
Accrued compensation	3,716,206	4,778,966
Other accrued liabilities	6,088,381	6,284,441
Income taxes	-0-	902,476
	30,345,601	35,391,741
DEFERRALS		
Deferred liabilities	10,834,741	10,296,244
Deferred income taxes	2,504,000	2,129,000
	13,338,741	12,425,244
STOCKHOLDERS' EQUITY		
Common stock, par value $5 a share, 50,000,000 shares authorized	65,377,975	68,294,765
Retained earnings	222,417,127	225,718,704
Unrealized holding gains, net of tax	3,686,000	4,890,000
	291,481,102	298,903,469
	$335,165,444	$346,720,454

Times Interest Earned

Another significant factor in gauging a company's financial strength is their ability to pay interest on their debt. Since the interest must be paid on a regular schedule and those payments come out of the income, it is interesting to see by how much the gross operating income exceeds the interest repayment required. After revenue is collected, a company covers operating expenses and costs of goods sold. The next item for attention should be the interest payment. If they have plenty of money left for interest payments that is good. This is usually measured by comparing the income before the interest payment with the interest payment. The income before the interest payment is just net earnings plus taxes paid plus interest paid.

The times-interest-earned ratio equals the income before interest payment divided by interest payment.

For the Alpha Beta Publishing Company, the net earnings value was $4,606,000 (see p. 72). They paid $2,100,000 for taxes and $198,000 for interest. So before the interest payments and taxes they had a total of $6,904,000 in income to work with.

Their debt ratio (as a percentage of shareholders' equity) was $2.81 million ÷ $66.14 million = 4 percent; times interest earned = $6,904,000 ÷ $198,000 = 35. They found it very easy to meet the interest payment.

At the end of 1995, Unisys Corporation had a debt ratio of 45 percent, and their times interest earned was only 1.3. This should have indicated two problems to the potential investor. First, there was so much debt, 45 percent of total capital, that Unisys would have trouble borrowing much more money if they had a crisis, as the banks would be skeptical of their ability to repay further loans. Second, if they suffered any significant downturn of revenues, then there might not be enough to cover the current debt payments, and there would be a risk of default.

> **Lesson:** When the debt ratio is too high, which depends on the industry for comparison, that may be a sign that the company is flirting with financial trouble. They would have trouble borrowing any more money. If the times-interest-earned ratio is too low, say less than 1.5, then the company is close to having trouble making their interest payments. In either case, if you find the debt too high or the times-interest-earned ratio too low, then you should either reject the stock

as a candidate to buy, or study the financial reports very carefully to see if the company situation looks like a short-term problem.

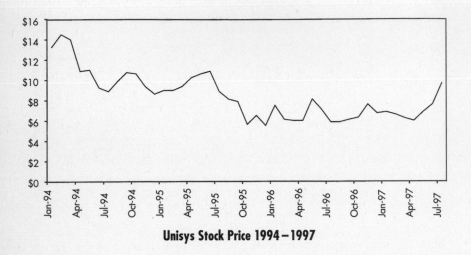

Unisys Stock Price 1994–1997

The debt ratio and the times-interest-earned ratio are never sufficient evidence by themselves that you should buy a stock, but they may be sufficient reason to reject it.

Review and Summary of the Basic Concepts

A number of things should be coming into focus if you fought your way through to this point. Let me reemphasize some of them.

What we have covered in this chapter and the last is just the beginning of financial analysis, but it is enough to help you make some serious and dependable decisions. For example, you know now a few things that you could look at on the balance sheet and income statement that might help you decide that a company is definitely not attractive for your investments. You know that a great deal of information is available in a neat summarized form if you are considering one of the 3500 stocks that the *Value Line* includes in either their regular or extended editions. All of this information is available through the SEC data bases for every publicly traded company.

The financial analysis involved in buying and selling stocks can become quite complex, but you can do a number of things to reduce that labor without giving up on smart investing. In chapter 13 we are going to focus on the search for simplicity. It turns out there are some useful and productive things you can do without getting into a lot of complicated financial analysis.

If you just do a little financial analysis on a company you are interested in, then that little bit might be enough to warn you away from the stock, but should never be enough to persuade you to buy the stock. A little bit of trouble may be reason enough to back off, but a little bit of good news is not reason enough to buy. If you are looking at a few or a lot of the financial facts on a company, it is quite often a good idea to compare other companies in the same industry. A company with 50 percent debt may be reasonable and average for one sector, as it is for the air transport industry, but a sign of weakness for another, as it would be for the semiconductor industry.

"Sure I bought it. Guy said it's risk free."

Finally, as you might expect, a great deal more could be said on the subject. If you find this stuff appealing, as I do, then get a book that goes into it further. The more you know about financial analysis and the more of it you work on, the better and more successful an investor you will be.

A Word on the Use of Ratios

Financial analysis is difficult stuff. If you are going to make money in the stock markets, then you must plan to do some work. It requires experience and good judgment to draw the right conclusions from the ratios that we calculate. Usually each separate number that you look at contains a little bit of good news and a little bit of bad. If you don't see the bad news, then you are missing something; go back and look again. Your job and challenge as a stock picker will be to decide which bits and pieces of information you want to look at, and then how to balance the positive or negative interpretation of each. We will have examples of that as we move ahead.

Recommended Further Reading

Graham, Benjamin, and David Dodd. *Security Analysis*. New York: McGraw-Hill, 1996.

*The policy of letting a hundred flowers blossom
and a hundred schools of thought contend is
designed to promote the flourishing of the
arts and the progress of science.*

—Mao Tse-tung

Different Strokes for
Different Folks

You do not need to manage your investments in the same way as anyone else. Try to find a way that is appropriate for your needs. This chapter focuses on ideas that are useful and appealing to some investors, but
not to others. We will return to the PIG principal and study several
approaches to finding protection, income, and growth.

This chapter will describe some different styles of stock selection. Each
of these is a broad and general style, and the section does not contain all
the details of how you will actually choose individual stocks. Think of the
investing styles as political labels like liberal or conservative. Those labels
tell us something about a politician's attitudes, but they do not tell us how
he will vote on each issue.

Diversification

When a sergeant in the army leads a patrol, he may tell the troops to spread
out so they won't make an easy target for the enemy to crush with one quick
attack. That is the essence of diversification. Diversification serves the purpose of spreading out your investment risks so that one event will not crush

your entire portfolio. It would be negligent of the sergeant to fail to warn the squad about the risk of bunching up. It would be negligent and foolish of us to fail to diversify our investments. Diversification is one of the most important tools of the investor who is seeking protection. Some ideas of diversification are relatively easy, and others are complicated. Find the method that works for you, and do not neglect diversification.

The central theme of diversification is to select and buy a group of stocks that will react differently if various risks come to reality. To achieve fair protection through diversification, it is probably necessary to buy at least ten different stocks. Opinions differ on that, but most experts will say somewhere between ten and twenty stocks.

A good example, if we start with a very small portfolio, can be seen if we consider a small investor named Jack who owns only one stock, Exxon, and is ready to buy more. Two primary risks to Jack's Exxon stock are that the world price of oil will fall substantially, or that the American economy will have a recession. What can he do to oppose those risks? He could buy the stocks of a trucking company and a large grocery store chain. The trucking company is strongly exposed to the risk of recession, but in case of falling oil prices, they should benefit from lower costs. The grocery stores are somewhat exposed to the risk of recession, but might actually withstand it very well. Even if times are bad, people still buy groceries and collect their unemployment compensation. They might even quit eating out, and spend more money in grocery stores. It is safe for Jack to decide that a stock portfolio composed of stocks of Exxon and a grocery store and a trucking company stock would be better diversified than just the Exxon alone.

Notice that the example did not tell Jack which trucking company or which grocery store stock to buy, but it does give him some ideas on where to start looking for his next stocks. He could also use mutual funds for part of his diversification scheme. Suppose Jack knows about a trucking company stock that he finds attractive, but he feels insecure about evaluating grocery store companies. Then he might buy the trucking stock and put an equal amount of money into a mutual fund that specializes in food retailing businesses.

As you begin buying stocks, you may become interested in one particular segment. You may buy stock of a large bank, and then think for many of the same reasons that another large bank is attractive, too. Resist the urge to buy another stock for the same reasons. If the two stocks have the same attractive features, then they also have much of the same risk. By buying both of them before you diversify, you run the risk inherent in bunching up. A swift rise of short-term interest rates might severely damage both stocks.

The practice of diversification is an art, not a science. There is no exact formula for deciding what to buy next. At all times, try to evaluate the risks to your current portfolio and think about buying other stocks that are less exposed to those same risks.

Impact of Fees

The expense of brokerage fees will have some effect on your stock purchase and sale decisions. If you are using a discount stockbroker, then expect the brokerage fee on each transaction to run somewhere between .5 percent and 1.5 percent of the principal. For a full-service firm, it would probably be 1 to 3 percent of the principal. In either case, you could save something on fees by making fewer, larger trades rather than many small trades. For example, if you have $10,000 to invest in stocks, you might consider investing it all in one stock, or buying two stocks for $5,000 each, or buying ten stocks for $1,000 each. We can estimate the brokerage fee costs for each decision:

Investment	Estimated Fees[1] Full-Service Broker
$10,000 In one stock	$250
$5,000 each in two stocks	$400
$1,000 each in ten stocks	$600
	Discount Broker
$10,000 in one stock	$150
$5,000 each in two stocks	$200
$1,000 each in ten stocks	$400

[1] These are just rough estimates that do not refer to any specific brokerage firm; however, they are realistic estimates.

Tough luck! That is the cost of being in the game—a consideration that makes mutual funds more attractive. Mutual funds' fees are usually cheaper than buying a diversified portfolio of stocks. But if you buy individual stocks, this kind of expense will have some influence on your decision making and profitability.

> **Lesson:** There is an extra cost associated with diversification. It is a cost that you must pay, because you must diversify. Just keep your eyes open and think about the costs of excessive diversification.

Effect of Taxes

Taxes. Right. Thank you very much. Taxes are here to stay, even if the Libertarians get elected. They may have some impact on your stock investing decisions.

First the good news. If you do all of your stock investing through an *individual retirement arrangement* (IRA) or a 401(k) plan, then the current profits are shielded from current taxes. You can buy and sell whatever you want without worrying about paying capital gains tax whenever you sell a winner. In fact, within a tax-sheltered account, it is advantageous to buy investments that would be taxable for others. The implied higher yield is worth more to you than it is to them.

However, if you are going to have to report your trading results to the IRS, then taxes should enter into your planning. This book is not the right place, nor am I the right advisor, to be telling you about tax management. If your investment account will be subject to tax reporting, and if the amounts of money are enough to significantly affect your tax bills, then consult a qualified tax advisor about strategies you may use to minimize the tax bite.

Impact of the Broker

There are two extremes of how to use a broker, and some reasonable compromises in between. At the one extreme, which is not usually the right choice, people put their money into an account and then allow the broker to make all the decisions about what and when to buy and sell. Those people might even give the broker power of attorney over the account, so she may generate any trades she likes without telling the client. We can imagine some few people have received good results that way. It is more likely that many have not. The *Wall Street Journal* regularly runs columns full of stories about brokers, brokerage firms, or investment advisors who have been fined or barred from practice because of using such client arrangements contrary to the interests of the clients.

That happens in two ways. The broker or advisor may simply be incompetent. Not everyone who passes the exams and registration processes for those titles has any skill in handling money. The exams focus more on knowledge of the law, not knowledge of investing practices. If an investor turns his money over to such an incompetent broker, then at least half of the blame belongs on the careless investor. It is all too common that clients have told their brokers to follow a safe and conservative strategy and then found out too late that she had been putting the money into high-risk investments.

In September 1996, a California broker was fined $25,000 and suspended for fifteen days by the National Association of Securities Dealers. That broker was found to be conducting transactions for a customer's account that were unsuitable in terms of the size, frequency, and nature of the security, and also unsuitable in view of the client's other investments and needs. Another California broker was fined $10,000 and barred from practice because of charges that he took $10,000 that a customer intended for investments and converted the money to his own use. A New York broker was fined and barred from practice based on evidence that he failed to disclose a prior arrest and conviction on the appropriate securities industries forms. We could go on and on just based on the regular reporting of such cases in the *Wall Street Journal*.

The second source of trouble for investors is the practice of churning. Churning is the process where a broker who has control over a clients account makes a lot of stock transactions to generate excessive brokerage fees. If you give your broker the power of attorney, then the only protection you have against churning is regular close examination of your monthly statement.

If you are among those investors who decide they cannot or do not intend to do any of the analysis and stock-selection work, then it would be better to only use mutual funds. At least take some basic precautions to protect your money. Be very careful in your selection of a broker or money manager. Rely heavily on recommendations of friends who have worked

*"Look here Sisyphus, I know you love your rock —
but let's talk about diversification."*

with a broker for several years. Steadfastly review every monthly statement from the broker to ensure that you know about, and are satisfied with the fees, the type and size and frequency of transactions, and the progress of the account. If you do not regularly and carefully review the statements, then you might as well be throwing the money out of the window.

If you ever feel that the broker or money manager might not be conscientiously serving your interests, then throw the bum out! Perhaps you should discuss it with her first, but do not hesitate to change the account if you stay dissatisfied with the broker for more than a few months. Changing is as easy and as difficult as finding the first broker. You go through the search process again until you find a new person who seems to be better. If you set up a new account, then the new broker/advisor/manager can take care of moving the assets out of the old account. You do not have to go back to the first, unsatisfactory broker and explain or justify your decision. Let the new account manager take care of that. It is easy.

On the other hand, suppose you study this book and some other things and decide that you will take on some of the work and responsibility. Now the question is how to use the broker/advisor/money manager. At first, you must be careful about selecting the person to work with. Then you must also be equally careful about checking the account statements and insisting on full and clear explanations of anything that is confusing. Beyond that, you have two choices. You may use a discount broker, who will principally just take orders from you to buy or sell this or that stock. They will also answer questions about the current market activity or price change of stocks you are interested in. You may use a full-service broker, who will offer varied additional services, including research and advice. Even if you feel confident about making investment decisions, the brokerage firm has more resources and information than you, and the individual broker has more experience. It may be helpful for you to see their research[2] and discuss each decision with the broker.

You can reduce the broker question to three situations: First, if you will do no stock research or decision making at all, I recommend that you just use mutual funds. If you decide to use a broker, then be very careful and insistent about getting good monthly reports.

Second, if you will do some research and decision making, but feel that you want a broker's or advisor's guidance and support, then you probably want a full-service broker, or possibly a discount broker and an investment advisor.

Last, if you feel confident doing all of your own analysis and decision making, then you should use a discount broker. Check their prices and services, and which mutual funds they can sell. Before you hand over any money make them show you a copy of their monthly statement to see if you can understand it.

Investing for Income

Investing for income is the cornerstone strategy for many individual investors. Well it should be. For most small investors, the income criteria for which stocks to buy or sell should be heavily considered in all their decisions. Some investors require that every stock they buy must be a high-yielding stock. That may be going overboard. In the interest of good diversification, it is wise to use more variety. This section will focus on ideas that are important when you are strongly concerned about the income factor.

If a stock pays a good dividend, and your decision to buy is strongly influenced by the income yield, then you should realize that some risks come

---

[2] If your broker is reluctant to show you their house research, then fire him.

along with that yield. One risk is the competition from bonds. Every investor has a lot of choices about where to put his money. For the income investor, one of the prime choices is the bond market. Any time that general interest rates rise, investors have the choice of buying bonds that pay higher yield. For many investors, high yields make the bonds more attractive than dividend-paying stocks. The bonds might be more attractive because their interest payments are fixed and guaranteed, not subject to the whim of a board of directors, as the stock dividends are. The bonds also might be more attractive because they are senior to common shareholders' claims. In case of financial distress for a company, the bondholders get their claims satisfied before the stockholders get anything. The bonds also might be more attractive if they were guaranteed by the United States, or some other government entity.

The bonds might be more attractive to some investors because they carry a fixed face value that is not subject to the vagaries of the marketplace. That idea is misleading because a bond cannot always be sold at its face value, but some investors like the idea of fixed long-term face value. Beyond the fixed face value, the true market value of bonds is usually not as volatile as stock prices.

So we see that bonds are attractive to income investors. Sometimes bonds will become so strong that they pull money out of the stock market. Strong bonds were at least one contributing factor for the crash of October 1987. Any time that bonds become very appealing, then other investors might start selling high-yield stocks, or at least quit buying, and that is what lowers the stock price. The market value of your investment will fall, even though the dividend may continue. Then you must decide whether you will sell because of the loss of market value or hold on because of the good yield. In many cases, it will make sense to hold on. This is the prime argument for the buy-and-hold investor, but it will be nerve wracking if the market price falls very far.

Another risk to the high-yield stock is that the dividend may be reduced. Remember the FPL case in chapter 6. In that case, the directors had plenty of earnings and security to continue and even increase the dividend, but they decided to cut it, causing great damage to the financial plans of many of their stockholders who were primarily income investors. The dividend that you think you are buying is subject to the profitability of the firm and the intentions of the directors. If a previously high dividend gets the ax, that will almost certainly severely hurt the stock price, too.

Several arguments weigh just as strongly in favor of dividend-paying stocks. In fact, although the above paragraphs stressed the risk, on balance dividend payments lend greater safety to the investment. If a company has a history of paying a steady dividend each year, the stock is attractive to many investors even during a time of falling market prices. We mentioned earlier how the dividend reinvestments for Dayton Power and Light caused a very good total return. The same kind of behavior should be expected from any stock when a strong, secure dividend is paid.

Dividends also offer some security against a falling stock price. Look at what happens if the stock price does fall: Allegheny Power Systems (symbol AYP on the NYSE) has an excellent long-term record of paying a dividend and even raising it every year. You might have bought their stock at $28[3] in August 1993, when the prior year's dividend was $1.61. Due to a number of factors, like the flap over deregulation of utilities and higher bond yields, the AYP stock price fell to $20 in October 1994. But, by then, the dividend rate had been raised to $1.64. At that new lower price, the yield was 8.2 percent. That's a lot of yield. That surely was enough to attract a lot of investors to come back to buy AYP. Those who did buy or hold on were rewarded because, within little over a year, the price was back above $30, and the dividend had been raised again.

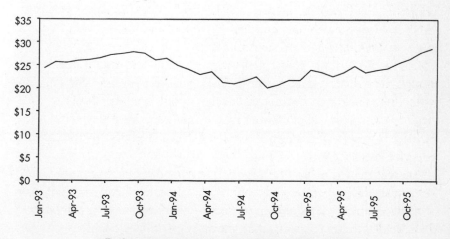

Allegheny Power Systems Stock Prices 1993–1995

---

[3] Price adjusted for split in December 1993.

Buying income stocks should have a place in the investment strategy of every small investor. The practice carries some unique advantages and risks, just like every investment strategy, but it should be included as an essential ingredient of your diversification plan. If you want to study this further, read *The Income Investor* and *What Works on Wall Street*.

Risk Avoidance

For some stock investors, protection of the principal is the most important criterion for investment. This is a bit of a dilemma because whenever you start buying stocks you must accept some risk of loss, and the potential risk is greater than you would have with bonds or mutual funds. However, let us suppose that you have made your own decision to accept some of that risk. The concern now for the intelligent investor is to minimize the risk. You should not expect to eliminate all risks, but to minimize them relative to the returns you expect from a stock investment using a few primary practices of risk avoidance.

The first practice is diversification; spread the risk so your portfolio will be somewhat shielded from a single shock to any one business or industry.

Second, buy yield. As we saw with Allegheny Power, yield tends to make a stock more attractive, even if the price might be falling, because the yield percentage increases. An important factor to consider here is whether the yield is secure. You should examine the company's history of both earnings and yield for at least the past five years to try to discern the directors' intentions. You should also make a judgment about whether the earnings are secure enough to continue the yield. If the company's profits are at risk, then so are the dividends. Another factor to check is the payout ratio. If that is high, say above 80 percent, then it may be difficult to maintain the dividend. If the dividend was 80¢ on $1 per share of earnings, then a decrease to 75¢ of earnings would put the dividend at risk.

Next, educate yourself. The more you know about financial markets, and any particular industry, the better chance you have of recognizing risks. If you can recognize the risks, then you have a better chance to either improve your diversification or simply stay away from a particular risky stock. This, by the way, is one of the great arguments in favor of investment clubs. If you work with an investment club, then you may be assured that the club members working together will always recognize and evaluate all of the risks in a stock better than you could on your own.

appropriate for the study of value investing. And remember that one of the ways to seek protection is through education.

What does the value investor do? Many things. We will discuss many valid methods of the value investor later, but here are some basics. The value investor distinguishes between a good company and a good stock. A good company is a prerequisite for a good stock buy but does not necessarily indicate a good buy. Any stock can be overpriced, regardless of how great the company is. Evaluate the company and evaluate the stock—two distinct but related jobs. Begin with the financial reports. The financial reports should tell some things about the management and intentions of the company, as well as its financial strength. More immediately, the reports should help you decide whether the stock price is attractive.

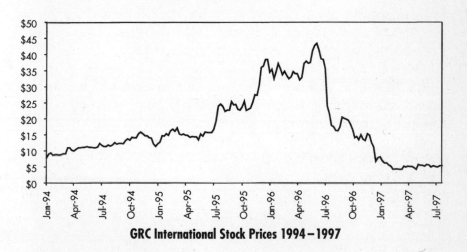

GRC International Stock Prices 1994–1997

The graph above shows the price of the stock of GRC International (stock symbol GRH on the New York Stock Exchange) for two and one-half years. GRC sells professional services and technical products, primarily to the government. They earned close to 50¢ per share in 1994 and 1995, but lost about $1.50 per share in 1996. Their long-term debt went from zero in 1994 to near 70 percent of capital in 1996. Their price-to-earnings ratio went from near 22 at the end of 1994 to 65 at the end of 1995. Based on the previous five years' performance, there was good reason to believe, in 1994, that the company was doing well. At that time, the stock (at $8 to $15 per share) was an attractive and promising buy. By late 1995 and early 1996, the price had raced ahead of reasonable expectations. At that time, it was overpriced and did not offer an attractive buy, even if the company had continued to improve. A confirmed buy-and-hold investor, who bought GRC in 1995 or 1996, probably would have a long wait for the long run to produce good results on this one.

So how shall you search for value? Here are some of the basic value-oriented indications of whether a stock price is reasonable, a good buy, or a good sell. No one of these indicators by itself is enough to lock in a decision to buy or sell, but each of them can offer some evidence pointing towards a decision one way or the other.

Price: You can look at just the price relative to how the stock normally sells. Look at Quanex Corporation (symbol NX on the NYSE), a maker of specialized steel and aluminum products. From 1991 to 1995, their stock price fluctuated between $11 and $32 per share. Here are the yearly highs and lows:

	1991	**1992**	**1993**	**1994**	**1995**
Year's high	23	32	21	27	27
Year's low	11	16	14	17	18

In early 1996, you could have bought this stock for $20. That price appears to be reasonably consistent with the prior years' range of prices. You might suspect that there could be a floor under this price around $15 or $16, and

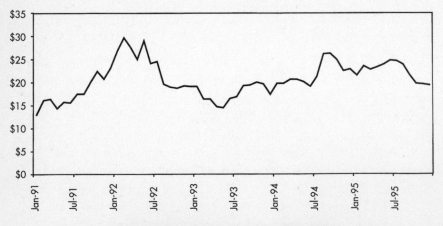

Quanex Corporation Stock Prices 1991–1995

you might reasonably expect that if things were going well, the price would be bid up to around $27. That range of prices looks like a favorable balance of opportunity. By looking at the price only, relative to prior years' history, this stock appears to be reasonably priced for purchase. That is not reason enough to buy it, but it looks reasonable.

Price-to-earnings ratio (P/E): A low price-to-earnings ratio is favorable for a buy. What is low? That depends on the company, the relative state of the market, and other companies in the same industry. Many investors set limits above which they will not buy a stock. You may commonly hear about other investors or mutual funds that will not buy any stock with a P/E ratio above 20. Others might say 12, 24, or whatever number works for them. If you set a limit that appeals to you, then stocks with P/E below that number will be relatively safer for your investments than those with P/E above.

There were seventeen companies in the same industry with Quanex, as reported by the *Value Line* in the spring of 1996. Two of them had losses in 1995, so their P/E ratios did not mean anything. Two of them had results in 1995 that were drastically out of line with their recent histories, so their P/E's probably did not mean anything. For the remaining thirteen, the average P/E was 14, and the median value was 12. The P/E of Quanex was 9. That is the lowest P/E value for the group, and so it indicates a good price for a buy. That P/E was also among the lower values for the entire stock market. The market-average[5] P/E at the time was close to 15.

What about stability of the P/E? Can we count on it staying attractive? The P/E's stability depends on the price and the earnings. Based on the information above, we were guessing at a price between $16 and $27 for Quanex for the next year or so. Their history of earnings (per share) for the past few years was

1991	$1.02
1992	$0.28
1993	$0.18
1994	$0.96
1995	$2.20

The *Value Line* estimate of earnings for 1996 was $2.25, and for 1997, $2.60.

---

[5] That means an average among the 1700 stocks that the *Value Line* covers.

Good news and bad news, right? The earnings had been volatile. The earnings history was not encouraging. However, if the estimate was any good, then the price was only nine times 1996 earnings and eight times 97 earnings. Both of those looked like low (i.e., attractive) ratios relative to the industry.

You could have done some optimistic projections. If the 1996 and 1997 earnings estimates were accepted as fair, and if you thought their P/E ratio might stay around nine, you might have estimated 1996 and 1997 share prices like this:

Estimated 1996 price equals P/E ratio x earnings,
9 x $2.25 = $20.25

Estimated 1997 price equals P/E ratio x earnings,
9 x $2.60 = $23.40

In analyzing stocks, you have to regard the P/E ratio as an indicator of the market's opinion about a stock. Stocks that are highly regarded have their prices pushed up, and the P/E ratio becomes higher. Stocks that are not so well regarded have their prices bid down, so the P/E ratio becomes lower. Now where is Quanex? Quanex is in the lower group of their industry. But earnings have been improving and are estimated to continue to improve. One might reasonably estimate that Quanex will be elected to the more favorable group among their peers in the industry. Let us say you make a leap of faith and guess that Quanex deserves a P/E ratio of 12, which is the mean of the group.

Now, using an assumed P/E of 12, we could do some estimating:

Estimated 1996 price equals P/E x earnings,
12 x $2.25 = $27

Estimated 1997 price equals P/E x earnings,
12 x $2.60 = $31.20

This appears to be an opportunity for some serious price appreciation. Take note, though. This analysis is strongly dependent on the estimates of earnings for 1996 and 1997, which we have seen is very tricky business. What else can we see? Are those estimates believable? Go back to the *Value Line*, and you can find their earnings for 1988, 1989, and 1990, which were $1.85, $2.11, and $2.03 respectively. This lends some credibility to the estimates for 1996 and 1997. The company is capable of earning $2 and more per share.

In sum, the price-to-earnings ratio analysis for Quanex appears to support both the value of the current $20 price and the opportunity for profit on share-price growth.

Yield: The current yield on Quanex in early 1996 was 3.1 percent. The industry average was about 1 percent. The overall market average was about 2.5 percent. For income and value investors, Quanex looked pretty good. What about the safety of the yield? Quanex had been steadily raising their dividend for eight years. The payout ratio in 1995 and 1996 was below 30 percent, which looked secure. The yield picture for Quanex was favorable for a buy.

Price-to-cash-flow ratio (P/Cf): Lower values of the price-to-cash-flow ratio are more attractive than higher values. A lower value of that ratio means that you can buy a dollar of cash flow cheaper. The trend is for investors to reward companies with low price-to-cash-flow ratios by bidding up the value of the stock, making these stocks more attractive investments.

The price-to-cash-flow ratios for Quanex and their industry peers can be found using the cash-flow-per-share numbers in the *Value Line*. For Quanex in 1995, the cash-flow-per-share was $4.59, so at the time of our analysis, when the price was $20, the price-to-cash-flow ratio (P/Cf) was $20 \div 4.59 = 4$. Of the seventeen companies in the group, three had untrustworthy cash flow values because they lost money in 1995, so we just looked at the other fourteen. The average P/Cf ratio was 8. The median was 8. The minimum was 4, and the maximum was 13. This made Quanex look good in terms of price to cash flow. From 1991 to 1995, their cash flow had been consistently going up, and was predicted to continue to rise for 1996 and 1997. The P/Cf was the best for the group, and it appeared that it was only going to improve. This, then, made another point in favor of the value investor buying Quanex.

Price-to-sales ratio (P/S): The price-to-sales ratio is regarded by some as among the most critical ratios for determining the value of a stock. Lower price-to-sales ratios are generally more attractive, and the market tends to reward the lower-value stocks by bidding up the price until the ratio is at least in line with their industry peers.

Just like with price-to-cash-flow ratios, we work with per-share values and use the *Value Line* to determine industry averages. For Quanex in early

1996, the price-to-sales ratio was $20 ÷ $66 = 0.3[6]. In general, any value below 1.5 is pretty good. For the seventeen companies in Quanex's industry group, one had a P/S ratio that was ridiculous (9), and the average for the other sixteen was P/S = 0.6. From the view of price-to-sales ratio, Quanex appears attractively priced. You should always question the dependability of such numbers, so let's look at the history for 1991 through 1995, and forecast for 1996 and 1997. The five-year history of sales per share showed $50.18, $41.95, $46.28, $52.27, and $66.09. The *Value Line* estimates of sales for '96 and '97 were $66 and $71. With these kinds of numbers, it is easy to have a lot of confidence in the current price-to-sales ratio, and believe it could get better.

Return on assets (ROA): A higher value of return on assets is favorable. The return on assets is in some sense a judgment on the management of the company. It indicates how much profit they are earning with the assets they have to manage. The ratio is also an indicator of the quality of the assets. For example, if two companies had $1 million of inventory, it is possible that one company might be selling the inventory rapidly for a 40 percent markup, while the other was selling it slowly for just a 20 percent markup. Then the first company would be making a much larger return on that $1 million of assets.

The average return on assets for Quanex's industry group in 1995 was 8 percent. The 1995 value for Quanex was 7 percent. There is not much to learn there. One might possibly infer that Quanex was slightly less efficient than the industry average, but that would be reaching for conclusions.

Return on equity (ROE): The return on equity measures how much the firm is earning relative to the amount of the owners' (the shareholders) value in the firm. A higher value of return on equity is favorable for future return to the investors. The average for Quanex's industry group in 1995 was 18 percent. The 1995 return on equity for Quanex was 20 percent. This looks pretty good for QNX.

---

[6] Nearly all of the calculations here get truncated to one or two significant figures because, for our purposes, it doesn't matter whether the ratio is 0.28 or 0.33. We just round off to 0.3. We will continue that practice throughout the book.

The return on assets and the return on equity measure somewhat similar things, but they are not quite the same. To illustrate that point, suppose there were two companies, the A1CO and the B2CO, that each had $500 million of assets, and in 1996 each earned $85 million. Then for each, the return on assets was 85 ÷ 500 = 17 percent. However, suppose that A1CO had no debt and B2CO had $200 million of debt. Then for A1CO the equity was $500 million, and for B2CO the equity was $300 million. Now we see for A1CO the return on equity was 85 ÷ 500 = 17 percent, but for B2CO the return on equity was 85 ÷ 300 = 28 percent. Both companies are doing equally well with the assets they have to manage, but the B2CO management is earning higher returns for the investors. It is worthwhile to look at both of those value-oriented ratios and see what they mean for your investment needs.

Let's take another view of A1CO and B2CO. We said that B2CO has the more attractive return on equity, but there is a trade-off for this: they also carry an extra risk factor, the higher debt. As an investor studying these two companies, you would need to decide whether you were concerned more with the return on equity factor or the debt factor. Two intelligent investors might make different decisions as to whether the stock was an attractive investment, depending on their point of view.

Current ratio: From the *Value Line* we can see, as of late in 1995, the current assets of Quanex were $242 million and the current liabilities were $165 million, so the current ratio was 242 ÷ 165 = 1.5. This is okay, but not really great. The other members of the industry generally had current ratios closer to 2 or 3, but 1.5 is not really bad. It shows they could cover their bills but did not have much room to spare.

Times interest earned: You should usually like for times-interest-earned value to be greater than 4, but this has to be tempered in comparison with what is normal for the industry group. Quanex had enough earnings to cover their interest payments 6.4 times over. (The *Value Line* gives you that number directly.) That is solid. No problem with the interest payments.

The value investor also looks at debt service. In addition to paying the interest on all of the debt, the company also needs to eventually pay off the long-term debt. A high level of times interest earned may be good enough to take care of the debt for a few years, but what if $100 million of debt has to be repaid in principal in six years? Does it look as if the company can pay that? They may have to establish a fund to set aside money to repay the debt, or they may have to roll over the debt into a new loan within six years. In either case, you need to look at the balance sheet and judge whether they will be able to do one thing or the other. If they plan to roll over the debt in a new loan within six years, then how can they deal with the risk of higher interest rates at that time. If the old debt interest was 8 percent, then how will they manage if the new debt has to be funded at a rate of 11 percent?

Quanex had $55 million of debt that had to be repaid within five years, but they had $45 million of current cash and were generating an additional $30 million per year of retained earnings. It appears that they would have no problem repaying the debt.

Leverage: At the end of 1995, the long-term debt for Quanex was $112 million, which was 40% of their total capitalization (the *Value Line* gives that number directly). That is a relatively high level of long-term debt, which is not good. Because of the preceding items on current ratio and times interest earned, Quanex appears to have no current problem with debt repayment, but if they wanted to borrow money to upgrade facilities or start a new product line, they might have difficulty convincing a bank to lend them more.

A Value Investor's Conclusions on Quanex

A typical value-oriented investor who wanted to get into the numbers would examine the ratios and values that we have just looked at. Some might draw differing conclusions about some of the numbers than what was stated here, but these are the kinds of things that value investors should study.

Can we make a definite conclusion about whether Quanex is a buy? Not yet. The calculations seem to show that the price is fair, and the investment should probably be safe. However, they do not show enough about the future prospects of the company beyond the *Value Line* estimates on earnings and cash flow. If you were to consider this stock, you should examine whether it would help diversify your portfolio. You should also examine recent news about the company and seek to learn how their sales were going and what their competitors were doing. If you use a full-service broker, get a copy of their company research on Quanex and a few of their competitors. After your investigations, you should review everything that looks favorable about the company and try to see what could go wrong.

In particular, in this case, the market is trying to tell you something. The market has priced Quanex at what appears to be a bargain price, based on all the value criteria. When that happens, it means that, on balance, other investors do not find it a compelling buy. Otherwise, they would push the price up. You should always respect the consensus opinion of the market. The rest of them may know something you do not. Quanex may be a good buy, but there is something out there that we have not yet seen. Try to figure out what it is before you buy the stock.

On balance here, I would have guessed (March 1996) that for a typical value investor, Quanex was a good buy at $21, but this guess still needed more work. In the fullness of time we learned something. In January 1997, the stock price was $25, and the 1996 earnings came in well over $3. Quanex was probably still a good buy then.

Investing for Growth

Investing for growth is not a whole new world; it is merely a different emphasis from value investing. The growth-oriented investor is usually more absorbed in a search for profits from share price increase rather than "value" and income. The growth investor will look at a lot of the same numbers we just worked with, but instead of stopping there, he might look at the history of everything over the past five years. He would also make a very serious effort at estimating values for the next couple of years. The growth investor would not be as concerned about the absolute level of current price. He would try to analyze the prospects for the company to increase its markets and sales or improve its margins on sales. He would look at the likelihood that the market might give the company a higher price/earnings ratio (the market does that by bidding the price higher).

To use Quanex as an example (although it is not considered a growth stock), a growth investor might look at all of the numbers above and decide that it is a good enough company that the market should give it at least as high a P/E multiple as most of its peers making the P/E estimate equal 15. Suppose that our growth investor was so sharp that she estimated the 1996 and 1997 earnings as $3.00 and $3.60. Then she would estimate the 1996 and 1997 prices as 15 x $3.00 = $45 and 15 x $3.60 = $54, respectively. That is a whole lot of share price appreciation! These numbers are based on estimates, but they do not appear to be wild estimates. They appear to be rational. That is the way of the growth investor.

The growth investor compares the P/E ratio with the rate of growth of earnings. Some investors have a rough rule of thumb that the P/E is reasonable if it is less than the percentage of annual increase in earnings.

Example: If the P/E ratio was 25, that looks pretty expensive, but if the average compound rate of growth in earnings over the past five years was greater than 25 percent, then that P/E of 25 might still show a reasonable price.

Second example: Olsten Corporation is a provider of temporary help services. From 1991 to 1995, the earnings per share of Olsten were $0.41, $0.58, $0.77, $1.08, and $1.39. In February 1996, the stock sold for $27 to $30. Based on the higher price and 1995 earnings, that gave a P/E ratio of 30 ÷ 1.39 = 22. The investor must wonder whether that is too high a price to pay for Olsten's stock. The four preceding year-to-year changes of earnings were 41 percent, 33 percent, 40 percent, and 29 percent. That gives an average well above 22, so based on the rule of thumb, one would think that the stock was not overpriced. If the earnings went up as much as 25 percent in each of the next two years, earnings would equal $2.17 in 1997.

There are two ways to look at that: First, if the price stayed fixed, then the P/E ratio at the end of 1997 would be 30 ÷ 2.17 = 14, so the price would look like a real bargain.

Second, if the P/E ratio stayed at 22, then the price would go up to 22 x $2.17 = $48, for a substantial profit.

In either case, a sustained high growth of earnings compensates for what might appear to be a high P/E ratio. That is the way of the growth investor.

The growth investor wants to buy growth stocks. That seems fair doesn't it? But how do you identify growth stocks? It requires a lot of estimations and projections, but generally a growth stock should have a history

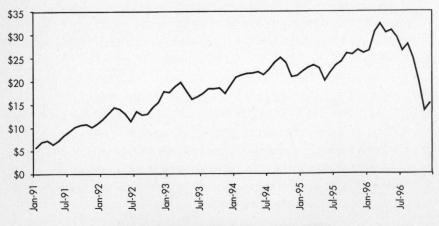

Olsten Corporation Stock Prices 1991–1996

of increasing earnings, sales, stock price, and market share. The critical issue for the growth investor is: At what price does the stock become too expensive to justify even the growth characteristics? That is always a tough call, and many investors will make different decisions depending on how they estimate the continued growth. Our guideline (the rule of thumb) is that the price-to-earnings ratio should be less than the percentage of earnings growth rate over the last five years. It is also critical, but difficult, to estimate how that history projects out over the next two or three years.

The computer software and services industry is a growth industry. The rate of increase of the group's revenues from 1991 to 1995 has been 21 percent, 15 percent, 20 percent, and 22 percent. There were thirty-one companies in the group with average P/E ratio equal to 30. Our guideline might suggest that the group as a whole was overpriced. That assumption would need to be tested through examining individual issues if you considered buying any of them.

One member of that group is Sybase, Inc. From 1990 to 1994, the yearly increases of earnings per share were 127 percent, 80 percent, 59 percent, and 55 percent. In early 1995, the price was $45 per share and the preceding year's earnings per share were $2.22. That gave a P/E ratio of $45 \div 2.22 = 20$. On our first guideline, the price appears to be not too high. Also, the sales had been up strongly each year. If a growth investor wanted to project the strong results on into the next two years, he might have felt comfortable paying $45 for Sybase.

In 1995 Sybase's earnings per share fell by 48 percent on flat sales for the year, and the growth investing community lost their faith in Sybase. The stock price fell from $45 to $30. At one point it was down as low as $20. It paid no dividend, so there was no salve for the hurt.

Another member of that computer software group is Microsoft (symbol MSFT on the NASDAQ market). In 1987 the P/E of MSFT was 20, and some value investors said, "No, thanks, too expensive." Some growth investors bought it anyway. In 1988 the P/E was 25, and it was the same story. In 1989, 1990, 1991, 1992, 1993, 1994, and 1995, the situation was the same. The company's sales and earnings went up substantially each year, and the stock price increased sixteen times over those eight years. In 1997 the same situation continues, and the value investors and growth investors still disagree about Microsoft. The company did not pay any dividend, so the income investors were shut out of that ride, too.

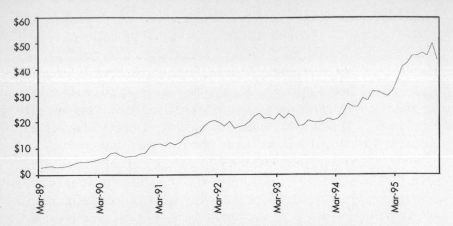

Microsoft Corporation Stock Prices 1989–1995 Adjusted for Several Splits

Getting to Know the Company

Many of the preceding lessons have been based on the numbers. That has to be, but there is another side of the picture, too. If you are going to buy a stock, or sell one, you must form some kind of opinion about the prospects of the company over the next two or three years. The numbers tell a lot of the story, but not all of it. You can and should also come up with opinions about the management, the products or services, the marketplace, and the competition. Many excellent publications[7] offer detailed analyses of different companies' current situations and whether they are attractive buys or not.

If you consider buying Chrysler stock, then you should go out and drive some of their cars. Check their showrooms and ask your neighbors what they think about Chryslers, Dodges, and Plymouths. A magazine like *Forbes* might run a detailed examination of the company's recent past and prospects for the next few years.

If you consider buying Food Lion stock, go out and shop there a few times. Ask your friends and neighbors about them, too. What do you think about their products and stores? Form your own opinions about their prospects.

Do you trust your own opinions about these things? If not, then you probably don't want to buy the stock. There are plenty of companies and

---

[7] Mentioned throughout this book.

products out there that you do understand. It may be too risky to buy the ones you do not. For example, I will confess that I buy stock in tobacco companies. I understand that business. I do not buy stock in gaming companies because I do not understand that business. My guess, without counting, is that out of the stocks listed in the *Value Line* or traded on the NYSE or NASDAQ, there may be half of them for which I feel some understanding of the business. That gives me a lot of companies (over 3,000) that I could be dealing with. I don't need any more than that. Neither do you.

One extension of that idea is to use your professional or business experience. If you have ten years' experience in telecommunications, sports management, gaming, or whatever, then that gives you at least one area (probably more than one) where you are way ahead of the crowd in terms of evaluating the prospects of companies. You can take advantage of that edge. Work the section of the market that you know.

Technical Methods

Technical analysis does not just mean using computers or doing a lot of calculations. It refers specifically to methods of studying a stock's history and market history to predict where they are going next. Since you are reading this book, you are not ready for technical analysis. The potential for results from technical analysis is highly controversial and will not be settled for years to come. The difficulty and challenge of using technical analysis are universally agreed on as quite demanding. Do not even think about using technical analysis, or relying on the recommendations of technical analysts, until after you have read this book and many other references, and practiced investing with real live money and real live risk for a couple of years. If there is any possibility for using technical analysis to get ahead of the crowd, it requires a great deal of experience to apply it successfully.

Recommended Further Reading

Smith, Charles W. *The Mind of the Market*. Lanham, MA: Rowman & Littlefield, 1981.

Krefetz, Gerald. *The Basics of Stocks*. Chicago: Dearborn, 1992.

O'Shaughnessy, James. *What Works on Wall Street*. New York: McGraw Hill, 1997.

Some men can make decisions and some cannot.
Once a decision was made, I did not worry about it afterward.
If you can't stand the heat, get out of the kitchen.

—HARRY TRUMAN

Decision Making and Conflicting Information

Your Money

The money you have set aside for stock market investing is important to you. It may be $5,000 or $20,000 or $300,000, but whatever the amount, it is important to you. If you lost 30 percent of it, you would be distraught. Could you deal with the psychological challenges of investing in individual stocks?

Suppose you had $20,000 and made these ten investments over a couple of years:

Stock Type	Invested	Total Return	% Gain or Loss
Computer company	$3,000	$1,500	+50 percent
Retail clothing stores	$2,000	– 400	– 20 percent
Gas and water utility	$4,000	800	+20 percent
Biochemical	$2,000	– 1,000	-50 percent
Grocery chain	$3,000	500	+17 percent
Automobile	$2,500	800	+32 percent

Stock Type	Invested	Total Return	% Gain or Loss
Bank	$3,000	-800	– 27 percent
Health maintenance	$3,500	700	+20 percent
Airline	$3,500	900	+26 percent
Telecommunications	$2,000	– 200	– 10 percent
Totals	**$28,500**	**$2,800**	**+14 percent**

That's a profit. Good for you! But along the way, you also had a chance to buy another computer company that went up from $36 to $72 in the two years, and every step of the way you thought it was overpriced and did not buy it.

While you were holding your bank stock, it fell from $68 to $60, and you couldn't decide what to do; it fell to $53, and you couldn't decide what to do; it fell to $44 and you could not decide; and at one point it fell to $38 before coming back to $50. Then you sold. After you sold, it went up to $65.

The biochem stock was purchased at $18. In a month it went up to $22, in two more months it went up to $28, and you wanted to buy more, but you couldn't make a decision until after it had risen to $31, so you did not buy more. It went up to $33 within eight months after you bought it, and you bragged to all your friends about your stock-picking prowess. You were looking at an 83 percent gain in eight months! That's equivalent to 143 percent gain per year. At that rate, you could turn your $20,000 into $1.7 million in five years. You should consider opening your own mutual fund and share your expertise with the masses. Meanwhile, while you were congratulating yourself, the stock fell to $31, but not to worry—any highflier can have a temporary correction. Three months later, it was down to $27, but you still had a large profit, on paper. Again, no need to worry, because you were sure of your stock-picking prowess, and anyway, you couldn't sell for a measly 50 percent gain. The next day the stock price fell to $23, but you knew that many investors had been buying at $27, so you waited for it to come back up around $30, when you could sell for a great profit. For the next six weeks, you couldn't sleep, you snapped at your wife, mistreated the dog, and neglected your job. The stock price fell to $19, $17, $14, and $11, and luckily your therapist convinced you to sell the stock, which left you with a 50 percent loss in a year. Immediately after you sold, the price went up to $12, then $13, then $14. And your buddies want to know how you are doing.

You think that's cruel? Forget it! That's nothing to the way you'll feel when there is real money out there that you need for retirement. But all right, maybe your broker will hold your hand and console you. However, your broker will also expect to collect his fees for the twenty trades, maybe a total of $1,800, maybe more, and he will not offer to help cover the losses. The burden of the decisions and losses is on the individual investor. If you can't stand the heat, get out of the kitchen!

Choices

Here, at last, is the entire secret to successful investing. Basically, just three things: look at the choices, decide on which may be good investments, place your buy or sell orders. The whole business really is that simple. If that is perfectly clear, then you may skip the rest of this chapter.

A few weeks ago I received my copy of one of the magazines that advises readers on money management. There was an article by a columnist that advised readers about how to figure their risks when investing their 401(k) money in the stock market. Sounds good so far, right? The only problem is that he evaluated the risk relative to the dumbest possible alternative that was available. It's like evaluating the risks in the state lottery and figuring it was pretty good compared to just spending all the money on a cabin cruiser,

taking the boat out to sea, and sinking it. Well, yes, I suppose so, but aren't there some better choices?

The analysis in the magazine article was weak because it compared one investment plan with the worst alternative. What he should have done was to compare the first plan with three or four other reasonable ways to handle the money.

I am indebted to Drs. Richard Bandler and John Grinder, who co-authored some books touching on neurolinguistic programming applied in psychotherapy, notably *The Structure of Magic* and *Frogs into Princes*. They helped me learn some lessons that have been applicable to making money, as well as other things. In 1977, I was on an airplane coming into Washington, D.C., National Airport. I will never forget the moment, approximately fifteen seconds before the plane touched down, when I read the following lesson:

> *People sometimes do things that subsequently cause them to be unhappy. Given the same circumstances later, they may repeat the same faulty decisions and actions. Some even repeat those errors after they know that the behavior is self-destructive. When they repeat the same self-injurious behavior it is because they do not understand that they have other choices for their behavior in that situation.*

I remember feeling a sudden enlightenment when I read that. What a way to live! This is truth! I thought that every other civilized adult had known that since the age of five; how come I was just learning it after completing my Ph.D. and being married and starting a family and all the other truck? No matter, it was a lesson. We don't learn to live, and we don't live to learn, we live and learn.

> This is an important lesson to apply in your investing. Any time that you consider buying any investment, consider your choices. If you don't consider the choices, then you will make a lot of mistakes that could be avoided.

Any time you think you have found an attractive stock investment, pause and consider that there are 8,000 or so other stocks you could be buying. You should have actively considered four or five of them. You might also invest in bonds, bond mutual funds, or stock mutual funds. Insurance, annuities, home improvements, and vacations are also to be considered. If you make your decision on one stock in the absence of options, then you will find some grief.

Decision Making and Decisiveness

Your success or failure as an investor will be determined by your decision making and your decisiveness. Those are two different things.

In 490 B.C., a few thousand Greek soldiers opposed an army of over two million Persians and their allies at Marathon. That may have been questionable decision making, but heroic decisiveness (the Greeks won, which is why we use the Greek letter Beta for volatility). At the battle of Gettysburg in 1863, Robert E. Lee decided to send his army, in the face of strong odds, to attack the opposing Union Army. That was probably questionable decision making, but brave and historic decisiveness. In 1990, I watched the price of Unisys fall from $15 a share to $1 and figured it was a bargain. I did not buy. I let the trend spook me, and I waited and waited and waited. That was good financial analysis but poor decisiveness. Two years later, the price was back up to $12.

Decision making is an intellectual quality. It deals with whether you can analyze and gather information and compare and judge factors to determine the probable value or likely return from a stock. In investing, as in life, one of the valuable attributes of good decision making is to figure out what the other choices are. Most of this book is dedicated to helping you acquire tools to help with your decision making.

Decisiveness is a moral and visceral quality. It deals with the ability to commit. People on Wall Street have a figure of speech: Can he pull the trigger? If you find a good deal in a stock, can you call your broker and say buy 500 shares at $23? Can you do that knowing full well you are spending a substantial part of your retirement account and that the market doesn't care if you live or die? I can't help you much with decisiveness. It is too much of an internal and personal quality. Your decisiveness in stock investing will probably change some as you go along and hit a few major winners or losers.

Your personal level of decisiveness will reveal itself by how you feel after you call your broker and say "buy 200 GM at the market" and watch $12,000 move out of cash into stocks. It will be revealed when you analyze a stock carefully and all the numbers look good, but you just have a hunch that the stock doesn't quite smell right to you. So you don't buy, and over the next eight months the price goes from $18 to $29 and back down to $16. It will be revealed after you sell your biggest winner and take a 60 percent profit after eighteen months, but the stock stays at its high price level for a few more months. If you start trading individual stocks, then something like those situations will happen to you.

Peter Lynch[1] is or was perhaps the greatest stock miner of them all. He said, "Everyone has the brains for investing. The question is whether you have the stomach for it." Everyone can do some credible decision making, but not everyone can take the decisive action. In order to be successful in stock market investing, you will have to bring both qualities to the job. That is one of the ways that a full-service broker may be worth the expense. If you can handle the decision making but have trouble with decisively putting in the buy or sell order, then a broker might coach you into the commitment. If you can't abide doing the research or analysis yourself, but don't mind stepping up to the risk, then the brokerage firm will have a world of recommended stocks for you to try. That is, they supply the decision making, and you supply the decisiveness. If you cannot handle either the decision making or the decisiveness, then do not invest in individual stocks, buy mutual funds.

Decision Making Never Guarantees Profit

Decision making on stock investments is difficult. It is not like high school algebra, where you could be sure of getting the right answer if you carefully applied the correct formulas. At any time, and for any stock you may consider, there will be many conflicting opinions. Any stock that is being traded each day is considered by the buyers to be a good buy and considered by the sellers to be a good sell. There is an instructive column that appears in *Smart Money* magazine each month that illustrates this. They call it the Face-Off. It serves to remind us there is never unanimity of opinion about stocks. In the Face-Off section, *Smart Money* presents opposing views of investment professionals about one stock each month. Let's review a couple. The point is not to criticize the analysts, but rather to illustrate that there is always room for interpretation and differing points of view.

---

[1] Commonly (and appropriately) referred to as Peter the Great.

In May 1996, two analysts looked at IBM, then selling at about 110. One said to buy because the company was in a turnaround, their management team was renewed and refreshed, the PC division would not damage profits, and mainframe size and power was growing. He said, "IBM has changed . . . into a growth company." Remember, growth companies, for growth investors, derive their appeal from projections about sales and earnings growth, and higher P/E ratios to be assigned to the company.

The other analyst said don't buy. He said the economy and competition and foreign currency pressures would prevent the company from raising prices. The PC division would hurt revenues and earnings. He didn't believe the projected demands for new mainframe computing power, and there was a risk due to a slowing economy.

Notice here that there was not much that they directly clashed on except the importance of the PC sales, and both analysts thought that division would remain weak. Both of those analysts had available all of the financial reports for IBM's last few years, and they were aware of what else was going on around the industry. They could hardly have disagreed on the past financial results—that was history. Where they disagreed was in the strength and certainty of future sales growth, and the economy's need for new mainframe computers. IBM stock had appreciated to $110 from $80 a year earlier. The price would go on to $160 within eight months after that article appeared. In February 1997, the buy/don't buy controversy on IBM continued.

In December 1995, the Face-Off showed conflicting opinions on Bankers Trust Company (symbol BT on the NYSE). This stock is different because we all think we know something about IBM, but nobody knows anything about Bankers Trust. Their stock price had a sharp run-up from $40 in December 1990 to $64 in December 1991, and was still at $64 in December of 1995. Earnings per share had been $9 in 1992, $12 in 1993, $7 in 1994, and $2 in 1995. The future appeared to be risky and difficult to predict. There had been some negative publicity related to unfortunate derivatives investing by some customers. The optimistic analyst said to buy it. He thought the bad image situation was behind them, the company had innovative solutions to financial services, and the derivatives trading would return to being very profitable. The discouraging analyst said don't buy because too many customers had gone sour on the bank, the derivatives business would not become strongly profitable again, and the stock was probably at a peak, presenting a high-risk investment.

These two analysts had access to the same recent financial reports, but they had completely different views of the bank management's ability to deal with their problems and capitalize on the strengths. The disagreement here was clearly about the degree of harm in the reputation issues and the degree of strength in the derivatives business. At the end of 1996, Bankers Trust stock had gone up to $88 with a 4.5 percent yield. (4.5 percent yield was very strong at that time.)

Don't worry about the losing analyst in each case. They are pros who know that you win a few and you lose a few. The lesson in this is that even these experienced professionals can go wrong.

> Do not get too carried away with the brilliance and insight of your own stock analysis. You, too, will be wrong on occasion.

Decisiveness Is a Two-Edged Sword

Someone has to make the decision. Someone has to say buy, sell, or I'll pass at this price. If it's you, then sometimes you will lose money or fail to grab an available profit. Sometimes you will be wrong because you were decisive and sometimes you will be wrong because you were not—as I was on Unisys. Decisiveness is an essential quality of the successful investor, however; it is also, like bravery, a quality that will occasionally get you in trouble.

So what about some real decisiveness? What about when you find a stock that you study and research and think about for six weeks, and decide that it is the greatest thing since cheese grits? Why not go on and put your entire pile of stock market funds into that one? Why should you have four investments that are going to average 11 percent return, when you could have one that gives 75 percent total return? After all, if decisiveness is the key to the kingdom, then let's get decisive! The answer is that you may be wrong. It may be that your one greatest stock turns out to suffer because the rest of the companies in its industry group all decline. When that happens, even the good, solid members of the industry group may be cast off by investors. On the other hand, one of those other stocks that you thought was just a fellow traveler may take off. If you thought the stock was good enough to buy, then probably a number of other people did, too, and for the same reasons. Maybe one of those other stocks will be the big winner. Decisiveness is necessary for success in the markets, but just like anything else, it can be overdone to the point where it hurts you. Diversify!

Being decisive does not equate with being in a hurry. It will be extremely rare that you find any investment, or that your broker finds one, where a difference of a few days in making your decision will make a huge difference. Even when that does happen, the few days are just as likely to help you as to hurt you. Remember that one of the true disadvantages of the individual small investor is that we do not expect to get the genuine hot tips on new developments. That may change in some cases, perhaps if the new development is in your employer, or their competitor, or customer—but generally we don't expect to hear hot critical news. Therefore, don't invest on an assumption that you are to reap a quick, large reward; you cannot expect to do that. Invest on the expectation that you have identified a company with good financials, sound history, and sound markets and management—a company that will fairly consistently reward you over the next year or two.

Looking at the Risks

Here are two more basic ideas of stock analysis. Find the good stocks. Avoid the bad ones. Which bad ones? Nobody knows. Essentially, every stock that is traded is a good buy for someone and a good sell for another. Otherwise there wouldn't be much trading. You cannot expect to clearly separate the good stocks from the bad ones. That theory is a myth. Here is another idea: Find some stocks that work for you and avoid some others that do not work for you.

Just for now, let's focus on avoiding the stocks that are not right for you. Almost every stock from every company will have some features that appeal to you. They do, after all, have hard-working, dedicated employees and managers who are doing their best to make the company profitable. Your challenge when you look at a stock and a company will be to understand the risks that threaten to offset the appealing features of the stock investment.

When any ten investors analyze a stock for possible purchase, it is likely that they will see pretty much the same reasons why the stock is attractive. My experience when talking to different investors about a company is that most people see the same arguments to buy, but they generally see different reasons why not to buy. They see different risks and appraise the risks differently. I think we have been taught a list of potentially favorable indicators and have not been disciplined to look on the reverse of each point. Let's examine some of those issues.

Some of the most obvious factors in favor of buying a stock are low price, low price-to-earnings ratio, or low price-to-sales ratio. Consider this example of a company that has a price of $14 per share, last year's earnings of $1.50, and last year's sales of $11. So the P/E ratio is $14 \div 1.50 = 9.3$, and the P/S ratio is $14 \div 11 = 1.3$. Both of those would be regarded as good by many analysts, and let's say that the average P/E in their industry group is 12, and the average P/S for the group is 1.9. What is wrong with this picture?

A low P/E ratio can be attributed to a high earnings rate (good news) or a falling price (bad news). Any time the P/E ratio and the P/S ratio are low for the industry group, other investors generally do not think that the company has the power to maintain those sales and earnings. You should check further to see if some threat to sales has been discovered. The lower ratios also mean that other investors have more confidence in the other members of the industry group and are willing to pay more for a given dollar of earnings or sales from the others. Do not lose sight of the fact that eventually the price of the stock you buy is determined by the actions of other investors who buy or sell the same stock. If the price ratios are low for a company, the market is trying to tell you something about the stock. Think about it.

Suppose that you have examined the new products that the company is offering this year. You think they will take their market by storm. On the other hand, don't you think that the competitors have looked at those products, too? Before you make an investment based on one company's new product line, check to see what the competition is doing.

Suppose that you like a good growth stock. You invest based on well-established trends of rising sales, earnings, stock price, and strong ratios. Okay, fine. The trend will continue for however long it continues. At some point the price will top out, and the wisest investors will have sold. The Greater Fool, as usual, will be left holding a "growth stock" as the price falls.

Here are some charts. Rhone-Poulenc Rorer was a growth stock from 1985 to 1992. The stock price went up from $8 to $12 to $24 to $32 to $40 to $48 to $64, with hardly a blip over seven years. In 1991 the price doubled, from 32 to 64. At the end of the year, the P/E ratio was 27. The

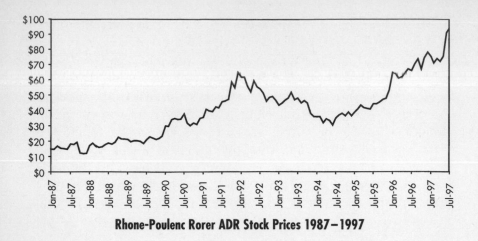

Rhone-Poulenc Rorer ADR Stock Prices 1987–1997

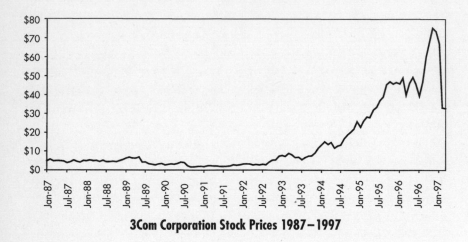

3Com Corporation Stock Prices 1987–1997

earnings even went up 26 percent in 1992. However, in 1992 the stock price fell from $64 to $48, and three years later was still at $48. Even the best of growth stocks may eventually become overpriced. Even the best of them will eventually burn someone.

You don't think so? You point at Coca-Cola and Microsoft, and say those babies will never stop going up. Could be, but I wouldn't bet the ranch on it. People use to say the same things about Hewlett-Packard and 3Com Corp.

We have looked at several different views of risk. Let's consider how each of those may affect your decision making and decisiveness in buying or selling stocks.

The market risk is the risk of a general trend of falling prices throughout the market. We call that a *bear market*. The historical and statistical records are clear that if a bear market catches you, then you must expect your stocks to fall along with all the rest. There are three ways to view that danger: (1) ignore it, (2) sell, (3) buy defensively. Some investors will ignore it because they know that the long-term trend of the markets is up, and eventually[2] any general losses in prices will be recovered. Maybe so, but for the people who bought the DJIA at average prices in 1930, it took twenty years for prices to recover (they did, however, collect some good dividends along the way). This may be the way of the buy-and-hold investor who plans to keep her money invested for a long time. Holding during a bear market is extremely tough on the nerves and difficult to maintain as you see your investment values eroding.

Another way to greet the bear is to sell. Then, you can be a bear, too. Good strategy—buy low and sell high. When you hear the bear then start selling or lighten up on your stock exposure. That's a fine idea, but it will be difficult to put into practice effectively. Most theoreticians would say that you cannot foretell the approach of the bear market. It is certainly true, that very few people can demonstrate long-term success at guessing the market's turning points. Market timing is either impossible or extremely difficult.

The third defense against bear markets is to buy what are called *defensive stocks*—that is, stocks that generally don't go down as much as the overall market (low beta), or perhaps even go up during bear markets. The last class of stocks may include real estate investment trusts (REITs). Their behavior is frequently not in step with the rest of the market. When paper assets—stocks and bonds—are falling, then sometimes real assets, such as property and buildings, rise. Some other possible candidates for defensive stocks include electric utilities and grocery chains. Diversify!

Of those three plans to fight off bear market risk, the last is most practical. It doesn't give you any guarantees, but it may help. Keep it in mind when you are working out your diversification plans.

Another risk is the risk of the competition. Your decision making should include more than just looking at the company you are interested in. For almost any company you should be able to identify a few competitors. It would be unwise to buy the one stock before looking at the others.

---

[2] In the long run, which may be two years or forty-eight years.

Then there are risks in the economy. Say you like Ford. Consider that 35 to 40 percent of their automobile revenues come from outside the United States. If the dollar becomes stronger against foreign currencies, then those sales are at risk, or at least would not be worth as much in dollar terms. If the U.S. economy went into a severe slump, then domestic sales would certainly suffer. You cannot evaluate Ford and the risks without thinking about both foreign and domestic economic factors.

Perfect Information

Decisiveness in itself entails risk. How and when will you know if you have done enough research into this stock and the company behind it? You never know. When you are ready to make your decision, then you effectively quit gathering the last little bit of new information that might effect your decision.

The obvious solution to that problem is not a solution. It is a trap in itself—the search for perfect information. You can imagine a case where some investor is so bright, so industrious, and so determined that he is committed to finding and analyzing all of the information on the company, their market risk, and their competition. That attempt paralyzes decisiveness. There is no perfect information. As you study and review all available information, more developments are coming over the horizon. The company does not stand still, nor do their competitors, nor does the market.

Investment Clubs

Help is on the way. One risk we haven't discussed yet is the social risk. It's like the great occupational hazard of computer programmers, who fall in love with their machines and forget to live in the world of people. The same thing can happen with investing. A lot of folks[3] get so absorbed in the quest for profits that they run a risk of becoming misanthropic hermits. There is a miracle cure for that, and it will make you a better investor also. It is the investment club. Every inexperienced individual investor would be well advised to consider joining an investment club. I have mentioned the advantage of better risk recognition. The investing that you do through a

---

[3] This problem is growing worse with the spread of computerized methods and online resources for investors.

club of conscientious working members will invariably be safer than what you might do alone. In addition, the club offers the advantage of discipline in your investing work. It is easy (at least it's easy for me) to let the financial research slide for a week or two and fail to keep up with your reading or fail to review the current situation of each of your current stocks. Investment clubs help with that. If you have made a commitment to ten other people to show up on Tuesday night with some analysis and insights on the stock of the month, then you are unlikely to go in unprepared. You will discipline yourself to do some work. You also get the probable reward of meeting other people who share some interest in stocks with you. Of course just about everybody shares your interest in money, but the club members are fairly serious about it.

Call the National Association of Investors Corporation (810-583-6242). They will send you a fine package of materials (free) that will help you find or begin a club, and a copy of their excellent magazine, *Better Investing*. The package will contain guidelines to their own investing method, which I am not going to review in this book. It is well worth looking at.

Sources

Your investment results will be no better than your decision making. Your decision making will be no better than your sources of information. (Remember, Peter the Great said everybody is smart enough to invest in stocks.) I am extremely biased and opinionated on these issues. If you have read everything to this point, then you already know several of my favorite sources of information.

Let's review and try to organize our sources of information. What sources of information? These:

1. General business news, both U.S. and worldwide

2. Business news specific to an industry group/sector

3. Business news specific to one company, and their financial reports

4. Education in investing, or particularly in stocks, bonds, or funds

5. Education on specific methods of stock selection

6. News about and analysis of the people and firms in the market

The first thing to understand is that you cannot read it all. Not even I can read it all, and I try; I enjoy the stuff. Too much very good information is available, and it is being updated and changed so fast that we cannot keep up with it.

For general business news, there are many excellent sources. My own prejudice is that the best general business reporting that anyone can find comes in the *Wall Street Journal* (WSJ). Try to plan to read the *Journal* every day for a couple of months, and then at least two or three times a week after that. That is the essential cornerstone of every plan for financial education. If you don't have time to read my books and the *Journal*, then read the *Journal*. Other outstanding choices include the business sections of some major papers like the *New York Times*, the *Washington Post*, the *L.A. Times*, and some of the other papers that put substantial resources into business reporting. One interesting special case devoted to financial news is *Investor's Business Daily* (IBD). IBD deserves your consideration for its excellent reporting of the financial markets but does not have as much coverage of general worldwide business news as the WSJ. The IBD will also give you a free two-week home delivery subscription if you ask. That is too good a deal to pass.

For reporting of general business news as news, magazines are useless. Everything is too late by the time you read it. However, for reporting of business situations as in-depth analysis, some of the magazines are better. In that class, look at *Forbes* and *Barron's*.

When you are evaluating a specific industry group or sector, or just one company in a sector, there are several good sources. *Forbes Annual Review of American Industry* gives comparable values of financial ratios for an industry group and for most of the prominent firms in the group. The *Value Line* gives a study of the situation of each industry group that includes the average values and ratios for financial analysis going back about ten years. All of the previously mentioned newspapers will also contain occasional in-depth studies of particular sectors. You can also find more such articles in the financial periodicals like *Smart Money*, *Money*, or *Kiplinger's Personal Financial Digest*. Another interesting source for a company or industry group is the professional journal of their industry. For example, if you were planning to get very serious about investing in the petroleum group, then you might read the *Oil and Gas Journal*. Every industry has its own professional or trade journal that will help you understand what is important for them.

When it is time to focus on one company, you should get copies of their annual and quarterly reports. The *Value Line* has telephone numbers to use to call each company's investor relations office. They are always happy to send out whatever you request. Otherwise, go into the Securities and Exchange Commission's Web site, using keyword EDGAR. EDGAR is a large database that has copies of the financial reports of all American publicly traded companies. It is very easy to use if you have access to the Web, and it is free.[4] Beyond those reports, the *Value Line* has excellent analysis, opinions, and summaries of the data. If you are not going to read the financial reports, then the *Value Line* is your best friend.

Standard & Poor's has a stock reports service that will sell you in-depth analysis, data, and recommendations on any of the companies that they normally follow (there are a lot of them). You can order their reports for fax or mail delivery by calling S&P Reports on Demand, 800-642-2858.

Caution: I have told you about twenty times so far that the *Value Line* is a valuable source of data and opinions. However, *the* Value Line *does not do your thinking for you.* Nor do any of the other sources that we are considering. Many of them offer specific recommendations on what to buy or sell, or the fair value of a stock, but none of those writers know you or your needs, or your total financial situation. You have to make the advice and analysis serve your needs. They will not do that for you.

Standard & Poor's publishes a bi-weekly called *Standard & Poor's Outlook,* which has detailed analysis and recommendations about a few stocks, and ratings on many more. It is also well written and useful, but does not contain as much information as the *Value Line*. S&P also sells a stock guide, chart guide, and earnings guide that will supply more details about individual firms. If you contact them, or your broker, you can probably get free copies to review.

All of the above sources comprise a veritable graduate library of investment education. In addition, your public library is your friend. Read the books that I have mentioned in the references at the end of each chapter in this book and read *The Small Investor*. There are a great many fine reference books for new investors, and some that are not so fine. I have endeavored to sort through many of them and recommend the ones that will be most helpful to you, without being excessively demanding. There

---

[4] This is a significant rebuttal to the arguments of the pure Libertarians that the government cannot do anything worthwhile.

are special cases, such as *Winning on Wall Street* by Marty Zweig and *Security Analysis* by Graham and Dodd, that are demanding on the reader but are so good and so well written that you might give them a try, too.

By the time you finish this book, some of you will want to see more on specific stock-selection methods. Almost all of the previously mentioned references will regularly run columns by some visiting guru who wants to promote his own method. Most of those are interesting and informative. None of them is guaranteed to work for you. Check your library and bookstore.

There are a few more books that demand special mention. In the first place, *What Works on Wall Street* by James O'Shaughnessy. In 1998 and beyond, you cannot consider yourself to be a well-informed and serious investor without having reviewed his research findings. The presentation may be a bit dry or too technical for some readers, but the bottom-line conclusions are of immense significance. This book will have major, and as yet unforeseeable, impact on the entire investment community.

Beating the Dow by Michael O'Higgins and John Downs (Harper-Collins, 1991) is probably the best thing available for finding an approach that is easy and practical, and yet really works (that means the historical evidence is strong, though it does not mean that it will work for you next year).

For immediate news about companies and people in the markets, television has a lot to offer. CNBC carries current market reports, plus interviews with company executives or investment professionals all day while the markets are open. Just keep in mind when they start giving advice that the CNBC staff are "talking heads," not professional investors. Some of their guests are among the best informed investors in the world. Another good cable offering is *The Money Line* on CNN, which is on weekday evenings. Public television offers *Wall Street Week* and *Nightly Business Review*. All of those programs are educational and interesting.

Investment newsletters are usually expensive monthly publications that contain one person's opinions about particular stocks or mutual funds that you should buy or sell. You may find that your local library carries some of them. Many of these newsletters make good reading, but few of them give advice that justifies putting your money behind them. The *Hulbert Financial Digest* is a publication that will help you sort out which investment newsletters are worthwhile, and which have given advice that proved to be reliable over a period of years. The *Hulbert Financial Digest* is probably in a library that has a strong business section. You may want to check your local university library.

. . . to regulate imagination by reality, and instead of thinking how things may be, to see them as they are.

—Samuel Johnson

The Income Investor in the Real World

Stock Selection

So far, we have covered a lot of complex material. This chapter and the next two are going to review some main points and demonstrate how they are applied in practical cases. We are going to look at several examples of stock selection. Because of the different needs of the investors involved, each will emphasize different selection factors. However, just as a reminder, lets say again that all investors need to keep these things in mind (the PIG principal):

1. How much should you emphasize protection of your principal?

2. How much should you emphasize income?

3. How much should you emphasize growth?

All of those factors are important to investors, but we emphasize different ones at different times as we have different needs and different diversification plans. You will adjust these factors to suit your own preferences for value or growth stock selection and the level of risk you choose to accept.

Now, the examples ahead will illustrate the needs and work to be done by several investors. In this chapter, we will emphasize income, in the next chapter, value, and in chapter 12, growth. Those are three approaches to stock selection that are widely practiced.

Income investing emphasizes the current dividend yield paid to the shareholder and the prospects for the future safety and predictability of that yield. Some of the primary benefits of income investing are the continuing stream of income and the protection that is attached to income-paying stocks.

Value investing emphasizes the attributes of a stock that can be measured by generally accepted accounting principles. Those include the yield, the earnings, the cash flow, and other values that are reported in the financial statements of the company. The value investor also looks at the history of how those values have changed in recent years and estimates of how those values are likely to change over the next couple of years. Value investing also depends on judgments of how high a price is reasonable to pay to acquire a share of those attributes. The value investor must be concerned not only with finding a great company, but also with finding the stock at an attractive price. The specific price that makes each stock attractive will forever be debated among different investors.

Growth investing emphasizes the profit that may be realized from share price appreciation. Growth investors like to buy stocks with both a history and a strong likelihood of continuation of earnings growth, share price growth, and price-to-earnings–ratio growth. The growth investor wants to identify stocks for which the earnings and P/E ratio will increase, because that will give a double boost to the share price. The growth investor is often in favor of the company retaining all the earnings to finance future growth and willing to forego dividend yield.

All investors, regardless of their emphasis on certain types of stocks, need to consider the safety of their overall portfolio of stocks and other investments. Three useful approaches to protection in stock investing are to (1) hold on to the money until enough work has been done to reliably identify the potential risks and rewards from a stock; (2) gain enough education and experience to recognize good sources of company information and how to evaluate the information; (3) diversify.

There are many useful approaches to diversification. Here are some that you may want to try:

1. **Diversify through method.** Buy some stocks with an income emphasis, some with a value approach, and some with a growth approach.[1]

2. **Diversify over business lines.** Buy stocks from different industries.

3. **Diversify the primary risks.** Buy stocks that have different kinds of primary risks.

4. **Diversify over time.** Spread your stock purchases over a period of time to catch different market conditions (dollar cost averaging).

5. **Diversify through geography.** Buy stocks of companies that have their main markets geographically diverse.

6. **Diversify your research.** Use many different sources for your investment information.

7. **Diversify the advice you accept.** Listen to many different stock market experts, but be ruled by none.

8. **Diversify your financial foundations.** Manage your stock market investments as an integral part of your overall financial planning; it should be affected by all of your other financial circumstances.

9. **Diversify through broader experience.** Work with an investment club (or perhaps a broker or investment advisor).

---

[1] Some writers and professional investors will disagree with that plan; they say that you should adopt one strategy and stick with it until it is proven deficient. I say that using several methods at different times can be a useful part of your diversification plan, but we all agree that you should adopt rational methods, not just a hit-or-miss approach.

"This is a great 'buy and hold.' You can put it away and forget about it."

Income Investing

Now we are going to focus on the needs and practices of an individual investor who was primarily concerned, at the time, with investing for income.

In early 1997, Eric had two years experience in stock investing. He held six stocks and cash:

Kind of company	Amount invested	% annual yield
Computer software	$4,000	0
Automobile	6,000	1
Drug	4,000	1
Electric utility	5,000	5
Electric utility	6,000	6
Book store chain	5,000	0
Cash (money market fund)	8,500	4
Total value	$38,500	

Eric's annual dividends and money market yield added up to $1,050, for a 2.7 percent yield on his portfolio. He made a decision that he wanted to buy one more high-yield stock to boost the income on his portfolio and increase both diversification and growth opportunities. His idea of high yield was 5 percent or above. To improve diversification, he ruled out buying another electric utility. Eric had a firm prejudice against high price/earnings ratios, because he thought they were too risky. His idea of a high P/E was 20.

Eric's first task was to find a group of companies, excluding electric utilities, with the annual yield above 5 percent and the P/E ratio below 20. A good place to start is the *Value Line* weekly Summary and Index, which has lists of high-yield stocks and lists of low P/E stocks. He could have read through the 1750 individual companies in the Index, looking for the right combinations. That is not difficult. You can do it in ten minutes. If Eric had a full-service broker, then he should have told the broker to produce a list of firms that satisfied his criteria. The *Value Line* list of high-yield stocks showed 100 stocks with yield over 6 percent.[2] Among those 100, 49 were electric utilities, 13 were investment companies, 10 were real estate investment trusts, and 14 were other kinds of utilities. That did not appear to be a broad enough selection to choose from, and it only included very high yield stocks.

Eric decided to look in the index and read through the lists of companies. Let's look over his shoulder at the process as Eric went through his stock selection analysis.

After searching the *Value Line* Index and reports for a couple of hours, and ruling out a few candidates, he made a few compromises on the required yield rate because of a shortage of candidates. He produced this list of companies:

Company	Industry	Yield (%)	P/E (using last year's earnings)
AGL Resources	gas utility	5.6	13
ARCO	chemical	5.3	10
Alliance Capital Management	investment	8.8	11
Aquarian Co.	water/diversified	6.8	12

---

[2] These facts refer to a particular date when Eric did this study. They would be different today.

Company	Industry	Yield (%)	P/E (using last year's earnings)
Atlantic Richfield	petroleum	4.7	15
B.A.T. Industries	tobacco	5.9	10
British Columbia Telecom	telecom	5.2	15
British Steel	steel	5.0	7
Brooklyn Gas	gas utility	5.5	13
Connecticut Natural Gas	gas utility	6.2	13
GenCorp	diversified	5.0	10
Great Northern Iron	steel	10.3	9
Jacobsen Stores	department stores	5.6	14
Kimco Realty	REIT	6.1	18
Lance	food	6.0	21
Merry Land & Investment	REIT	7.0	17
Moore Corp.	office supplies	4.9	14
Nash Finch Co.	wholesale food	4.1	11
National Presto Corp.	small appliances	5.3	15
Ogden Corp.	facilities services	6.3	16
PENN REIT	REIT	9	16
Perkins Family Restaurant	restaurant	10.8	9
Reliance Group Holdings	insurance	4.3	9
Shell Transport	petroleum	4.5	18
Piccadilly	restaurant	5	14
Plum Creek Timber	wood/paper	7.3	15

REIT = Real Estate Investment Trust

This is a nicely diverse group of candidates that has been gathered for further consideration.

Notice: The rest of this analysis depends on real data and conditions for these companies, but it is old data. If anyone analyzed the same companies at the time you are reading this, they would see different information and presumably reach different conclusions. This discussion is not intended to show you a stock to buy at the time you are reading this.

Now Eric wanted to review all of these twenty-six companies and reduce the list to a smaller set to study. The reasons for eliminating a company from further consideration can be anything you like or don't like. You do not have to justify to anyone else your reasons for not buying a stock. The reasons given here may appear arbitrary or shallow to some readers. So be it. If these reasons worked for Eric, then that is good enough.

Companies to remove from further consideration (this can be based solely on studying in TVL or the S&P Stocks on Demand reports):

- Piccadilly Cafeteria—the earnings are not stable enough.

- Perkins Family Restaurant—high debt and the *Value Line* forecasts a cut in the yield.

- Shell Transport—Atlantic Richfield in the same industry looks better.

- Brooklyn Gas and Connecticut Gas—AGL in the same industry looks better.

- Great Northern Iron—peculiar trust structure and tax situation, confusing.

- BC Telecom—trades on the Toronto Stock Exchange.

- Kimco Realty—Merry Land in the same industry looks better.

- Ogden Corp.—too much debt.

- PENN REIT—payout ratio is too high, debt is too high, and Merry Land looks better.

- Aquarian—too much potential trouble and cost in water resource management and potential new state and federal regulation.

- Lance—payout ratio too high (at or above 100 percent) and dividend not safe.

- Jacobsen Stores—too much debt.

- Reliance Group Holdings—can't understand what their business is.

That left twelve companies.

The *Value Line* gives three ratings on each stock. One is for timeliness, which is for estimated price growth potential over the next six to twelve months. Eric was not concerned about short-term profit, so he ignored that rating. Another rating is for technical performance. Eric doesn't care for technical analysis, so he ignored that rating. The third rating is for safety. Eric likes to use that rating. He decided to refine his list by looking at the *Value Line* safety rating, the beta rating for volatility[3] of the stock price, and the Standard & Poor's rating of safety of the common stock. The *Value Line* safety rating is from 1 (best) to 5 (worst). The S&P rating goes from A+ to D (nr = not rated). The *nr* means that S&P , for some reason, could not do a reliable rating. For the twelve stocks left, Eric found these values, using the *Value Line* and the *S&P Stock Guide*.

Company	Yield %	P/E	Value Line Safety	S&P Rating	Beta (VL)
AGL Resources	5.6	13	2	B+	0.75
ARCO	5.3	10	2	B+	0.80
Alliance Capital Mgt.	8.8	11	3	nr	1.25
Atlantic Richfield	4.7	15	1	B+	0.75
B.A.T. Industries	5.9	10	3	nr	1.10
British Steel	5.0	7	3	nr	0.85
GenCorp	5.0	10	4	B	1.25
Merry Land & Investment	7.0	17	3	nr	0.75
Moore Corp.	4.9	14	2	B-	0.95
Nash Finch Co.	4.1	11	3	A-	0.65
National Presto Corp.	5.3	15	2	B+	0.70
Plum Creek Timber	7.3	15	3	nr	0.85

[3] Recall that volatility roughly indicates how much a stock's price moves up and down, beta measures volatility, and beta = 1 is average volatility.

He decided to require that the safety rating be 3 or better, the S&P rating should be B+ or better, and the beta should be 0.80 or lower. That narrowed the list down to these five.

Company	Yield %	P/E	Value Line Safety	S&P Rating	Beta (VL)
AGL Resources	5.6	13	2	B+	0.75
ARCO	5.3	10	2	B+	0.80
Atlantic Richfield	4.7	15	1	B+	0.75
Merry Land & Investment	7.0	17	3	nr	0.75
National Presto Corp.	5.3	15	2	B+	0.70

Now the hard work begins. It would be easy to pick one of these stocks to buy. They all have some appealing features, but what other information could he dig out, and how should that affect the decision? First, he looked at diversification. All six of the above companies were in different industries from anything that he currently owns. None of them shared any special risk attributes with the current six holdings, except for the threat to high yield stocks. Any stock that has a high-yield is strongly subject to the influence of the bond markets, but since Eric decided to buy high yield this time, he decided to accept that.

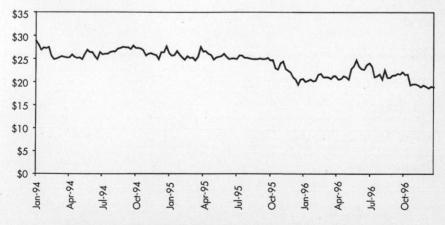

AGL Resources (Parent of Atlanta Gas Light) Stock Prices 1994–1996

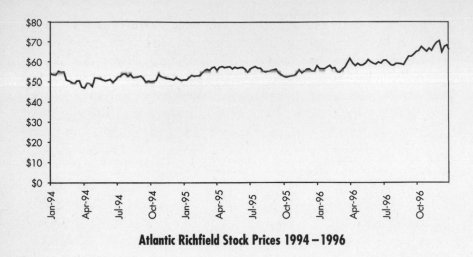

Atlantic Richfield Stock Prices 1994–1996

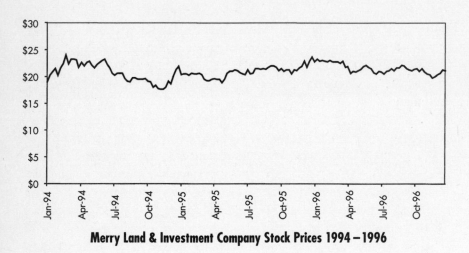

Merry Land & Investment Company Stock Prices 1994–1996

He obtained copies of the most recent annual and quarterly reports for each of these five candidates. (If he had a full-service broker, he should have asked for their research recommendations on each company.) It would also be worthwhile to buy copies of the S&P reports on each (S&P Reports on Demand, 800-642-2858). He could have called the SEC or accessed EDGAR through the Internet to get copies of their most recent 10K and 10Q reports. Let's say he did all of that. There was no great hurry about making the decision. There is no shame in holding cash for a couple of weeks longer.

National Presto is safe and secure in their niche of inventing and selling small appliances, and has no debt. They even had enough cash on hand to cover $29 dollars per share of the $41 share price.[4] The dividend was not predictable because they apparently just pick a number to pay once a year. The payout ratio is 82 percent, but in other recent years has been lower than that. They have not done much this year in the way of exciting new products. National Presto did not appear to have any readily identifiable problems, or qualities to make the stock look attractive. Eric made a tentative judgment to set them out of consideration.

Atlantic Richfield is an integrated oil producer[5] with a current payout ratio of 68 percent, but in the previous two years, that ratio was over 100 percent. The dividend was good and might even be increased if the earnings stayed up. The stock price had stayed between $100 and $120 for four years. The current price was $116 when Eric looked at it. If the price of oil and gas rose much, then ARC would be a major beneficiary. Eric liked that play on energy prices. They had $4 billion of long-term debt to be repaid within five years. If interest rates went up much, that might be a problem. The market capitalization[6] was over $18 billion and they had over 100 million shares outstanding. This was appealing, since Eric likes large-cap companies.

AGL Resources sells gas to Atlanta and some other southern communities. Eric preferred it over Brooklyn Gas and Connecticut Gas because of the location, size, and growth of the market. AGL also would profit from an increase in energy costs—for instance, if the price of crude oil went up much. The debt was not too high for a utility (49 percent). Revenues had slacked off a little in recent years, yet earnings and cash flow had grown consistently. This occurred during a period of fairly restrained energy costs. The payout ratio was 78 percent, but for the preceding four years, it was near or above 90 percent. It appeared that there was a fair chance of a dividend increase here. This company had a $1 billion market cap and solid financial stability. That, along with the share price stability (low beta) and growing earnings and dividends, made AGL look good to Eric.

---

[4] This is analogous to Alpha Beta Publishing having too much idle cash sitting around.

[5] They produce gas and petroleum, and refine petroleum products.

[6] Recall, capitalization is the total market value of all of the common stock.

Merry Land & Investment Company is a real estate investment trust (REIT) that specializes in upscale apartments in the southeastern United States. The market capitalization was $800 million. REITs measure and report *funds from operations* (FFO) instead of cash flow. The FFO number stands in place of cash flow for that industry but must be treated by comparisons within the industry. For Merry Land, the FFO and earnings and dividends had been steadily growing for five years. This appeared to be another candidate for good growth of dividend if the FFO held up for the next few years. The total debt was low by REIT standards. Officers and directors owned about 10 percent of the common stock, which gives them a good healthy stake in further success of the company. Merry Land had one apparent problem; for two years the payout ratio had been greater than 100 percent. REITs are forced to pay out most of earnings, so the ratio should stay close to 100 percent. Eric decided that the payout ratio was not a large problem because of the financial strength (relatively low debt) and growing FFO of the company.

ARCO is a major worldwide chemical business. The market capitalization was then $5 billion. Total long-term debt was about 32 percent, which is near average within this industry. Sales, cash flow, and earnings had shown good strength over the preceding five years, but the dividend had remained fixed. The payout ratio was only 50 percent. There was a clear opportunity here for the dividend to be increased, perhaps increased a lot, but it appeared that the directors were not interested in that. There had been one small increase the latest year, but it had been a while before that. The *Value Line* analyst speculated that a dividend increase might be in the works for the next year. The company was financially quite solid. Much of ARCO's stock is held by the company or other large investors. Only about 10 percent was among public investors. The risk/reward potential in having the stock owned by large investors is that if one of the large traders decided to either buy or sell any significant amount, it would have a dramatic impact on the trading price of the stock—which might turn out to be good or bad. Eric decided the other choices were more interesting for him.

Nash Finch Company is a large food wholesaler. Their revenues had shown good growth over the past ten years, but the cash flow and earnings had not. The stock price was near the lower limit of its past five year history, which had fairly consistently stayed between $16 and $20. The financial strength and debt ratio were reasonably strong compared to others in the food wholesale business. The dividend had grown consistently but slowly for the past ten years. The payout ratio was only 50 percent, but it appeared that the directors meant to keep it at or below that rate. There was not much here to attract an investor's attention.

After completing those reviews, Eric reduced his considerations to these companies:

Company	Yield %	P/E	Safety (VL)	S&P Rating	Beta (VL)
AGL Resources	5.6	13	2	B+	0.75
Atlantic Richfield	4.7	15	1	B+	0.75
Merry Land & Investments	7.0	17	3	nr	0.75

And the winner is: Merry Land! Why? It offers diversification, safety, and high yield, plus the clear possibility of higher dividend to come in the near future. Either of the other two companies would probably serve Eric well also.

There are other risk considerations on Merry Land. There is no S&P rating, so Eric had to study the 10K statement very carefully to look for potential problems. He found nothing worth worrying about. The big open question is stability of the real estate market. Eric felt that it had been flat for so long that it should pick up in the next few years. Also, Merry Land concentrates their assets in the Southeast, which appeared to be a safer, growing economy. The payout ratio will bear attention. Eric should review the quarterly financial reports and ongoing news reports on Merry Land to see that no problems arise. What would be hints of problems? Lower FFO, or the payout staying above 100 percent, or a slump in real estate values in the southeast, or a significant increase in their debt.

What about the risk in inflation, which is always a threat to the stock markets? With Merry Land, there might be a little cushion against inflation. They would try to raise rents. That works unless there have been too many new apartments built in their market areas.

The ever-present market risk is unavoidable, but high-yield stocks always provide some protection against a general market slump. In summary Merry Land looks like a good buy for Eric. The stock price was $23, so with his $8,500 cash, he could have bought 200 or 300 shares, which would nicely complement his other holdings. The potential reward is

exactly what he started out looking for, and the risks are reasonably clear and easy to track.

This analysis is the result of about ten to fifteen hours work, two trips to the library, and four telephone calls, or Internet access to the financial reports.

In chapter 15, we will reconsider Eric's stock search when computers and online services are called into play. That will make the work faster and easier, and will also produce more candidates for consideration.

Recommended Further Reading

Knowles, Harvey, and Damon Petty. *The Dividend Investor*. Burr Ridge, IL: Irwin Professional Publishing, 1992.

Nichols, Don. *The Income Investor*. Chicago: Dearborn Financial Publishing, 1990.

I have been a selfish being all my life, in practice,
though not in principle.

—JANE AUSTEN, PRIDE AND PREJUDICE

The Value Investor
in the Real World

Value Investing

Many people say that all investing is value investing, or should be. It's like buying a car; some folks select a car for speed or comfort, but they still should look for good value. The income investor that we just looked at was a value investor too, but his idea of value was expressed in dividend payments coming back to him. Dividend payout is one of the ways that we measure value. But for this section, when we talk about value investing, we mean something a little broader. We mean focusing on the financial attributes of the company and the qualities of their products, markets, or sales that can be reasonably measured and considered in terms of the price of the stock. And there is another point of view: to most value investors, things that can be measured count more than things that can only be speculated about as future developments. To be more precise, the typical value investor is more impressed with current financial reports than with predictions about new products in development. We are going to look at some work done by a typical value investor. She is particularly interested in earnings, cash flow, total debt, yield, and the stability or predictability of those factors over the years.

Value Investing: Case 1

Lillian was single and an electrical engineer. She had an aggressive investment plan with the intention of finding growth and value, but value first. She had an investment portfolio holding ten well-diversified stocks with total market value of $124,000, and $22,000 in cash. Her total financial situation was secure enough that she wanted to invest aggressively (accept reasonable risk). The total dividend yield on her ten stocks was only 1 percent, but that was not a concern for her. In mid-1996, the market capitalization of each stock she held was over $3 billion. She was interested in trying some smaller companies that might offer diversification and more growth potential. This stock selection example is based on data that Lillian used in mid-1996.

The "value investor" can use many different standards of value. Some people depend on price-to-earnings ratio, price-to-sales ratio, debt-to-capital ratio, or a combination of any of the other financial indicators that we have looked at. Lillian was particularly interested in P/E and price-to-cash-flow ratios. Her criteria for beginning her stock selection analysis were these:

1. The market capitalization should be $1 billion or less.

2. The P/E ratio should be 14 or less (based on current price and 1995 earnings).

3. The company reported a profit in 1993, 1994, and 1995.

4. The price-to-cash-flow ratio should be 5 or less (using current price and 1995 cash flow).

5. The total debt should be not more than 35 percent of capitalization (meaning the long-term liabilities plus shareholders' equity on the balance sheet).

6. The return on assets should be 12 percent or more.

7. The stock should improve diversification of her portfolio.

8. The company must offer products or services that she understands.

How does one find such stocks? This is a screening process. She could have approached it by reading in the *Value Line* or the *S&P Stock Guide*, or using some of the software and database methods that we will look at in a later chapter on computer methods. The computer methods could make the work go fairly easily, but just to show what you can do with a little elbow grease, let's watch how Lillian worked it out by hand.

She started by reading through pages in the *Value Line* and focusing on the P/E ratio shown there (using the preceding twelve months' reported earnings). If the P/E was 14 or less, she looked at the market cap. To get the market capitalization from the *Value Line* page requires an extra step. You multiply the current price shown by the number of shares outstanding. That takes a little arithmetic, but after doing three or four equations, you can probably estimate the result in your head. Notice here that she doesn't have to know the exact market cap. She just wants to see if it is under $1 billion.

Examples of determining market cap:

Price	Shares Outstanding (M=million)	Market Cap ($)	Less than 1 Billion?
25	14 M	25 x 14 M = 350 M	yes
48	1,200 M	48 x 1,200 M = 57,600 M	no
17	150 M	17 x 150 M = 2,550 M	no
4	42 M	4 x 42 M = 168 M	yes

The calculation is on the product of the two numbers on the left. If that product is less than 1,000 then the market cap is less than one billion.

For each stock that had P/E less than 14 and market cap less than $1 billion, she then checked to see if the earnings were positive in 1993, 1994, and 1995. This was the initial screen. With a few hours of reading through the *Value Line*, she was able to find a rich list of candidates. The following is actually less than half of the candidates that she found.[1] They are grouped by industry to show the diversification of the companies available.

---

[1] The data used is from 1996.

Company/Industry	P/E Ratio	Market Cap ($ million)
Automobiles/Parts		
Navistar	12	700
APS Holdings	11	266
Republic Auto	12	59
Standard Motor	10	184
Wynns	12	264
Tires and Rubber		
TBC	9	160
Home Appliances		
Toro	12	438
Precision Instruments		
Esterline	11	224
Kollmorgen Corp.	12	100
MTS	13	194
Medical Supplies		
Bindley Western Industries	12	207
Bio-Rad Labs	11	360
Spacelabs Medical, Inc.	13	200
Transportation		
Rollins Truck Leasing	12	484
Maritime		
American President	9	583
Food Service		
International Dairy Queen	13	441
Luby's Cafeterias	12	483
NPC International	11	183
Perkins Family Restaurants	10	137
Piccadilly Cafeterias	14	97
Ryans Family Steak Houses	11	396

Company/Industry	P/E Ratio	Market Cap ($ million)
Industrial Services		
Buckeye Partners	9	460
PHH Corp	11	905
Petroleum		
Holly Corp.	10	198
Tesoro	6	225
Specialty Chemical Companies		
Furon Co.	13	200
LeaRonol, Inc.	14	231
NCH Corp.	12	426
Defense Industry		
Moog, Inc.	13	139
Metal Fabricating		
Allied Products	8	215
Amcast Industrial Corp.	9	149
Fansteel	14	51
Lawson Products	12	253
TransTechnology Corp.	8	76
Steel Industry		
Ampco-Pittsburgh Corp.	11	107
Carpenter Technology	11	175
Cleveland-Cliffs, Inc.	10	510
Home Building		
Hovnanian Enterprises	8	148
Kaufman & Broad	13	548
Pulte Corp.	11	650
Retail Building Supply		
Hughes Supply	13	214
Wolohan Lumber	13	71

So far, this work required no special skills but it did require judgment in deciding on which criteria to use. She decided what conditions to impose on stocks for the first three screening tests and spent a couple of hours in the library with the *Value Line*.

What had she accomplished? This process discovered about 150 companies and eliminated about 1600 from the *Value Line* listings. Lillian then had to check these companies for her other criteria. The quickest things to check next were the price-to-cash-flow ratio and the long-term debt ratio. The *Value Line* showed the cash flow for 1995 and the debt ratio. When she checked those values, she had to divide the price by the most recent year's cash flow per share. Her criterion that the price-to-cash-flow ratio must be 5 or less eliminated almost all of the companies she had found first. The remaining candidates were reduced to these:

Company	P/E Ratio	Market Cap ($ million)	P/CF Ratio	Debt Ratio
Navistar	13	700	3.4	11%
Piccadilly Cafeterias	14	97	5.4	19%
West Company	13	381	5.5	29%
WHX Corporation	7	325	2	21%
Nash Finch Co.	12	198	4	31%
Springs Industries	14	903	5.1	19%

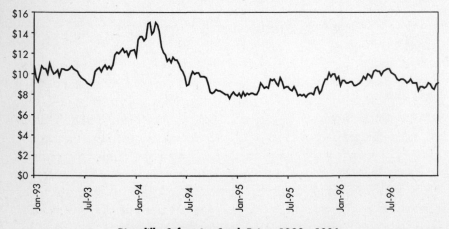

Piccadilly Cafeterias Stock Prices 1993–1996

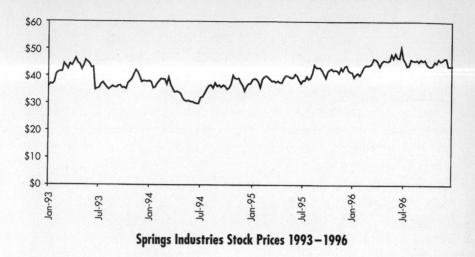

Springs Industries Stock Prices 1993–1996

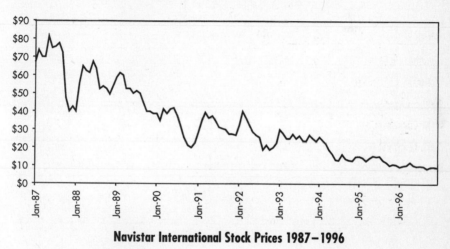

Navistar International Stock Prices 1987–1996

A few things have happened here. She imposed such a strict criterion for the price-to-cash-flow ratio that very few companies passed that test, and she decided to accept a few that were slightly on the high side. A few other companies passed the cash-flow test, but they failed the debt-ratio test. Lillian should have considered whether her criteria were altogether sound since so few companies passed the tests to this point. Either her criteria were too tough and she missed out on a number of promising companies, or possibly she found a couple of truly special cases to study further. Rather than deciding at that point that one of those companies was nec- essarily a strong candidate to buy, she could only conclude that they had passed some fairly strict screens.

The next screen is the return-on-assets test (should be at least 12 percent). The return on assets can be calculated by using the earnings divided by the total of all liabilities and equity, if total assets is not listed directly (using 1995 data). The *Value Line* gives that figure for each year. Lillian's research yielded the following results:

Navistar ROA = 17 percent
West Co. ROA = 9 percent
Nash Finch ROA = 8 percent
Piccadilly ROA = 6 percent
WHX Corp. ROA = 8 percent
Springs Industries ROA = 8 percent

After this screening only Navistar was left. Lillian still had two factors to check: did this stock diversify her portfolio? and did she understand their business? She decided that they did diversify her portfolio, and since they build and sell trucks and school buses, she understood their business. So then what? Did she have to buy this stock? No. She should have studied a number of factors closely. Navistar, at that time, appeared to be a classic mix of high risk and possible high reward. Navistar is in a business that is naturally subject to wide swings in profitability during economic cycles. They have to make significant expenditures in plant and equipment well before anyone can predict the business environment when that plant and equipment become productive. They were severely hurt by the recession in general business activity in 1990–91.

We have not yet reviewed all of the risks in Navistar. Most of the values she had checked to this point depended on price or earnings. What could she say about the stability and predictability of those factors? Look at the past price history:[2] The price of Navistar International stock had been very weak for the preceding eleven years. The highs and lows for the past eleven years were

	1985	1986	1987	1988	1989	1990	1991	1992	1993	1994	1995
High ($)	113	116	88	74	68	46	43	41	33	27	18
Low ($)	65	44	36	38	36	20	21	18	19	12	9

---

[2] The historic data for Navistar is adjusted to reflect a one-for-ten reverse split of the stock in 1993.

This is not a pretty picture. The market in general, and all of the people who held Navistar stock some time in the past ten years, had good reason to vote no confidence in the stock. The stock price could not recover to a higher level until that confidence was restored.

During those same eleven years, the book value of the company had climbed erratically from a negative $220 per share in 1985 to something over $10 per share in early 1996. At the time of Lillian's analysis, the stock was selling close to the book value per share. That was a good sign. Over the same period, the earnings had been terribly unstable. The eleven years' earnings were $7.70, ($1.80), $3.30, $6.40, $1.00, ($1.60), ($7.70), ($7.00), $1.43, $.99, and $1.83 (the parentheses indicate losses).

To get a clearer look at current prospects, Lillian decided next to focus on the past few years' financial results. Here is the data she found:

	1990	**1991**	**1992**	**1993**	**1994**	**1995**
Sales ($ million)	146	130	145	60	69	83
Earnings per share ($)	(1.60)	(7.70)	(7.00)	0.40	0.99	1.83
Book value per share ($)	23	13	3.66	7.10	7.71	8.49
Debt ($ million)	152	145	172	150	124	127

There is some reason here to imagine good prospects for Navistar, and also plenty of reason to see great risk. Lillian had to pause and refocus on what she was doing. She was considering an investment in the stock market; there were three major factors that would control her decision: protection, income, and growth. The income factor here was missing because Navistar did not pay any yield and had not for a long time. The protection factor was difficult to analyze. The stock was selling close to book value and had fairly low debt. Those were good protection factors, but it was clear that in case of economic recession, the company stood a fair chance of losing all of that book value quickly.

The growth factor was highly speculative. Growth in a stock price is entirely slave to the opinions of other investors. The price can only go up when buyers push it up. In the middle of 1996, the market at large had a poor opinion of Navistar. Even if they did everything right, it would probably take a few years of strong results to restore enough investor confidence to attract significant buying.

Navistar is a classic dilemma. The initial screening factors plus the price-to-book ratio may have been taken as reasons to buy the stock. The lack of yield and the extreme instability of the price, sales, and earnings all indicated strong reasons to believe that it was a risky proposition. For many conservative investors, Navistar would probably be entirely too speculative. Lillian decided that the lack of yield was not a problem, and she was willing to take the risk on a company that was selling close to book value. She bought 800 shares at $11 per share in the middle of 1996. At the end of that year it was selling at $10, and a year after her purchase the price was $9.75, which was equal to the book value at the time. The bad news was that the price had fallen. The good news was that the book value had increased. Lillian was holding on, and it was still a risky investment.

Okay, so Lillian found something that she called value. You may disagree. Based on the data she had available in early 1996, Navistar looked pretty risky. You might have, with good reason, decided that it was not attractive then. When you read this, check your *Wall Street Journal*; how is Navistar doing?

So you see, there is value, and then there is value. It's just like when we buy shoes or cars. What looks like value to one shopper may look like trash or luxury to another. To illustrate how much things vary, let's look over the shoulder of another value investor.

"I like the looks of this one."

Value Investing: Case 2

Richard was also a value-oriented investor, though a more conservative one than Lillian. In late 1996, Richard was looking for a new investment to improve the diversification in his portfolio of eight stocks. Those eight, at the time, had a market value of $67,000, and that plus the money market account gave him a yield of 2.7 percent. His eight stocks were in eight different industry groups: banking, electric utility, automobile, computer hardware, tobacco, home appliances, and home furnishings. His ideas of diversification included these industry groups: building materials, chemical, raw materials, drugs, entertainment, energy, and industrial services.

He decided to limit his search to those industries and apply two value criteria. The price-to-sales ratio should be not above 1.5, using both the previous year's reported sales and the average of the past three years' reported sales; and further, the price-to-book-value ratio must not be above 1.5.

In part of these calculations, Richard used some estimated earnings values for 1996. How dangerous is that? Not too. For those companies whose fiscal years ended in December 1996 or early 1997, the analysts' estimates on their earnings for those years should be pretty good. Estimating earnings is difficult, but by the time the company is 90 percent through the fiscal year, and the first three quarters have been reported, then the earnings for the year should be fairly clear. This may be questionable for a business like a toy company or a department store, whose results are so strongly dependent on the Christmas selling period. For the industries that Richard looked at, that should not be a major factor.

A quick read (about two hours' work) through the 1700+ stocks in the *Value Line* uncovered fifty companies that satisfied Richard's criteria. There was considerable concentration in certain industries. Nine of them were in building materials, eighteen in paper and timber, and six in metals. To simplify the rest of the discussion, we will assume that he managed to reduce those candidates by first focusing on each industry grouping and eliminating all but one in that group. That is a good way to get a grip on the decision-making process because it is easier to compare companies within one industry group than among different industries.

After searching for and reducing the number of candidates, Richard was left with these companies for further study. At this point, he did not know whether any of these companies would be a good buy for his needs—he only knew that they all passed two good value screens.

Company	Price/Sales (most recent sales)	Price/Sales (three yrs. sales)	Price/Book
Angelica Corp.	0.34	0.38	0.86
Total Petroleum	0.17	0.18	1.10
Furon	0.44	0.49	1.40
Wellman, Inc.	0.49	0.53	0.85
TJ International	0.52	0.53	1.31
Thomas Industries	0.38	0.41	1.13
International Paper	0.53	0.63	1.33
Westvaco Corporation	0.97	1.01	1.38
Destek Energy	1.50	1.41	1.14
Imperial Chemical	0.53	0.58	1.26
Rhone-Poulenc	0.59	0.59	1.44

This was a richly diverse group of companies to consider for investment. Probably any one of them could have been argued as a good choice for a conservative, value-oriented investor. Richard, however, could not buy all of them. He wanted to settle on one, which required further investigation and additional criteria to reduce the number of candidates.

He decided first to review the companies to see whether there was anything about any of them that would scare him away from an investment. TJ International, a building-materials company, was dropped from the list because their price-to-earnings ratio was over 50 based on the previous twelve months' earnings. The earnings were expected to improve, but even based on the past three years' trend of earnings, the P/E ratio appeared to be staying well above 20. The projected improvement of earnings for 1997 did not convince Richard. This certainly does not mean that TJ was a weak company, nor a weak investment. It only meant that it was not an attractive risk for Richard at that time. Each individual investor can reject a stock at any time for any reason. You don't have to prove that it is a bad investment.

Destek Energy, a coal and energy company, was dropped because of the price-to-earnings ratio, too. Using 1995 earnings, the P/E was 36; using 1996 earnings, it was 27; and using 1997 projected values, it looked like close to 23. The company also did not pay any dividend. It had a number of attractive qualities, including passing Richard's first screens, but he decided it was too expensive based on earnings. Rhone-Poulenc was dropped for the same reasons. That left Richard with these eight companies:

Company	P/E Ratio[3]	Price/ Sales	Price/ Book	Yield %[4]	Market Cap[5]	Debt/ Capital
Angelica Corp.	21	0.34	0.86	4.8	185M	33 %
Total Petroleum	**	0.17	1.10	2.7	429M	54 %
Furon	11	0.44	1.40	1.2	182M	24 %
Wellman, Inc.	21	0.49	0.85	1.7	562M	34 %
Thomas Industries	14	0.38	1.13	2.0	216M	28 %
International Paper	19	0.53	1.33	2.4	1.25B	43 %
Westvaco Corporation	12	0.97	1.38	2.8	3.06B	36 %
Imperial Chemical	15	0.53	1.26	4.7	9.20B	23 %

*** Total reported a loss for the recent twelve months*

Richard decided to scratch Total, and he was not thrilled with International Paper because of the P/E and the debt ratio. He decided to drop International Paper because it appeared that the others suited his value criteria better. He decided to check the *Value Line* financial strength rating and S&P rating on the remainder.

Company	Value Line Financial Strength	Standard & Poor's Rating
Angelica Corp.	B+	B
Furon	B	B+
Wellman, Inc.	B+	B+
Thomas Industries	B+	B
Westvaco Corporation	A	B
Imperial Chemical	A	B+

---

[3] Using most recent twelve-months' earnings reported.
[4] Using dividends paid in preceding twelve months.
[5] M for million $ and B for billion $.

Probably any of these six companies would have been a decent investment for Richard. He felt that any one of them would improve diversification of his portfolio. No matter how much research he spent on the question, there would never be a perfect guaranteed answer. But for the final step, he decided to get into the details of how each company did business and what their prospects were (based on mid-1996 information).

Angelica had two main lines of business: textile and laundry services for health-care businesses; and uniforms and shoes. Sales had been slowly increasing for five years, but the earnings had been falling. Forecasts were

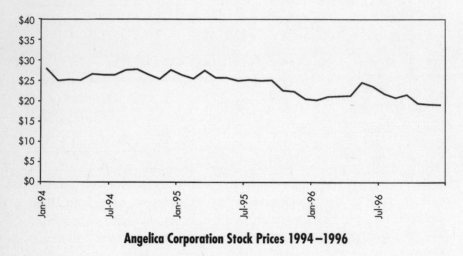

Angelica Corporation Stock Prices 1994–1996

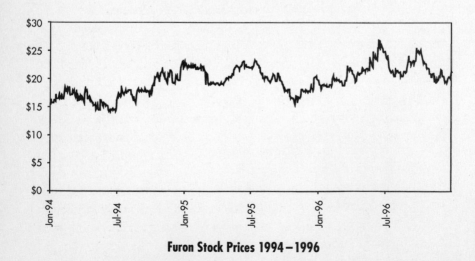

Furon Stock Prices 1994–1996

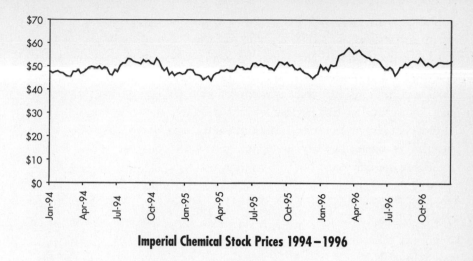

Imperial Chemical Stock Prices 1994–1996

that earnings would not improve much soon, so the P/E ratio was likely to stay up around 20. Richard decided to drop them.

Furon manufactured industrial components using specialized polymer chemistry. The stock price had been very erratic for the past two years, but over a six-year period, it had a definite upward trend. Sales were improving significantly in 1996 and were projected to improve strongly in 1997. The book value had steadily improved for the past six years. Their gross profit was sufficient to cover interest payments ten times over. Furon was completing the acquisition of another company that would enhance their markets and product lines, but would also roughly double the size of the company. That was a good news/bad news situation, since such a large acquisition would certainly put strains on their management and sales organizations. Furon looked very attractive with the only major question being how they would handle the changes.

Wellman was the leading recycler of synthetic fibers from soda bottles. Over the past six years, their sales had grown steadily, but the cash flow and earnings had not kept pace. With the combination of erratic earnings, relatively higher debt, and recently falling stock price, Richard decided to pass on Wellman.

Thomas Industries manufactured and sold residential and commercial lighting. Their past five-year history of sales, cash flow, earnings, and book value had been strong. The stock price had been on a general upward trend for most of the preceding four years.

Westvaco Corporation was in the paper business. Over the past three years, their sales, cash flow, and earnings had all shown improvement. The book value had also shown steady growth. In 1995 and 1996, the stock price appeared to have hit a plateau around $28 to $32. Richard thought that if the financial factors all kept on improving, then the stock price would have to respond to that. He also felt that the value factors he had checked at first—the P/E ratio, price to sales, price to book, and yield—all offered some insurance against any significant loss of the stock price below the $30 that he was looking at.

Imperial Chemical is a large and diversified worldwide chemical business. Their sales, cash flow, earnings, and book value had also been increasing handsomely for four years. Richard felt that with the Japanese and European economies being in a slump at the time, then worldwide sales prospects should only get better for Imperial. There was one odd factor with Imperial. The "shares" were not true shares in the company, but were ADRs (American Drawing Rights) set up by an American intermediary to serve as proxy for the English shares of Imperial Chemical. Dealing in ADRs meant that the shareholders' rights and ownership were not in fact guaranteed by the company, but rather by the intermediary, with some reassurance from the NYSE since it had decided to list them for sale. Some people don't like that arrangement. Some do. It depends on the level of trust you have in the NYSE and the U.S. Securities and Exchange Commission. Richard was not worried about ADRs, so that was not a consideration for him.

He had four candidates left. Probably any one of them would have been a fair selection. He decided to base the final choice on a weighted evaluation of five factors. He assigned each company a score of 1 to 5 (1 = poor, 5 = very attractive) on five factors. The factors selected were

1. yield

2. price-to-earnings ratio

3. four-year history of improving the financial data, sales, earnings, cash flow, and book value

4. ratings by *Value Line* and S&P

5. debt-to-capital ratio

The scores were tabulated as:

	Furon	Thomas	Westvaco	Imperial
Yield	1	2	3	5
P/E	4	2	3	2
History	5	5	4	4
Ratings	3	3	3	4
Debt ratio	3	3	2	3
Total score	16	15	15	18

That didn't settle much. It just illustrates that all four of these companies have some attractive qualities. Richard finally decided to go with Imperial Chemical (symbol ICI on the NYSE) based on their higher total score, the size of the company, and the international presence, all of which were attractive to him. Another investor could have very reasonably decided to buy another one without having to apologize for it. Richard bought Imperial Chemical for $50 per ADR in December 1996.

What risk was he accepting? There is always the risk of simply being in the market. If the market took a severe fall, then it wouldn't matter how clever his analysis was. His stocks and ADRs would probably fall as much as the market averages. With ICI, he had a little extra protection because the good yield offered some protection from falling along with the market. He also had the risk of being in a major basic industry. In case of an American or worldwide recession, ICI would certainly suffer. He had the risk in trusting his own judgment: No matter how smart and hardworking he was, there was always the chance that he may have over-looked something or misunderstood some of the reports. He accepted the risk of late-breaking developments. If ICI had a plant blow up the morning after Richard bought the stock, then that would be in the risk category known as *tough luck*. There is no escaping the risks from the competition: A number of other well-managed and aggressive businesses would like to take away ICI's customers and profits. These risks come with the markets. If Richard could not recognize and accept the risks, then he had no business buying individual stocks. He might have been better advised to stick with mutual funds.

Nothing in this chapter should be taken as a recommendation that you either buy or sell, or refrain from buying or selling, any of the named stocks. All of this data and analyses will be old information by the time you read this and no longer appropriate for your decision making. Only the methods and general approach are important to you now.

In chapter 15, we will return to Lillian's and Richard's searches, this time using computers and online resources. This will make the work go faster and also allow us to screen sets of 5,000–8,000 stocks, rather than the 1700 or so we used from the printed version of *Value Line* data.

Recommended Further Reading

Train, John. *The Midas Touch*. New York: HarperCollins, 1988.

Graham, Benjamin. *The Intelligent Investor,* 4th rev. ed. New York: HarperCollins, 1986.

We dance round in a ring and suppose,
But the Secret sits in the middle and knows.

—ROBERT FROST, "THE SECRET SITS"

The Growth Investor
in the Real World

All investors would like to have value now and growth later. The "value investor" generally has more confidence in audited current financial reports that show value now. The "growth investor" generally has more interest in studies of a company or a market that foretell growth later.

Look at this record of sales and earnings reported for the past four years and projections of the next three years.

| Year | **Past Four Years** | | | | | **Projections** | | |
	1	2	3	4	Today	5	6	7
Sales ($mil)	200	220	290	310		330	370	400
EPS ($/share)	1.20	1.28	1.35	1.47		1.65	1.80	1.99
Stock Price ($)[1]	22	25	29	37	39			
P/E ratio[2]	18	20	21	25	27			

---

[1] End-of-year stock price.
[2] Uses end-of-year stock price and that year's earnings per share.

While the value investor may look at the current P/E ratio of 27 and conclude that the stock is just too expensive, the growth investor would more likely say that the trends of growing price, earnings, sales, and P/E make it a good buy even though the current price is pretty high. The growth investor looks at a glass that is half full and says that the current price is only twenty-four times next year's earnings, and only twenty times the year seven earnings. Since the market has enough respect for the stock to maintain a P/E ratio above 20, this is a good deal. The argument that the price is too high could have been used in year one, two, or three, and each time it would have been wrong. The value investor who turned away from this stock in year one or year two passed up a great opportunity. The value investor says, "Yeah, maybe, but we don't really know where it is going next year, and I see enough good, cheap opportunities to keep my money busy." That's why there are markets. People buy and sell because they have different opinions about the value and fair prices of things.

A Growth Story: Pittway Corporation

Here is a growth story. Early in 1993, the Pittway Corporation spun-off (sold) one of its major divisions. The price, sales, and earnings before that year cannot be properly compared with later years. We begin our study of Pittway (symbol PRY on the NYSE) with 1993 data. Pittway is a diversified business that makes and sells burglar and fire alarm systems, publishes business magazines, and invests in real estate.

	1993	1994	1995	1996	1997[3]	1998
Sales ($M)	651	777	945	1,100	1,280	
EPS ($)	1.01	1.58	1.93	2.41	2.85	3.33
Book Value ($M)	293	328	363	441		
Dividend ($)	0.37	0.33	0.33	0.33	0.33	0.33
Stock price[4] ($)	16	24	32	44	53*	
P/E ratio[5]		24	20	23	19	
Growth of EPS from previous year		57%	22%	25%	18%	17%

* Actual early-1997 price

[3] Figures for 1997 and 1998 are estimates.

[4] Middle of each year.

[5] Mid-year price divided by last year's earnings.

The value investor might have looked at these numbers in 1996 and decided that the P/E was too high and the yield (less than 1 percent) too low to make the stock an attractive buy. The growth investor, on the other hand, would be very impressed with the long-term increases of all the measurable financial traits, and the steady maintenance of the high P/E ratio.

Here is how a growth investor might have analyzed Pittway. Suppose that in January 1997, the growth investor decided to either project the earnings trend out into 1997 or accept the earnings estimates from the *First Call Earnings Estimate Guide*. That would lead to a fairly firm estimate that the company should produce $2.80 to $3.00 earnings per share in 1997. Then the current (January 1997) price of the stock, $53, would be about eighteen to twenty times the 1997 earnings.

Now, the growth investor would estimate the future price:

> *Estimated future price = estimated future EPS x estimated P/E ratio.*

So if the P/E ratio were to stay around 20 to 23, as it has been for three years, he might decide that the stock was due to go to a $56 to $69 price range. That comes from an estimated earnings times an estimated P/E ratio ($2.80 x 20 = $56, using the lower estimates, and up to as high as $3.00 x 23 = $69 using the higher estimates).

There is one fly in the ointment for the growth investor. Stick with me now, this is complicated. Many growth investors use a rough rule of thumb that a price for a stock is attractive if the P/E ratio is no higher than the percentage rate of growth of the earnings per share. In this case, that rule said to buy Pittway in 1994, 1995, and 1996. In 1997, the question becomes more difficult and debatable. If you use the $2.85 earnings estimate, the P/E ratio was 23, but the estimated percentage growth of EPS was just 18 percent. However, using the higher estimate of $3.00 for 1997 earnings, the P/E would have been 18, and the percentage growth of earnings per share would have been 24; so the rule would indicate a buy. A lot depends on the guesses we make about where earnings will be for the current or next fiscal years. Many growth investors would have found Pittway to be interesting in 1997, but they would not all have reached the same conclusion about whether to buy it.

The data that we looked at would be the starting point for a growth investor's investigation of Pittway. The prudent growth investor would also go beyond these figures and check a lot of other information. In this particular case, the other data are encouraging, too. The long-term debt ratio is 17 percent, which is a healthy value. The times interest earned is 12, which is strong and safe. The book value and the rate of return on common equity have both been increasing steadily. The *Value Line* safety rating was 3 (average), their financial strength rating was A, and the S&P rating was (surprise!) *not rated*. The reason that Pittway was not rated in 1997 was the spin-off in 1993. That spin-off changed the company and changed the comparable financial data so much that it caused S&P to discontinue the rating until they had ten years of data with the new company structure. That is by no means a strike against the company or the stock.

Pittway represents the kind of stock that probably would be appealing (early 1997) to many growth investors, or people who were simply looking for a growth stock, but might have been considered as overpriced by the value investors and not of interest to the yield investors. All of them would have regarded Pittway as a fine company with a great record in their businesses. The question in each case was whether it suited the individual investor's needs. Different folks would have had different answers to that.

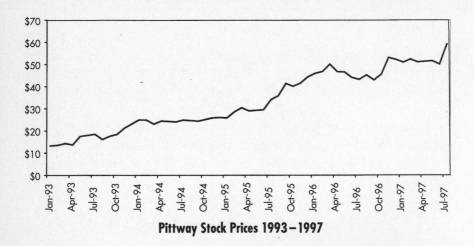

Pittway Stock Prices 1993–1997

Looking for Growth

If you are the growth investor, or at some time looking for growth stocks to round out your portfolio, then how do you find them? There is no exact formula, just as there was no single exact method for value investors.

There are a number of guidelines for growth stocks. You can apply one or more of them as suits your research needs.

1. Look for stocks that have a three- to four-year history of increasing stock price or earnings per share, and some reason to expect those trends to continue.

2. Look for stocks for which the latest analysts' estimates of earnings and revenues are going higher. Consult *First Call Consensus Guide* or *Zacks Analyst Watch*.

3. Look for companies that you believe have good opportunities to enter new markets.

4. Look for companies that have new products that will create new markets or sweep the competition out of existing markets.

5. Look for companies that are doing something new in the way they run their businesses that will cause them to attract much larger market share or significantly reduce their costs.

6. Look for companies for which the percentage growth rate of the EPS is larger than the P/E ratio.

One way to begin is by looking at history. You can do that by reading the S&P reports, the *Value Line*, the stock charts and earnings reports that may be given in *Investor's Business Daily*, or by using online resources and computer databases. You can also read *Smart Money*, *Barron's*, *Kiplinger's*, or your local business newspapers. All of them will sometimes have articles that may point out good growth prospects.

One example of good-looking history was Pittway. Another one, in early 1997, was Barnes & Noble.

A Growth Story: Barnes & Noble

Barnes and Noble sells books, magazines, coffee, and atmosphere[6]. They have practiced a successful strategy of establishing new stores that their customers will regard as nice places to visit, whether they want to buy a book or not. They have a dedicated corps of customer relations coordinators whose

---

[6] Disclosure: At the time of writing this, the author owns stock in Barnes & Noble.

"You pay your money and you take your chance."

full-time jobs are to ensure that there are things going on at the stores that will make them attractive destinations for singles, families, children, scholars, and everyone else. The senior management is aggressive in opening new stores wherever they can sniff any business, regardless of what the competition may be doing.

Barnes & Noble (symbol BKS on NYSE)

Year	1993	1994	1995	1996	1997[7]
Sales ($ millions)	1,340	1,620	1,980	2,448	
Earnings per share	0.30	0.81	1.10*	1.48	2.27
Book value ($ millions)	329	358	400		
Cash flow per share ($)	1.23	2.06	2.49	3.45	4.00
Dividends per share	0	0	0	0	0

*Excludes a one-time special restructuring charge.

[7] 1997 values are estimates published in *First Call* (and subject to revision).

This is what a growth story looks like.[8] There is, of course, a price for growth. The long-term debt at the end of 1995 was $262 million, and that went up to $290 million the next year. The rapid growth of new superstores and related closings of some of their smaller B. Dalton stores in malls may cause personnel strains on both the growth side and the shrinkage side. Other companies see the same opportunities and are trying to pursue a similar strategy to Barnes & Noble's. It is not yet perfectly clear whether B&N will be successful in dominating their target markets.

What are the risks that might impede the growth plan? The competition is strong and active in targeting the same markets. Several other companies are following a similar strategy. Barnes & Noble's business obviously depends on discretionary spending. People don't have to go to coffee shops and bookstores. The rapid pace of growth of B&N puts a strain on their infrastructure. Just because they can successfully manage a string of 200 stores doesn't mean that they can manage 1,000 stores with proportionally larger employment, debt, cash flow, and internal management issues. The 1997 price/earnings ratio was about 24. That might look high to many investors. If the stock markets turned down across the board then a stock with P/E of 24 and no dividend would be at high risk for a sell-off, too. If they simply failed to boost the earnings significantly for a year or two, then the stock might no longer be viewed as a growth vehicle, and the markets might devalue it down to a P/E of 10 to 15, causing a significant slide in the stock price.

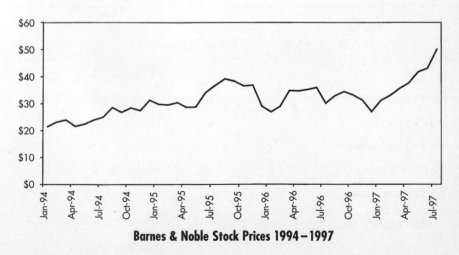

Barnes & Noble Stock Prices 1994–1997

---

[8] Reference point for the Barnes & Noble story is mid-1997.

On balance, in early 1997 many growth-oriented investors decided that the history of growth and the estimates of continued growth were strong enough to outweigh the problems of the high price/earnings ratio and lack of yield. For the first half of 1997, that appeared to be a good call. The astute Barnes & Noble shareholder will keep his eyes on the company and watch how the growth and profits develop.

Looking for Growth

There are more places that you might look in search of good growth candidates. The *Value Line* has something to offer if you want growth but do not like assuming much risk. Some people think that looking for growth automatically means accepting high risk, but maybe not. In the *Value Line*'s section called Selection and Opinion, they sometimes run a short section called Growth Stocks with Low Risk. That section will show ten or fifteen stocks that they think might be attractive if you need growth and safety. That list is worth your time and attention. For instance, in the spring of 1997, they looked at stocks that had at least a 10 percent compound rate of growth of earnings for the past five years, and an estimated 11 percent rate of growth for the next five years. They also required at least a two (second best out of five) rating for safety, and financial strength rating of B++ or better, using their own ratings methods. After adding in two other technical restrictions, they found that only twelve out of 1700 stocks in their system met the requirements. Those were presented (May 16, 1997 issue) as good candidates for consideration by investors who wanted growth and safety. The list included these, among others:

- Becton-Dickinson—medical supplies
- Home Depot—building supplies
- Hong Kong Telephone—telecommunications
- Sysco Corp.—food wholesale

In this way, the *Value Line* does us a great service and helps us get started looking for growth. They also have another, more specific, suggestion. The Selection and Opinion section always contains a stock that is chosen specifically as a growth candidate. That stock gets a full-page write-up with a description of the company, selected financial data, an analysis of the growth prospects, and a chart of the past few years' performance. That stock is always something worth thinking about. Just remember that the *Value*

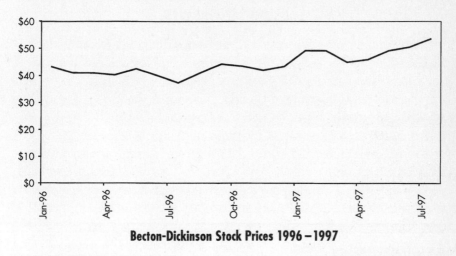

Becton-Dickinson Stock Prices 1996–1997

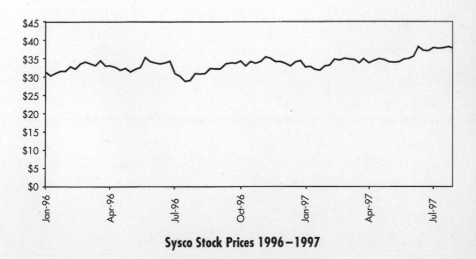

Sysco Stock Prices 1996–1997

Line editors do not know you or your investment parameters. They did not volunteer to do your thinking for you.

Another valuable source for the growth investor is the *First Call Consensus Estimate Guide*. It presents current results of earnings estimates and other investment research by a large sample of professional financial analysts. It is not generally available in libraries because it is written more for a professional audience, but if you use a broker, they should make their copy available for your study. In it you can find companies that have had the greatest positive or negative changes in earnings estimates. These selections are further separated into companies that are widely followed (a lot of analysts' attention) or underfollowed. You can find companies that have recently announced earnings that were the greatest positive or negative surprises compared to previous analysts' opinions. Those summaries of best and worst are the kinds of places that growth investors may go searching for companies that should get favorable attention in the markets.

Beyond the lists mentioned above, *First Call* also shows useful financial data and analysts estimates for over 5,000 publicly traded companies. For each company they show the stock symbol, the industry, the current average of analysts' recommendations, the prior month's average recommendation, the prior year's actual earnings per share, and the current years average estimated earnings per share. They show the actual reported earnings per share for each of the past four reported quarters, the estimated future growth rate of earnings, and the past five years' actual growth rate. They show more than I can list here. *First Call* deserves your attention if you wish to look for growth candidates or just track the latest facts and opinions on the stocks that you own. It is a valuable publication for the buy-and-hold investor because it will help to remind you when one of your investments demands reconsideration.

Another useful source for the growth investor is Standard & Poor's *Current Market Perspectives*. This publication is a bird of a different feather. It presents graphs of the price and volume history of over 2,000 stocks over the past five years. Here is an example:

YEARLY RANGES	Sysco Corp (SYY)	OPTIONS

NYSE
SP500
★★★

FOOD
Food distr & service systems

CBOE

F.M.A.N.

5

		40
		35
		30
		25
		20
		15
		RSR
		10
		VOL THS
		6000
		4000
		2000
		0

S O N D J F M A M J J A S O N D J F M A M J J A S O N D J F M A M J J A S O N D J F M A M J J A S O

1994	1995	1996	1997

CAPITALIZATION MIL		YEAR JUN	SALES	EARNINGS	DIVIDENDS	EARN EST	S&P RANK	CURRENT P/E
L T DEBT	623.0	1995	12118.0	1.38	.44	1.93	A+	21.0
PFD	NO	1996	13395.0	1.52	.52	INSTIT HOLD	SHRS	%	CURRENT YIELD
COMMON	174.4	1997	14454.6	1.71	.45	596	107	61	1.6 %
BK VAL/SHR	6.79	INTERIM EARNS		N/A (N/A)	DIV. INDIC. RATE .60			

Reprinted from Standard & Poor's Current Market Perspectives,
by permission of Standard & Poor's Corporation.

Some investors will use charts such as this to try to foretell trends or changes in trends. Specifically, if they see a stock rapidly changing price, either up or down, accompanied by higher-than-normal sales volume, then they might conclude that this change is significant and is the start of a trend. Of course, anyone who could accurately forecast changes in trends would be a very successful investor indeed. As we have seen before, all such methods to forecast market action are highly debatable and difficult. However, many investors like to use the charts in conjunction with their other methods of analyzing stocks. The S&P *Current Market Perspectives* publication also contains some financial history on each firm, but the most interesting information is in the charts.

Another useful source for the growth investor is the publication *Analyst Watch* from Zacks Investment Research, Inc. *Analyst Watch* is a monthly publication with a midmonth update on significant recent developments.

It contains a lot of information that parallels the *First Call Consensus Estimate Guide*, but has additional useful data and ratings.

Analyst Watch contains Zacks proprietary ranking system, which is a very short-term price-forecasting method. It only forecasts prices three months ahead, but has been proven productive for those who choose to practice a lot of short-term trading. Short-term trading is not a good practice for us because the brokerage fees on many short-term trades would be likely to offset the potential profits. The main value in *Analyst Watch* is in their reporting on estimations and forecasts of earnings of over 5,000 firms from 2,500 industry analysts.

They publish a Zacks Recommended 100 list of stocks that differs from the short-term top-rated stocks. The Recommended 100 stocks are chosen with a view to value and stability, in addition to the short-term prospects. This list would serve as one place that the investor might go searching for growth candidates.

In addition to those listings, Zacks includes lists of best current average recommendations, largest changes in recommendations, stocks with high dividend yields, stocks with the best changes of their long-term growth estimates, and more lists of various groups that many investors would find interesting.

Zacks also includes details on 5,000 stocks, such as the industry, the company's rank among their industry group, the details of buy/sell recommendations among all the analysts who follow a given company, the fifty-two-week high and low prices for the stock, the current and next-quarter estimates of earnings, and other data.

The growth-oriented investor who needed some companies to study could very well pick up the latest issue of *Zacks Analyst Watch* and turn to the list of "Best Change in Long-Term Growth Consensus Estimate." There she would find over fifty companies for which consensus opinion among professional analysts indicates the greatest improvement in long-term earnings growth. She can find one that is followed by ten analysts, so the consensus is based on a lot of research, or she can find one that is followed by only two or three analysts, so there is a chance of getting into the stock before it is widely studied by a lot of brokerage firms. Either approach might be helpful to some investors. In May 1997, that list included Westinghouse Electric, Public Service Company of New Mexico, Airborne Freight, and American Power Conversion. There was a lot of choice among them in terms of industry, size, and history. Any investor could find something in that list worth considering.

In chapter 15, we will look at the online information available from *First Call* and the software and database systems available from Zacks and the *Value Line*. That will show you a couple of ways to gather information quickly when looking for growth.

Footwork

The search for growth is almost by definition a search for something that most other investors have not yet discovered. If you confine yourself to the published and most popular financial news, then it is unlikely that you will find much that is truly special and original. You may still find some good investments, but you probably won't get there first.

Another approach is to look where the financial analysts are not looking. While they are all stuck in New York or Boston or Chicago reading financial reports, you could get out and do some original research. Visit some stores, malls, or auto showrooms. It is possible for you to discern trends or improved products and sales long before they are ever reported if you look around.

If a local supermarket goes through a remodeling and brings in some new and appealing products, then pay attention. If they are part of a national or regional chain, then they are probably doing the same thing in all of their stores (you could ask the manager—it's easy). If you think the changes are smart and appealing, the chances are that other shoppers will, too. If you visit that store once a week for a couple of months, you will probably be in a better position than any of the financial analysts to forecast their growth prospects. You should still review their reports in the publications, but you could then expect to make a reasonable appraisal of their prospects six months before the data hits their next financial reports.

Recommended Further Reading

Lynch, Peter. *Beating the Street*. New York: Simon & Schuster, 1993.

Facts which at first seem improbable will, even on scant explanation, drop the cloak which has hidden them and stand forth in naked and simple beauty.

—GALILEO

The Search for Simplicity

In this chapter, we will look at some methods that require less work and less experience from the investor. Some of these simple methods may produce good results but have potential problems, however. By the time you finish this chapter, you may well wonder why the rest of the book was necessary. There are many simple approaches to stock selection. In this chapter, we are only going to look at a few that have good supporting evidence. Each method presented here has been practiced by investors over many years and has been found useful.

Nevertheless, just as in all the other cases of stock picking, there are no guarantees. There is a fair amount of dissenting opinion and evidence. The high priests of the efficient market hypothesis claim that such methods as these are worthless. Others, selling the modern portfolio theory, claim you cannot make investing this simple without ignoring risks. We will try to give fair consideration to both sides of the argument. Each section of this chapter comes with some warnings as to why the method might not be right for you, and what kinds of risk/reward trade-offs are involved if you use that method.

But just to make it clear where I stand—I believe there is overwhelming statistical and historical evidence that some of the simplest methods

*"But Hekava—look, the guy said five will get us ten,
and ten will get us twenty."*

are productive and reasonable choices for the small investor.[1] For further
evidence, proof, or history, refer to the references listed at the end of the
chapter.

As a final warning before we dive in, even the best and most appealing
of these methods do not excuse you from the obligation to diversify. If you
someday practice one of these simple methods and find three stocks that
are attractive and are all large banks, then you probably should not buy all
three of them. Look at the stocks and other investments that you already
own, and see how you can manage to diversify with your new investments.

Dollar Cost Averaging

Individual small investors often have two problems that can be helped
through dollar cost averaging. Big-time professional money managers
probably suffer from the same problems, but they have other ways to deal
with them. Those two problems are fear and lack of discipline.

---

[1] O'Shaughnessy's book *What Works on Wall Street* presents overwhelming
statistical evidence that some of the simple methods work for money managers who can buy hundreds of stocks with fairly low transaction costs.

A certain amount of fear is essential to be a smart investor, but too much can paralyze you. Investors sometimes have trouble deciding whether they are buying at too high a price or selling too low. You never know. If you don't want to practice market timing, which is trying to predict where the market will go next, the easy way out of that problem is to make a plan to buy a certain dollar value of securities on a regular basis.

That plan also resolves the self-discipline problem. It is all too easy to make a few investments, and then say to yourself, "Buy and hold, that's the thing." So you may put your money in the market and not think about it for six months. A commitment to a regular investment amount will help you develop a habit of watching your investments.

Dollar cost averaging is a practice where the investor decides on an amount of money and a regular schedule to consistently add to her investments. It may be $25 each month, as would be common with an investment club, or it may be 4 percent of salary each payday, as you might do with a 401(k) plan at work. You may pick out one stock that you like and get into a dividend reinvestment plan with that company, adding $50 each month to your stock holdings with that one company. There are several ways to approach dollar cost averaging, and each of them should help you resolve the problems with fear and lack of self-discipline.

In order to fully illustrate this method, we will look at three examples with buying stocks. The first has a stock that fairly steadily increased in value, the second a stock that fairly steadily lost value, and the last example a stock that was quite volatile in price.

A fellow named Gerry was a pretty smart operator, but he had a thriving small business that kept him from spending a lot of time studying the market. We are going to assume in three cases that Gerry had found a company that looked like a good long-term holding in which he could buy an even $50 worth of stock each month, beginning the stock purchases in June 1994 and continuing the dollar cost averaging plan until June 1995.

Example One: Graco, Inc. builds equipment for moving liquids, such as pumps, spray guns, meters, and valves. In June 1994, Gerry could have bought Graco stock for $13 per share. The stock had been in a slump lately, but the earnings and cash flow appeared to be very healthy. They also paid a quarterly dividend that Gerry converted into more shares. Most dividend reinvestment plans and some brokers will work with fractional shares to allow dividend reinvestment.

Here is how Gerry's investment in Graco grew:

Month	Share Price ($)	Dividend Per Share ($)	Amount Invested ($)	New Shares Bought	Total Shares Owned
June 1994	13	0	$50	3.9	3.9
July	12	0.093	50	4.2	8.1
August	12	0	50	4.2	12.3
September	12	0	50	4.2	16.5
October	12	0.093	50	4.3	20.8
November	12	0	50	4.2	25.0
December	13	0	50	3.9	28.9
January	13	0.093	50	4.1	33.0
February	14	0	50	3.6	36.6
March	16	0	50	3.1	39.7
April	17	0.107	50	3.2	42.9
May	17	0	50	2.9	45.8
June 1995	19	0	50	2.6	48.4

At the end of a year, Gerry had invested a total of $650, and he held stock worth $920. And this is real-life, folks. Anybody as smart as Gerry could have done it. Besides returning a good profit, this approach overcame the fear of starting in Graco while the price was falling, and it gave Gerry the discipline to keep at it during the first few months when it was going nowhere. The disadvantages were that anyone who had the nerve to simply put the entire $650 into the stock at first, and reinvested the dividends, would have ended up with 51.5 shares worth $979. On the other hand, the person who waited until February to buy $650 worth would have ended up in June with 46.8 shares worth $889. Gerry's way was a wise, conservative approach for the investor who did not want to charge out onto a limb.

Example Two: Next, we will look at the situation if Gerry made the same decision to use dollar cost averaging to buy Quixote Corporation beginning in June 1994 (and reinvesting the dividends). Quixote makes highway safety materials and compact discs for audio systems. Before June 1994, their stock price had been very strong for three years.

Here is how Gerry's investment in Quixote grew:

Month	Share Price ($)	Dividend Per Share ($)	Amount Invested ($)	New Shares Bought	Total Shares Owned
June 1994	22		$50	2.3	2.3
July	21		50	2.4	4.7
August	21		50	2.4	7.1
September	20		50	2.5	9.6
October	18	0.11	50	2.8	12.4
November	16		50	3.1	15.5
December	13		50	3.9	19.4
January	11		50	4.6	24.0
February	10		50	5.0	29.0
March	10		50	5.0	34.0
April	11	0.11	50	4.9	38.9
May	12		50	4.2	43.1
June 1995	12		50	4.2	47.3

Gerry wound up with holdings worth $568 after investing $650. Dollar cost averaging does not guarantee that you make money. But a bolder fellow who might have invested all $650 in June 1994 would have ended up with 30.1 shares worth only $361, a far worse result. By dollar cost averaging, Gerry avoided the worst result on Quixote.

Example Three: Here is one more case that really illustrates another good feature of dollar cost averaging. Suppose that Gerry took the same approach to buying Sequa Corporation in June 1994. Sequa is a manufacturer of aerospace products, metal coatings, and specialty chemicals. Over the two years before June 1994, their stock price had been in a long-term downward trend, with one intermediate rally to higher prices in late 1993. Sales were falling, cash flow was falling, and they paid no dividends. Goodness knows why Gerry wanted the stock, but just suppose he had his reasons. Over the thirteen-month span while Gerry was buying more stock, the prices each month were $31, $30, $29, $28, $25, $24, $23, $24, $25, $30, $31, $31, and finally $31 in June 1995. Gerry finished the period with 23.6 shares worth $732. The price of the stock went nowhere in the thirteen months, yet Gerry finished with a profit on his $650 invested. The two clear benefits of dollar cost averaging were that Gerry had the discipline (say nerve) to keep with it during the worst months, and he actually was acquiring more stock at the lower prices than he was at the higher prices.

That is a variation on buy low–sell high. With dollar cost averaging, you buy more at lower prices and buy less at higher prices. In conclusion, dollar cost averaging is a good practice for most small investors who do not want to make large commitments at one time. Just remember our second example—in case of generally falling prices, you can still lose.

Mutual Funds

This is a book about stock selection methods. I assume that you have already figured out how mutual funds fit into your investment plans. However, it would be foolish of us to lose sight of the fact that we always have choices in our investing. Any time that you consider making one kind of investment, it would be best to pause and consider your choices. In this chapter, we are concentrating on the easier ways, and that certainly means we should consider mutual funds.

The three great benefits of investing through mutual funds are:

- professional analysis and management

- greater diversification

- less work for the individual investor

Those benefits should look appealing to you, even if you want to do some individual stock selection. Say you had a nicely diversified portfolio of seven stocks, but you decided that you wanted to invest another $5,000 and that a bank stock would improve your diversification. If you didn't know anything about the banking business, and also thought that bank stocks were generally pretty expensive, it might require a lot of heavy research to find a single good bank stock. But you have the option of looking in the *Morningstar Reports* to find several funds that specialize in the financial industry. Selecting one of those would be far less work than finding a stock, and probably less risk if you don't know anything about the business.

At the risk of boring you: *Any time* that you consider making an investment, you should consider the other options that are available. Even if you are a committed stock picker, mutual funds may still offer some attractive choices.

Buy Yield

We have seen that the selection of good stock investments requires some forecasting and prognosticating—always difficult and risky. Is there a way to reduce the risk in forecasting the potential rewards of a stock investment? Yes. Buy yield. That means buy stocks of sound companies with good dividend payments.

In buying yield, you should consider all the information you can find about the company and its markets, but place a higher emphasis on the dividends paid and the dividends history.

One legitimate point of view is that the final determination of a stock's value lies solely in the future dividends that the company will return to the investor. This belief is based on the assumption that the future growth of stock price is strongly influenced by investors' forecasts of the dividends. It is. The yield-oriented appraisal is also an expression of the cash-flow point of view, which says value depends on things that can be measured in dollars, in an accounting sense. The thing that can be most directly and immediately measured is dividend payment.

There is another point of view, as we discussed in chapter 3 in the section on the special role of income. Some investors emphasize that the greatest gains we see in stock investments frequently come from share price appreciation. That is true, but it depends on a more speculative approach to investing.

In the interest of good diversification, every small investor should at some times, perhaps most of the time, buy yield. Earlier I mentioned my investment in Ford. That investment has turned out to be quite profitable. It was based on an appraisal that the company was sound and committed to paying good dividends to the shareholders, and that the history seemed to indicate that the directors would try to get the yield back up to where it had been before the recession of 1990. The profit in the investment came largely from their improved earnings, which led to good share price increases, but the factors that gave me the confidence to buy early and count it as a safe investment were the yield and the company's history of paying good dividends.

Here is a chart to illustrate what would have happened if an investor bought yield and used dollar cost averaging. She invested in Ford stock at a rate of $100 per month for three years from 1990 through 1992, reinvested all dividends, and held the stock until the end of 1996. The lower line shows how much she had invested up to that date. The top line shows the value of her investment. The total amount of money she invested was $3600.

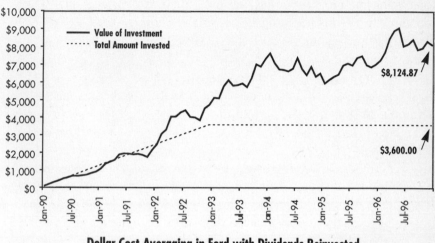

Dollar Cost Averaging in Ford with Dividends Reinvested

In 1991, I bought Potomac Electric Power at 23⅜ for those two good reasons: safety and yield. The safety judgment was based on the industry, their position in their market, the good yield, and the company history of dividends. The dividend at the time was $1.56 per year, for a yield percentage of 6.7 percent. They had steadily increased the dividend for ten years in a row, and the payout ratio had generally stayed below 80 percent. I figured that the worst that could possibly happen would be a drop to where they fell in the 1987 crash, $18 per share. If that happened, then the yield would be 9 percent, and I could probably make up the loss in three years' dividend payments. This seemed about as safe as it gets. That's what yield does for you. As events developed, I sold it two years later at 27⅜, when the yield on that price was 6 percent, and bought it back a year after that for 22. By that time, the dividend was up to $1.66, yield = 7.5 percent.

Buying yield will strengthen your portfolio in several ways. It will provide regular income, which you may use for further investments. If the yield is rock steady and reliable, then it provides safety, because if the price fell significantly, the yield percentage would go up to a level that would certainly attract other investors. And finally, investing for yield helps to provide diversification. The good yield stocks should be considered like a sector of the market that behaves differently from the low- or no-yield stocks.

Suppose you bought 200 shares of a stock at $20 that was paying a $1.24 annual dividend. And suppose, also, that you had studied the company and its history so that you felt the dividend was very safe and sustainable. Then how badly could you get hurt? How about even if the stock price fell, say to $18 and $17, and then $15, in three years. If you reinvested your dividends each year at the end-of-year prices, then after the three years you would hold 248.4 shares worth $3,726, and yielding 8 percent on the current price. You invested $4,000, so the pain on the loss can't be too bad. And if the dividend was still safe, then it would be certain that other investors would be attracted by that yield to come back in and buy the stock.

Is it all that easy? No. There is a dark side to yield investing, just as with every other scheme that man devises for making money. First, you have to estimate the security and dependability of the yield. Without those estimates, the whole calculation goes out the window. Remember FPL Group from chapter 6. Their history had demonstrated a strong dividend and gave every expectation that they could and would continue it. Surprise, surprise. The directors decided to cut the dividend and some shareholders were badly hurt. Second, yield investors are subject to the impact of the bond markets. High-yield investments are at some times competing with bonds. Yield investors always watch both stocks and bonds to see where the best deals are. When bond yields go up, as they do from time to time, then some investors sell their stocks to buy bonds, and the share price of your high-yield stock might drop. When that happens, you have the option of holding on and taking your quarterly dividend, but sometimes we get in positions where we need the money. If you have to sell when the price is down, then you may take a loss.

Summary on buying yield: Buying yield is a good idea and should be part of every investor's diversification scheme.

"Hey Mister, that's a funny looking dog!"

The Dogs of the Dow:
The Dow Ten, or Five, or Four, or Nine

Here is a yield-oriented plan that will help you avoid the potential problems in buying yield. The plan is this: Buy yield, but also buy another factor that will provide a little extra safety and insurance. The general name of the plan is "Dogs of the Dow." It's too easy, but it appears to work much of the time. For a detailed explanation of the plan and various ways to modify it, I recommend the book *Beating the Dow*, which is listed in the references.

The basic plan is to buy yield among the stocks in the Dow Jones industrial average. Doing this helps to reduce the risks that we mentioned above. The risk of yield being reduced or discontinued is less because those large and well-established companies can better predict their markets for a longer period of time. They can better plan the future course of dividend payments and work towards a stable, consistent yield. The risk of many investors selling the stock and lowering the market price is reduced because many investors buy these stocks as long-term core holdings. They do not expect to sell under any normal circumstances. Beyond that, many mutual funds have objectives that say they must buy some or all of the DJIA stocks. Index funds that are advertised as blue-chip, DJIA, or S&P 500 funds must buy and hold those stocks. The result is that by buying the stocks in the DJIA, you get some protection against rude surprises.

There are several ways that people buy yield in the DJIA. I will show some of them here, and there are other variations, but they all play to the same safety and predictability factors that we saw above. Any of these methods are sometimes called the "Dogs of the Dow" strategy. The reason for that name depends on the arithmetic of calculating yield. Sometimes high yield means the price has been beaten down. Yield is dividend divided by stock share price. When the price falls, the yield percentage rate increases. Look at these two examples:

1. *The dividend stays fixed at $0.70, but the price of a*
   share increases.

Dividend	0.70	0.70	0.70	0.70
Price	$14.00	15.75	17.00	19.00
Yield	5.0%	4.4%	4.1%	3.7%

2. *The dividend stays fixed at $1.00 per share, but the*
   share price falls.

Dividend	1.00	1.00	1.00	1.00
Price	$22.00	20.00	18.50	16.50
Yield	4.5%	5.0%	5.4%	6.1%

Consequently, the DJIA stocks with prices falling will tend to become those with higher yields, or the DJIA stocks that lag behind in a general price increase among the group will also tend to have higher yield. In a word, stocks tend to become higher yielding after a prolonged period of poor share price performance. Hence, those among the thirty DJIA companies with higher yield are sometimes called the Dogs of the Dow. Of course, the Dogs of the Dow may also have gotten there just because the directors wanted to reward the shareholders with more dividends. The name Dogs is not entirely fair or accurate, but we are stuck with it.

The examples above also carry a warning: When you buy the Dogs, there is a reason why they got there. The reason may be that other investors have poor opinions of those companies. Remember that all investing carries some risk. Work hard to try to recognize the risks.

Here are some methods for buying the Dogs:

Dogs 1: Among the Dow Jones industrials, buy the ten stocks with the highest yield. Hold them for one year, and then adjust the portfolio by selling whatever is necessary and buying new ones to get the new ten highest yielding stocks. That is a simple and surprisingly effective method. All you have to do is look in *Barron's* or the *Wall Street Journal* at the table where they list the yields of all of the thirty DJIA stocks. Pick the ten highest yields and buy those stocks. Check the table again next year. Sell the stocks that have fallen out of the ten, and repeat the process.

Dogs 2: Among the DJIA stocks, find the ten with highest yield. Discard the one with highest yield, and use the other nine for one year. This answers a prejudice that the one stock with the highest yield must truly be a Dog.

Dogs 3: Among the DJIA stocks, buy the five highest yields.

Dogs 4: Among the five highest yields, discard the one at the highest yield and buy the other four.

Dogs 5: Among the thirty DJIA stocks, find the ten with the lowest price/earnings ratio, and then buy the five among them with the highest yield.

Dogs 6: Among the thirty DJIA stocks, find the ten with highest yield, and then among that group buy the five with the lowest price/earnings ratio.

You can see there are many variations available. All of those methods have some supporters and some claim to producing good results. I read a newspaper article a few months ago that said that Dogs 1 was the absolute guaranteed key to success in stocks investing and would never let you down. That was bad advice. There is no risk-free investing method.

> **Gard's Dog:** Here is an opinion that you get free with the book. There is no guaranteed method to profits and success in the stock markets, but among the simple methods that require almost no work and can be applied by any small investor, the various forms of the Dogs are pretty good.

But just how do they work? Do they produce profits? We can look at some history—the total return from following each of the six Dog strategies during 1990, 1992, or 1995. This assumes equal amounts invested in each of the stocks indicated by that strategy, and selling at the beginning of the next year. It also includes the gains from dividends paid during the year.

	1990	1992	1995
Dogs 1: ten with highest yield	−9%	8%	34%
Dogs 2: Dogs 1 with the highest yielding stock removed	−8%	11%	31%
Dogs 3: five with highest yield	−11%	−7%	31%
Dogs 4: Dogs 3 with the highest yielding stock removed	−10%	−2%	29%
Dogs 5: the five highest yields from among the ten with the lowest price/earnings ratios	−14%	7%	32%
Dogs 6: the five lowest P/E ratios from among the ten with the highest yields	−21%	7%	42%
DJIA with dividends	14%	12%	30%
S&P 500 with dividends	−5%	5%	36%
Russell 2000 with dividends	−19%	18%	50%

The *Value Line*

Many individual investors who search for simplicity have learned to rely on the *Value Line Investment Survey*. The *Value Line* has a strong long-term record for predicting stocks for investments, but it will not do your thinking for you.

They present data and opinions on about 1700 stocks in their standard edition, and another 1800 stocks in the expanded edition. The two editions receive slightly different treatment. The standard edition contains most of the best known firms in the American markets. Their computer product, the *Value Line Investment Survey for Windows,* covers more companies and has more data (see chapter 15).

Simplicity is both the blessing and the curse of the *Value Line*. They have one section in each report that reduces a complex analysis to a single number for a rating. That makes it easy for the reader to look to one source for a single, clear, and credible recommendation. That also makes it easy for the reader to forget to do his homework and to overlook other factors. The editors are careful to warn the readers that they should not buy and sell based solely on the *Value Line* Timeliness Ratings. However, we can be sure that more people read the ratings than read the warning.

There are three ratings that cover their standard universe of 1700 stocks. The Timeliness Rating is a number, 1–5, where 1 is best and 5 is worst. It is based on their own methods for analyzing the stock price performance and company earnings, and recent trends in both of those. The rating gives the *Value Line* opinion of the chances for growth in the stock share price over the next six to twelve months. The top 100 of the stocks they cover get 1, the next 300 get 2, the next 900 are rated 3, the next 300 are rated 4, and the bottom 100 get 5. They generally recommend that investors who are trading for short-term performance buy stocks rated 1 or 2 and avoid those rated 4 or 5.

The Safety Rating is also a number 1 (best) to 5 (worst). It gives their opinion of the safety of the firm and stability of the stock price. The Technical Rating, which they call Technical Rank, gives their opinion of each stock's likely performance over the next three to six months. It is based on their proprietary technical methods for analyzing the stock's recent price history.

The *Value Line* (TVL) ratings and data are helpful, but they do not relieve you from the responsibilities for managing your own money and making your own decisions. Their editors and analysts do not know you or your current portfolio of investments. They cannot consider your need for diversification or risk management. You have to take care of those things. You should never accept the *Value Line* ratings as determining your buy and sell decisions. You should accept them as good indications about which stocks may best deserve your further investigation. You can also use their reports to screen a large group of stocks and pick out a few for further study. That is how I used TVL in selecting a group of twenty-six stocks for further study in the case history of the income investor in chapter 9. It took me about an hour using their information to select those twenty-six stocks.

The *Value Line* also sends out a booklet called *How to Invest in Common Stocks: A Guide to Using the Value Line Investment Survey*. It focuses on using their publications to help with your stock investment decisions, and for that purpose, it is excellent.

You should go to your public library and spend a little time with the *Value Line*. Some individual investors may use it frequently, and some may not, but everyone should at least see what they have to offer. Look there if you want to know the telephone number to reach a company's investor relations office; if you want to know their earnings for the past five fiscal years, or their current debt; or if you want to see a brief and credible opinion of the company's prospects for the next year. But if you want to buy the stock after using the *Value Line*, read the annual report and the 10K or 10Q reports to the SEC, and check all the sources for recent news on the company. The opinions and data that you read in the *Value Line* may be one to three months old depending on which edition you have in hand. Be thorough in your research and decision making. The *Value Line* is an excellent and easy way to get started.

Blue Chips

Blue chip is a term used casually to indicate the largest and best known American companies or their stocks. These may be the companies in the Dow Jones Industrial Average, or Transportation Average, or Utilities Average. They may include all of the companies in the Standard & Poor's 500 list. No one agrees on one definition of a blue chip. You may assume that the term includes any American corporation that has been in business for thirty years, is publicly traded, and has a market capitalization of over $10 billion.

Some investors and some mutual funds prefer to keep their stock investments among blue-chip companies. That practice has some potential benefits: It reduces the number of companies that you need to watch, makes most of the research easier, and lends some element of improved safety to the investment.

With the blue-chip approach, the number of companies to study is reduced from well over 9,000 publicly traded companies to about 500 that qualify as blue chip. If you impose further restrictions on the group, such as only looking at companies with a price/earnings ratio below 17, then you could quickly reduce the number well below 500. That reduction may be comforting to some investors as they start looking for investments.

Most of the research on blue chips is easier because more of the national press will be reporting on them, and more financial analysts will be watching them. For example, any blue-chip candidate is very likely to be included in the *Value Line* Standard Survey of 1700 companies, so you know a good place to start looking for basic information. Any dramatic news about a blue-chip company is likely to be reported in the national news immediately, so you will have fewer surprises. You should hear any important news on a blue-chip company just about as early as most of the market watchers. For smaller and younger companies, it may take a good deal more digging to find all the information you would need to make a stock selection decision. Standard & Poor's reports will include detailed information and opinions on any blue-chip company.

Investments in blue-chip companies may be safer than others. If a company is large, widely watched, and has been in business for over twenty years, then there is a reasonable presumption that you will be able to see if they have any great troubles on the horizon. It is reasonably safe to assume that a blue-chip company is not going to go bankrupt quickly (although such things have happened). There is less likelihood of a sudden total collapse of the stock value. However, that does not mean that the stock is safe from normal market volatility. Stocks of blue-chip companies may go up or down just as wildly as any others if they are severely mis-valued. Certainly IBM is among the blue-chip stocks, and they took their shareholders on a wild ride through 1993–1997. There was never any question of IBM going out of business or losing most of their markets, but investors' opinions of the stock value fluctuated extremely.

The drawbacks to blue-chip investing are just the mirror images of the advantages. The reduced number of stocks to consider might eliminate some very good candidates. Because more analysts follow the blue chips, you are less likely to find a real bargain in pricing among that class. If you confine yourself to blue-chip companies, then you will never buy any initial public offerings (IPO's) or companies that are going through a rapid expansion of their markets and sales.

In 1995, 1996, and 1997, the investors who confined their attention to the blue chips of the Dow Jones Industrial Average or the S&P 500 were greatly rewarded with better than 20 percent annual total return. So we see that blue-chip focus can be highly profitable. On the other hand, as I write, it appears that those same blue-chip stocks are currently very highly priced. It is difficult to find many among them that look like bargains. It may require a strong stomach and a firm faith in forecasting abilities to continue to invest in that group.

Follow Your Broker

For those who use a full-service broker or investment advisor, one of the simple choices is to follow their recommendations on what to buy or sell. This, of course, requires great confidence in the broker, because you are the one at risk. That practice might be reasonable for someone who will not bring herself to do the work, arithmetic, or decision making. If you choose to follow an advisor on all your investments, then some checks and balances are in order.

You must check the monthly statements carefully to see if you are satisfied with the advisor's trading practices and the results. You must ask the broker clear, direct questions about anything that disturbs you in the portfolio report. You should go in slowly and limit the amount of money in the account until you have become well acquainted with the broker and her trading methods.

Don't hesitate to change brokers if you are dissatisfied with either the results or the answers you get. If you do decide to change brokers, don't let the first one bully you into apologizing for it or backing down on your decision. Just go find another broker that you hope will be better and ask him to transfer the account over to the new firm.

But finally, if you are not going to take any personal hand in either the work or decision making of buying stocks, then it would probably be cheaper, safer, and more profitable to simply look in *Morningstar Reports* and find a few mutual funds to buy.

Indexing

Indexing is the philosophy of going for average. That's not bad. Over the long-term, the average of stock investments is more profitable and safer than many of the alternatives. If you wanted to individually index your stock investments, then you would simply pick out a group of companies that you wanted to follow and then buy a representative sample of those stocks. Some people might decide to just follow the Dow Jones utilities stocks. They could just look at that list of fifteen companies and buy equal amounts of seven or eight of the stocks, maybe even all fifteen if they could afford it. Once a year or so they could balance the investments if a few of them had gotten well ahead of or well behind the others.

Indexing is not a bad idea. However, there is a simpler and cheaper way to do it. If you decide that you want to index, then use a mutual fund. You would have lower costs, and better diversification, than by doing it alone. There are many respectable and profitable mutual funds that are committed to indexing. You can probably find several that work in any area of the market that interests you.

Follow a Method

Remember, early on in the book I said choose a method. A method is better than no method. At least if you have a method you will sound like you know what you are doing. Your buddies will be impressed. We will look at some things that can happen if you choose a method and stick with it through thick and thin.

For an example, let's look at Charley, who is an intelligent and disciplined investor and has $50,000 he is willing to put at risk in the stock markets. So Charley has read this book and a few others, and he thinks the smart money bets on low price/earnings ratios. For him, that is the whole story of stock selection. In September 1991, he found eight companies with very low P/E ratios and he bought:

Company	P/E	# of Shares	Share Price	Total Cost
Salomon, Inc.	4.6	200	25	$5,100
Commodore	5.5	600	11	6,700
Fremont General	6.0	250	23	5,850
Thiokol	6.1	300	19	5,800
Travelers, Inc.	6.5	300	20	6,100
Town & Country	6.3	1,500	4	6,100
Grumman	6.8	300	19	5,800
Phelps Dodge	6.9	80	69	5,620
Total invested				**$47,070**

Each purchase carried a $100 commission included in the total above.

In January of 1993, Charley woke up from his holiday nap and reviewed the situation.

Company	New Price	# of Shares	Value	Dividends	Net
Salomon	37	200	7,400	160	7,560
Commodore	6.50	600	3.900	0	3,900
Fremont	34	250	8,500	195	8,695
Thiokol	17	300	5,100	141	5,241
Travelers	27	300	8,100	600	8,700
Town & Country	2.88	1,500	4,320	0	4,320
Grumman	25	300	7,500	375	7,875
Phelps Dodge	49	80	3,920	158	4,078
Totals			**48,740**	**1,629**	**50,369**

On the money invested, he developed a 7 percent total return over sixteen months. Not bad. During the same time, the S&P 500 index was up about 16 percent. Charley could have bought an index fund and done better with less fees and less work. But maybe that's not a fair test. Charley sold all those stocks and paid another $800 in brokerage fees, so he had left about $52,400. He waited until April 1993 and bought seven new stocks selected solely on the basis of low P/E.

Company	P/E	# of Shares	Share Price	Total Cost
R G Barry	3.4	800	7	5,700
Dime Savings Bank	4.2	800	7.875	6,400
Columbia Gas	5.3	300	23	7,000
SPI Pharmaceutical	6.0	400	16	6,500
Rohr	6.5	700	8.875	6,313
Sea Containers	7.1	250	24	6,100
DeBeers	7.4	400	16	6,500
Total				**44,513**

He bought and held until January 1997, whereupon he decided to check his monthly statement:

Company	New Price	# of Shares	Value	Dividends Collected	Net
Barry	11	800	8800	0	8,800
Dime Savings	16	800	12,800	0	12,800
Columbia	64	300	19,200	180	21,000
SPI[2]	22	400	8,800	320	9,120
Rohr	22	700	15,400	0	15,400
Sea Containers	17	250	4,250	720	4,970
DeBeers	30	400	12,000	772	12,772
Total					84,862

On the money invested, he has developed a 90 percent total return in just less than four years. Not bad. During the same time, the S&P 500 index was up about 77 percent. With dividends paid, it would have returned a total of about 85 percent. Charley could have bought an index fund and done almost as well with less fees.

These two examples are intended to illustrate that a simple strategy, such as buy low P/E, with no other judgment factors applied, may or may not produce any good results. For a more complete and reliable study of the situation, we need to look into a statistical analysis of what would happen if you applied this process to buy a small group of stocks on many different occasions. If the criterion of buying the fifty large-cap stocks with the lowest P/E ratios had been applied repeatedly at different starting times over the years from January 1986 to December 1996, the average annual return to be expected was 14.6 percent. Over the same time period, the average annual total return on the entire S&P 500 was 14.8 percent.[3]

A deeper analysis of the question has been done by James O'Shaughnessy and his associates and described in their book *What Works on Wall Street*.

---

[2] SPI merged into ICN Pharmaceutical in a one-to-one stock trade.
[3] These results are from the *What Works On Wall Street* software produced by James O'Shaughnessy and Standard & Poor's.

He has studied the results of buying the fifty stocks with lowest P/E from a larger population of stocks and holding them for one year. He has analyzed the results from applying that process consistently over the period from 1952 to 1994. You should read his book. To summarize and simplify one result of his statistical studies: Buying low P/E stocks has been an effective strategy over the forty-two year time span if you confine it to large stocks. Large stocks means roughly the 1,000 or so stocks with largest market capitalization. As a very rough rule of thumb, in early 1997, any company with market capitalization over $1 billion would qualify as a large stock.

You should recall that past performance is not necessarily indicative of future results, but O'Shaughnessy presents powerful evidence that the low P/E strategy has been effective over a long time period.

Warning: Do not take this as an endorsement of using the simple strategy of just buying low P/E stocks. The next year's market will be different from the market of the past fifty years. Among the low P/E stocks there will certainly be some losers. The discussion above says that *on average* if you bought *a lot* of low P/E stocks of companies with large market capitalizations *in the past forty years,* then the return would have been pretty good.

But you might not hit the average. You probably will not buy a lot (fifty or more) of the low P/E stocks. You will not be buying the market from the past forty years. Therefore you might not get the expected result.

There are no risk-free investments, nor risk-free investment strategies. The low P/E strategy is just one reasonable approach if you are looking for a very simple strategy and want to buy large-cap stocks.

There are other reasonable and simple strategies. With all of the above warnings and side-stepping repeated, you could also try some of these:

- Buy stocks with low price-to-book-value ratio
- Buy stocks with low price-to-cash-flow ratio
- Buy stocks with low price-to-sales ratio
- Buy large-cap stocks with high yield

These are strategies anyone can apply with a minimum of work, and that have a decent chance of being better than random guessing. O'Shaughnessy's book and his software give the results from applying many of these strategies.

In his famous book, *The Intelligent Investor*, Ben Graham also mentions one other attractive and simple strategy, which is to buy stocks for which the price per share is less than the net current assets per share. You can check those values using either the *Value Line* or *Standard & Poor's Stock Guide*. Both of those publications will show you the company's current assets and all liabilities. The net current assets equals current assets minus all liabilities. Divide that by the number of shares and compare it to the share price.

Example: We will look at Luria & Son Corporation in May 1991. The *Value Line* showed them with $95 million of current assets, $46 million of current liabilities, and $3 million of long-term debt. The net current assets were $46 million (95 − 46 − 3), and they had approximately 5.5 million shares. The net current assets per share is 46 ÷ 5.5 = 8.4. The stock would then appear to be a bargain at a price below $8.40. At the time, you could buy it for $6. Two years later the price was $10, and in July 1993 the price was $13.

This is an opportunity to find incredible bargains. If you find a company with the price less than the net current assets, it may be too good to pass up. It may be a no-brainer! It may also call for some caution and careful reflection. How could that be? You would want to take a hard look at the numbers and the condition of the corporation. Here are two examples of how those numbers might be deceiving:

(1) Current assets might be misstated. The current assets include inventory. If the inventory consisted of old products that might never be sold, but were carried on the accounts valued at the cost of production, that might greatly overstate the value of current assets. In such a situation, the net-current-assets-per-share figure would be unreliable.

(2) The liabilities might be misstated. For example, if the capital structure included preferred stock carried on the books at a par value of $1 a share, but it required dividends of 20¢ per share, then the true liability of that preferred stock would be something closer to $4 to $6 per share, depending on their cost of borrowing. Then the long-term liabilities would be understated. In such a situation, the net-current-assets-per-share figure would be unreliable.

In the case of Luria, there was no preferred stock, but most of the current assets value was in inventory. That situation would have required closer investigation in May 1991.[4]

There is a lesson in all of this. Most of the simple strategies that we have looked at involve a bias toward lower price relative to something. The something may be dividend, or book value, or sales, or something else. The lesson is that price is always important. It is essential to remember in all your stock selection work that it is not enough to find a great company. What you need is a great company at a great price. Buy low.

Recommended Further Reading

Cobleigh, Ira U., and Peter J. DeAngelis. *The $2 Window on Wall Street*. New York: Macmillan, 1986.

Malkiel, Burton G. *A Random Walk Down Wall Street*, 6th ed. New York: W. W. Norton and Co., 1996.

O'Higgins, Michael, and John Downs. *Beating the Dow*. New York: HarperCollins, 1992.

---

[4] You would look at the sales-to-inventory ratio to see how often they were turning around the inventory each year for one indication of how the inventory was moving or aging.

The Search for Something Special

Not every tool that serves one worker will serve another as well. I sit at my computer and type words. Some others would either not type at all, or type better words, or worse. There are a great many tools that might be useful to some investors and not to others.

In this chapter, we will look at some tools or methods of investing that might be good for you. These are tools of investors who are looking for something special. Some of these require more work, more experience, or more specialized education than you have. Don't worry about it. Many people try exercise plans or entertainment that are not right for them in order to discover what works. The same is true for investing tools. Read these methods and see if some of them look useful for you.

Value Criteria

We have already talked about value-oriented investing. What else is there to say? Plenty. There are many ways to select stocks for the value investor, and most of them have some rational basis to make the method appear worthwhile. There is a difference between the needs of the professional mutual fund manager and the individual investor. Some strategies have been shown to work well if you can consistently invest in the 50 or 100 stocks

---

[1] The tools to him who can use them.

that best fit the criteria, but might expose you to too much risk if you are only buying one stock at a time.

First, what criteria? There are many to choose from. Second, to what extent will the ratios and tests rule your decision making? If you find a stock or company that satisfies your value selection rule(s), then is it necessarily a good buy for you? There are different points of view on that, but I recommend that you adopt a policy that your value criteria will only help you to find candidates that look attractive. After that, you should still study the companies and find out what you can about their products, management, and competition. Remember that most of the value-oriented selection criteria start by using the stock price as part of the calculation (e.g., price-to-earnings ratio, or price-to-cash-flow ratio). Those ratios might look good just because the price has been driven to low levels. That is a reflection of the market's consensus opinion about the stock, and you should show some respect for the market's opinion. Think of market opinion as like a 900-pound gorilla: It may be wrong, but it demands respect. So even after you have found a stock, or a few, that satisfies some good value selection criteria, then still do some research on the company and its industry group. Chapter 11 illustrated that process. The value selection criteria may include any tests that you think point to a reasonable price for the stock. Some people like the following, and some would have stricter or looser criteria (for instance, see the ideas of Ben Graham later in this chapter).

Candidates for Value Selection Criteria

1. The price-to-earnings ratio should be less than some standard that you regard as safe (at times you might prefer less than 12, or 14, or less than the market average).

2. The price-to-cash-flow ratio should be less than a standard that you regard as attractive (6, or 8, or 9, or whatever you believe is good).

3. The company had positive earnings for the past four years in a row.

4. The price per share should not be above 1.5 times the book value per share (some very cautious investors might say less than 1 times book value).

5. The earnings have grown by at least 20 percent during each of the past two years.

6. The long-term debt to total capitalization ratio should not be more than 25 percent (or a little more).

Those are only samples of value selection criteria. Use any one, or a combination of them. You could think of others, and as we saw in chapter 11, investors may choose to use combinations of the criteria. You may want to refer back to the examples in chapter 11 to see how the value criteria might be applied in specific real-world cases. Chapter 15 has further examples.

In the summer of 1997, you might have applied the following six value conditions to the 5,000-plus stocks evaluated in the extended edition *Value Line Investment Survey for Windows*:

1. The price-to-earnings ratio should be less than 15.

2. The price-to-cash-flow ratio should be less than 7.

3. The company had positive earnings for the past four years in a row.

4. The price per share should not be above 1.5 times the book value per share.

5. The market capitalization should be above 200 million.

6. The long-term debt to total capitalization ratio should not be more than 25 percent.

This set of six requirements taken together is rather complex and rigorous. You would have discovered that, among the 5,000 companies, only six passed all of those strict value requirements.[2] They were British Steel, Tecumseh Products, Timkin Company, Avondale Industries, Cleveland Cliffs, Inc., and Mine Safety Appliances. Any one of those six companies may be looked on as something special. Each should give a serious value investor something to chew on.

---

[2] This is a complex search; it took about fifteen minutes, using their software and database, to write the requirements, run the screen, and look at the *Value Line* opinions.

One of the greatest books about investing ever written is *The Intelligent Investor* by Ben Graham. He encouraged value criteria for stock selection. Graham also encouraged some degree of confidence for the individual investor who was willing to work at and think about careful stock selection:

> *The policy of investing in high quality stocks does not require high qualities of insight and foresight to work out successfully. The danger lies in concentrating their purchases in the upper levels of the market, or in buying non representative common stocks that carry more than average risk of diminished earning power.*

Where Graham said "upper levels," he was telling us not to pay exorbitantly high prices just because a stock is currently popular and "everyone is buying it." Where he said "more than average risk of diminished earning power," he was telling us to take a careful look at the company and its products, markets, and competition.

His specific value selection method for the conservative investor was to buy large companies that satisfy all of the following conditions:

1. The quick ratio[3] should be greater than 2 and the long-term debt should be less than the working capital.[4]

2. The company should have paid dividends for the past twenty years.

3. The company should have been profitable every year of the past ten years.

4. Over the past ten years, the earnings should have increased by at least 33 percent.

5. The price per share should not be more than 1.5 times the net assets. The price per share should not be above fifteen times the past three years' average earnings.

---

[3] The quick ratio measures the company's ability to pay current liabilities without selling inventory; it is current assets minus inventory, divided by current liabilities.

[4] Working capital is current assets minus current liabilities.

That list makes up a severe value test. Any company that satisfied all of the criteria would probably look like a compelling buy to any investor.

To illustrate how severe Graham's value criteria list is, we will go back and reconsider the value selection cases from chapter 11. In those examples, our two value investors found seventeen stocks that satisfied their initial value selection tests and a few other considerations. I said that any of those might be an attractive investment for some value investors. They were

Angelica Corp.	Destek	Furon
Imperial Chemical	International Paper	Nash Finch
Navistar	Piccadilly Cafeterias	Rhone-Poulenc
Springs Industries	T.J. International	Thomas Industries
Total Petroleum	WHX Corp.	West Co.
Westvaco	Wellman, Inc.	

How do these seventeen good-looking companies do on Graham's criteria?[5]

- Six of seventeen companies failed the twenty-year dividend test.

- Seven of seventeen companies failed the ten-year earnings growth test.

- Eleven of seventeen failed the three-year average P/E test.

- Four of seventeen failed the ten-year profitability test.

Only two passed all four of those standards: Nash Finch and Springs Industries. Neither of them passed Graham's other conditions. It is a challenge to find a stock that satisfies all of the conditions, but if you do, it should be a good investment choice.

Earnings Criteria

We have discussed before the advantages and disadvantages of using the stock's dividend yield as the primary selection criterion. The same arguments might be applied to using earnings as the main factor. The company's earnings go into two channels. One is dividend yield for the shareholders, and

---

[5] Using 1996 data.

the other is retained earnings for the company to use for growth or paying down their long-term debt.

In 1993, Rollins Truck Leasing Corporation reported earnings of $30 million. They used $5.5 million of that to pay dividends to shareholders. That was about a 1 percent yield. They held the other $24.5 million for retained earnings. Their long-term debt was high and going higher, but without the retained earnings, it would have gone higher yet. In 1994, they earned about 16 percent on net worth. That means that the $24.5 million retained in the company's net worth was put to good use. It avoided additional interest payments and compounded the growth by an additional 16 percent. In 1994, they earned about $39 million and paid out $6.4 million in dividends. In 1995, the earnings on net worth were about 15 percent, so all of the retained earnings here were adding on good new value for the shareholders.

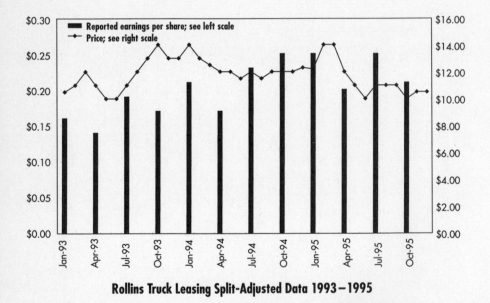

Rollins Truck Leasing Split-Adjusted Data 1993–1995

The point is that earnings benefit the shareholders even if they are not paid out in dividends. So how do you select stocks with an eye to good earnings? There are several possible rules. Any combination or variations of these will be of interest to some investors.

Tests to Indicate Good Earnings

1. The P/E ratio should be less than some specific cut-off level that you think is attractive. Some investors might say less than 10, or 11, or 15. You have to pick the value that works for you.

2. The earnings per share should be growing. You might say it has to have increased by 15 percent in each of the past three years. Some investors might say 20 or 25 percent, for two years, four years, or ten years. You may pick a level that seems reasonable and attractive to you.

3. The earnings per share should be growing faster than the average for the company's specific industry group. You have to check an industry report to see that industry average. You might get that from the *Value Line*, *Forbes,* or *Business Week*.

4. The projected earnings per share, using the consensus of analysts who follow the company, should be increasing by some specific level that you like—say 15 or 20 percent—or a percentage that is greater than the stocks current P/E ratio. You might find those numbers in *Zacks Analyst Watch* or the *First Call Consensus Estimate Guide*.

It may seem difficult or unrealistic to pick the values that seem right for you in some of those criteria, but you can do it. Start out and look at reports in the *Value Line*. Get a feel for what numbers are average or above average for the kinds of companies you like to study. Try a few selections using some specific selection criteria and see whether you are getting good candidates. Adjust the numbers to make the process productive for your needs.

Here's an example of a search for good earnings: We'll say that in mid-1996, I wanted to find a large American bank to invest in, and my earnings criteria were that the P/E should have been not above 14, and the earnings-to-net-worth ratio for the past year should have been above 13 percent. So I went to check some banks in my *Value Line*; it turns out that thirty-six of the fifty-four banks listed satisfied these criteria. That was not producing anything special! So I decided to make the criteria a little stiffer. Based on the numbers that I found in the first test, it looks like maybe P/E not above 12, and earnings at least 16 percent of net worth would be more interesting. Check it out. Then only ten of the fifty-four banks made the grade.

But that still was not sufficiently special for my investments. I fixed the criteria to be P/E not above 11, and earnings-to-net-worth ratio at least 18 percent! None of the banks made that grade. At this point, it might have been best to simply do some more reading and see what was there. It turned out that only three of the banks had a P/E ratio that rounded off to 11. Their ratios of earnings to net worth were 13 percent, 14 percent, and 15 percent. The best of that pack was NationsBank. Among the banks with a high percent earned to net worth and a P/E at 13 or lower were

Bank	P/E	Earnings/Net Worth
First Tennessee	13	19%
Bank of New York	12	18%
Citicorp	12	18%
Corestates Financial	12	19%
Wells Fargo	12	26%
Wilmington Trust	13	20%

A prudent and conservative investor might well have decided that any of those were good investment opportunities in mid-1996, and that all of them had something special to offer in terms of the earnings criteria.

Growth Criteria

What more can we conclude about growth-oriented stock selection? These methods are, from a certain point of view, always something special. The issue here is that growth selection requires some crystal ball to see into the future business and earnings of a firm. We know that is difficult. Very few people successfully predict earnings more than twelve months out. Besides being difficult, it is subject to an infinite variation of conclusions. The growth argument that makes sense to one investor may be logical, yet not make sense to very many others. There are too many reasons why we might predict that one company should do well next year, and too many reasons why we might conjecture that the new strength will prevail into the succeeding years. There are too many reasons why any other investor might strongly disagree.

Just for example, one investor might say that Procter & Gamble has long dominated the home nondurable-products market. Their strategy of discontinuing coupons on cereals and lowering prices will blow the competition away. That is a good sign for continued strong growth in their market share and revenues. Okay, maybe so. Another investor might say that the President's Choice product line carried by Ruddick Corporation and sold in their Harris Teeter grocery stores is becoming better, more diverse, and more widely accepted every day. Since they undercut P&G on price where they compete, this is going to be a major problem for all of the major brands and a good reason to expect continuing growth in Ruddick Corp. There is some logic in each of those arguments, and some contradiction between them.

The difficulty is that the growth investor must plan a strategy to change horses in midstream. In fact, he must argue that his analysis is apart from the common herd before buying the stock, but that the herd's opinion will come around to his view after buying the stock. Why? Before buying the stock, the growth investor must be convinced that the current price is attractive. That assumes that the market has not yet recognized all of the virtues in the company and that the stock is still undervalued. However, after buying the stock, there is no profit unless the market quoted price moves up, and that requires that a great many investors see the value and want to buy it then. That new state of grace among the other investors depends on their either seeing the potential in the company or eventually seeing new strong earnings. In either case, that is likely to take time. As we have seen, time is the enemy of the forecaster. The longer you wait, the more the possibility that something unforeseen will occur and the predictions become worthless.

Growth investing is a legitimate and potentially profitable approach to stocks. It is by definition, however, always a search for something special. It is also more difficult and riskier than some other methods. It requires more experience and risk-tolerance. Examples of growth investing are included in both chapter 12 and chapter 15.

Investment Clubs

An investment club is almost always something special for the individual investor. In the simplest possible terms, an investment club is a partnership among a small group of investors who agree to share the work and decision making of buying stocks. They could invest in anything, but by far the majority of them stick to buying stocks.

For information about investment clubs, or how to find one in your area, contact the National Association of Investors Corporation (NAIC) at 810-583-6242.[6] They can help you with advice about how to start or find a club. They publish an excellent magazine, *Better Investing*, which should be in your local library. They will help you with organizational work and provide some methods that they recommend clubs use in doing their own analysis on stocks.

An investment club will typically have between ten and twenty members and meet once a month. The members agree on a fixed amount that each one will pay into the club's holdings each meeting. That amount may be $20 to $50, or whatever the members agree makes sense for them. Each meeting will usually include some presentation by one or more members on stocks that they have studied, followed by a discussion of those stocks or any others of interest. If a member thinks that the club should buy or sell something, then that is decided by majority rule. The club may decide to follow the NAIC methods for studying and buying or make up their own procedures.

Investment clubs offer at least three distinct advantages to the individual investor. First, the club will help bring some discipline into your investment practice. If you are a member of a club that is going to meet on Wednesday to discuss a company that all the members have agreed to consider, then you are not likely to just go in empty-handed and look like a dunce. You will probably do some reading. If the club is reviewing their portfolio monthly, then that will serve as a reminder for you to do the same. For those of us who work alone, it is all too easy to let things slide for a while and not keep up on our research. A club will help guard against that fault.

The second advantage is education—especially for investors with limited experience (that's all of us, right?). In an investment club discussion, you will probably hear more useful approaches to stock selection and more interesting points of view on an individual company than you would think up on your own. Most investment clubs make a significant and generous effort to help educate the beginners.

---

[6] Or write to: Box 220, Royal Oak, MI 48068.

"I'm only taking this to my best customers—this is the deal of the century!"

The third advantage is the clincher: Safety. This author says that the stock purchases that you make with an investment club will *always* be safer than the purchases you make alone. What happens in stock selection work is this: Most of us will look at a company and see many of the same reasons why the stock might be appealing. I don't know why; it just works that way. People tend to look for reasons to buy. However, a group of ten people who study a particular stock will see a wide variety of potential risks in the stock due to their experience, education, how much work they did, what news they heard recently, or any of a hundred other variables. A group that comes together to discuss the wisdom in a stock purchase will always do a far better job of recognizing the risks than any one person working alone. That makes the final decision a safer process. To repeat: The stock purchases that you make with an investment club will *always*[7] be safer than the purchases you make alone.

---

[7] Well, all right—there is one potential fly in the ointment: A club where the members don't really share the work, where they depend on one or two dominate personalities to lead the rest around, may not be safer. Avoid clubs that work that way.

Bottom-Up

A lot of investment analysis begins with the financial statements of a company. This type of investment process is called bottom-up investing. It starts with the bottom line[8] of the company and works up to bigger issues, such as products, then markets, then competition, the economy, interest rates, and progressively larger issues. This process would typically begin with the investor hearing about some company that sounded interesting. That's the way I got into Ford. I did not start by considering world wide markets for consumer durables. I started by looking at one company whose cars I liked. Then I read financial reports, the *Value Line*, and the *Wall Street Journal*, and looked everywhere I could for news about Ford or their competitors. The focus was very much on one company.

Bottom-up investment research can be productive, but should not rule out other methods. Remember the rules of diversification. Don't restrict yourself to one approach unless you become very confident that you are going to make sound decisions that way. Even if you do like bottom-up methods, you should look at all other relevant information about the industry and the economy, too. If one company looks attractive to you, it is possible that others in the same industry may be better. Bottom-up analysis is a reasonable way to begin your investigations; it is not the end of the story.

Top-Down

The top-down approach starts with national or global economic factors, and then narrows the focus of study to perhaps one country or one industry, and then to a few companies. For several years, I have been convinced that the world has been just a stumble away from an energy crisis. Many people say otherwise, but my personal economic philosophy says energy is critical now, has been for ten years, and will be for the next ten years. This thinking has led me to interests in companies that produce energy or service those that do. For example, oil drilling or refining companies, gas production or pipeline companies, petroleum exploration companies, or those that make the tools for the preceding, all look interesting to me. The top-down investor might add to her portfolio using that kind of thinking by studying the lists of companies in those industries to find one or two

---

[8] The *bottom line* is the last line, or earnings line, of the earnings report; it also refers to the total financial statement of the company.

that are good, or by buying a mutual fund that specializes in that area. For the energy-wise investor, there are several mutual funds that would invest for you and provide diversification.

For the individual investor, there might be too much risk or work in trying to find a single stock to buy in the energy business. All of the ideas and methods we have studied so far could be helpful, but the industry is complex and not familiar to most of us. You probably understand a lot about Pepsi-Cola's business, but how much do you know about the major international oil firms? On the other hand, if your top-down studies led you to seek investments in the area of recreation, then you might be as well qualified as anyone to estimate the opportunities and risks. When you are looking at broad and complex issues such as energy, think about whether that is a job that you want to tackle on your own, or if it would be better to have a fund manager doing it for you. This is a book about buying stocks, but don't forget that you have other options, too.

Momentum Investing

Isaac Newton and Keith Jackson[9] taught us about momentum. Old Mo is not to be taken lightly. An object in motion is in motion, and all that sort of thing. Such concepts have their place in the study of stocks.

The trend is your friend, if you can see the trend. But there are many good reasons to believe that in the stock markets, there are no trends except the ones we see in the rearview mirror. Momentum investing is based on the belief that there are trends, that some people can see them, and that there are certain indicators that should help us identify the stronger trends. In the interest of helping the reader sort through the news and magazines and commentary, we will look a little at momentum investing.

But This is Very Tricky Business!

The reader is advised that the identification of trends, and investment practices that rely on that skill, are fraught with peril and probably best left to experienced investors who can judge and accept the risks.

Some momentum-oriented investors like to seek out stocks that have been doing well for a few weeks/months/hours, or whatever time frame seems

---

[9] Sports commentator (joke).

best to them. If the stock shows an upward trend in price, sales, or earnings per share over some time period, and particularly if that trend is accompanied by higher than average volume, then the momentum investor wants to jump on and ride that train. However, momentum sometimes is used as an excuse to avoid the basic research that we have discussed so much earlier in the book.

One of the central concepts of momentum is the effect of volume. This idea says that when a price change occurs with large trading volume, that is more important than when the price change occurs on light trading volume. Say you have been watching a company for a year, and the price stayed between $14 and $18 per share with average daily trading volume of 30,000 shares. Then for a week you see the trading at these levels:

	Mon.	Tue.	Wed.	Thr.	Fri.
Trade volume	40,000	45,000	60,000	80,000	100,000
Closing price ($)	17	18	20	21	22

That would be read as an indicator of strong momentum, confirmed by strong volume. If the daily prices had shown the same closing values, but with much lower trading volume, then some traders would say it was not a significant move. In the example above, you might say that just as many people are selling as buying, and that may be true; however, the sellers have good motivation to sell. Most of them are taking profits. The buyers only come in here if they believe the stock is still a good deal at these prices. The higher volume confirms that significant numbers of new buyers are convinced that the stock is a good deal at those prices.

Many traders also look at earnings momentum, which they think reflects a future trend in improved earnings, or sales momentum. In each case, this comes down to a forecast that the alleged trend will continue for a while and enrich the stock value. That is a reasonable point of view, and it will be of value if you can accurately foresee an earnings trend that will continue. However, we know that it is difficult to foresee such trends.

You may have noticed that momentum investing shares some ideas in common with growth investing. True, but there should be a change in approach. The growth investor should look at a lot of fundamental and industry factors, although he or she may use earnings growth and stock price growth as the starting points to select interesting stocks. The committed momentum investor is much less likely to spend her time and attention on fundamental and value factors. She may let the momentum factors decide the buy-and-sell questions.

Paccar is a manufacturer of heavy-duty trucks and mining equipment (Kenworth, Peterbilt trucks). From October 1996 through May 1997, their stock had a significant run-up in price accompanied by a large increase in trading volume (see chart below). Momentum investors who watched Paccar would have been impressed by the action, particularly because of the high volume sustained over several months. A sharp and aggressive momentum investor probably bought this stock in November or December of 1996 and made a handsome profit on it.

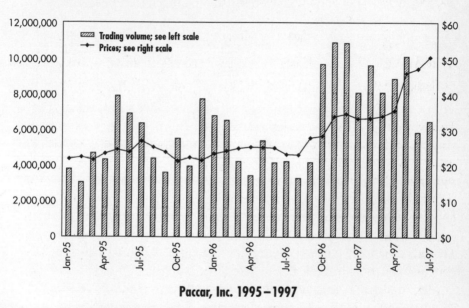

Paccar, Inc. 1995–1997

Foreign Stocks

The foreign markets and foreign companies offer you choices to diversify your investment portfolio. For that reason alone, they are worth consideration. There are, however, a few problems with investing in the stocks of foreign companies. Lets first look at the variety of ways you can make such investments:

1. Use a stockbroker who can deal directly in foreign markets.

2. Buy ADR's (American Depository Receipts) in the American stock markets.

3. Buy mutual funds or closed-end funds that invest in foreign countries.

4. Buy WEBs[10], which represent investments in foreign stock indices.

The ADRs are securities that entitle the owner to the rights and profits of ownership of shares in the foreign countries. They stand in the place of shares that are not registered in the American markets. The value and integrity of the ADRs are guaranteed by a bank that actually owns an equivalent value of the foreign companies' shares. ADRs are generally, but not universally, thought to be as good as owning the shares.

Buying funds for foreign investments has all the advantages, and more, that we expect from buying mutual funds for any kind of investment. The extra advantage is that the professional fund managers will presumably have better access to information about foreign companies and better expertise on using that information.

WEBs are a class of securities (actually, they are derivatives) that depend on the value of certain foreign stock indices. By buying the French WEB, you could buy an interest in the French stock market, but not an individual French stock. WEBs are traded on the American Stock Exchange.

Sad to say, foreign stock investments carry some additional risks. If you buy German stocks, then the value of the investment is represented in deutsche marks, not dollars. It is subject to currency fluctuations. Even if the stocks go up in value in Germany, they might lose value in dollars. That cuts both ways. It is equally likely to be either an advantage or a disadvantage.

It is more difficult to get good, reliable information about the foreign stocks or economies. Most other countries do not have the same strict controls on financial reporting that the United States has. There are greater risks of foreign financial reports being misleading or confusing. There is certainly greater risk that you will not hear about foreign business developments as

---

[10] World Equity Baskets—a type of security indexed to foreign trade markets.

soon as you would wish to hear them. Most of those new risks are best handled by letting mutual funds (or closed-end funds) handle your investments in foreign stocks.

There are some foreign companies that overcome those difficulties just because they are large, well known, and closely followed by American financial analysts. For those it might make sense to buy their stocks or ADRs on the American markets. In that class, you can place such firms as Royal Dutch Petroleum, Volvo, Telefonos de Mexico, Endessa, Toyota, and others.

Penny Stocks

The term *penny stocks* is used to cover the class of stocks that are priced quite low. Typically they are in a range of 1¢ up to $2 or $3 per share. There is always a good reason why they are priced so low: The market's opinion is that the price is fair. For such stocks, you should always expect greater risk, less reliable information, and greater volatility. Some individual investors like to sport with these mavericks because of the potential for great gains. If you bought $5,000 worth of a 25¢ stock and it then went up to $1.75, you would have a great percentage profit. That is an overwhelming lure to some investors. Resist it. Penny stocks almost always entail greater risk than the potential reward is worth. It is unlikely that you would obtain enough reliable and timely information to justify taking on that risk. The only exceptions should be the cases where you truly have access to special information before it is widely known. That, of course, will not happen very often. Penny stocks are an acceptable investment class only for those who have considerable experience and can accept high risks.

CANSLIM

William J. O'Neil is a well-known author, investor, teacher, and publisher. He owns and publishes the *Investor's Business Daily*, which we have mentioned repeatedly. He is the author of a respected book on stock investing, *How to Make Money in Stocks*. O'Neil has developed a method that he claims should be used by individual investors who are looking for something special. It goes by the acronym *CANSLIM*. If you want a more complete description of the method, refer to his book, or to the videotape *One Hundred Ways to Improve Your Investment Results*, which *Investor's Business*

Daily will send you free, along with ten free issues of the paper, if you call 800-831-2525. This section will just outline the main themes.

CANSLIM is a combination of ideas that you should recognize by now. It requires somewhat more work and judgment than many of the methods that we have mentioned earlier. However, it has the endorsement of Mr. O'Neil, which should count for something, and it is based on his study of stock market winners and losers over forty years. It consists of seven selection ideas:

1. **C is for Current:** The current quarterly earnings should be up 25 percent over the same quarter a year ago.

2. **A is for Annual:** The annual earnings per share for the past five years should show compound growth of 25 percent or more. (To test this, the most recent year's earnings should be at least three times those of five years ago, and the trend over those five years should be pretty steadily up; there may be some fluctuation.) Examples for A criteria:

   Earnings per share for five years($): 3.00, 3.70, 4.90, 6.50, 9.00 is good

   Earnings per share for five years($): 1.00, 1.97, 2.85, 2.75, 3.45 is good

   Earnings per share for five years ($): 2.00, 3.50, 4.00, 3.75, 4.90 is not.

   Even though that last example may look fairly good, it does not satisfy the "A" criterion for selecting something special.

3. **N is for New:** There should be something new happening in the company's business or industry that looks like it would stimulate favorable stock price action, or the stock should be hitting a new high or breaking out of a trading range that it has held for a while.

4. **S is for Shares:** The number of shares in circulation should be less than thirty million (this makes the stock price more responsive to buying interest).

5. **L is for Leader:** The company should be a leader in its industry, and the stock should be a leader in its industry group in the market. The relative price strength (as reported in IBD) should be 80 or higher.

6. **I is for Institutional:** The stock should be held by several major investment organizations (mutual funds, insurance companies, pension funds).

7. **M is for Market:** The investment should be in phase with major market trends. That, of course, is very tough to judge, but don't buy stocks while the market is in a major down trend, unless perhaps the one company's industry group is bucking the trend and going up. Mr. O'Neil has a chapter on this in his book.

Graham and Dodd

Ben Graham also worked on another book, with David Dodd, called *Security Analysis*. Good news–bad news, okay? It is a great book, but requires a commitment by the reader. It may be somewhat dated, but a lot of basic concepts and philosophy never go out of style. If you will make the commitment to read it, you will not be disappointed, although you may decide that some of the work is beyond your interest or experience.

This much is certain: One may not consider oneself to be a well-informed student of investing without having read *Security Analysis*[11]. If you will carefully consider and attempt to apply all of their ideas and methods in your investment decisions, then you will be on solid ground. That does not guarantee that you will make a profit, only that you will have as good a chance as most.

The Graham and Dodd methods require studious application of fundamental financial analysis, taken with good judgment about how to interpret the numbers for various industries and different market conditions. Their methods are generally in line with what we have called value investing, but they also look at the choices for investing with bonds or keeping cash on hand. It would be inappropriate to attempt to summarize their

---

[11] And, it says here, the same is true for James O'Shaughnessy's book *What Works on Wall Street*.

lessons here. Their book is too complex and serious to admit a brief summary. Read it.

Fads

In 1991, I talked to an experienced broker with one of the well-known national firms about what he was recommending to conservative small investors. He was all in a lather over biotechnology. It had been quite a hot fad, and many of those stocks had appreciated strongly over the past year. They would have appealed to momentum investors, but not to me. In 1996, any number of new stocks related to Internet products and services came to the market. They were getting all of the free publicity and attention that anyone could hope for, and many of them appreciated dramatically. Both of those fads turned out to be losers a year later (with a few special cases, as there must be). We have heard before about the Nifty Fifty of 1969 and 1970, another speculative fad carried to excess.

Such things will always be with us (refer to the ideas of Galbraith in chapter 1). The speculative excesses are in the nature of markets. The desire to go along and be part of the trend, part of the winning crowd, will always be in our nature. Fads have led millions to financial ruin in the past and will do so again. You must wear your strong armor of protection against the madness of the crowds.

In 1995 and 1996, one of the popular fads was "craft brewing." Handmade beer, if you will. A number of small private breweries with unique formulas and methods decided to offer stock for sale and use the funds to expand their markets. Much of that beer was pretty good. Not much of the investment opportunity was good. Pyramid Brewing went public at $19 per share and fell to $3. Pete's Brewing went public at $18 a share and fell to $6. Many of the other boutique breweries' stocks were just as bad.

When the crowd gets its teeth into a fad, then whatever they are buying is not something special. Not everyone is going to make money just by going along. Your job as the rational and disciplined investor is to know what you are doing. You must know the justification for your investment decisions in terms of market history, basic research, personal investment strategy, and stock selection method. The strongest armor you can own is to have a method. Know your method. Work at your method. Don't adopt the crowd's direction simply because everyone is doing it.

Gresham's law in economics tells us that bad money drives good money out of circulation. For much the same reasons, bad investing drives good investing out of the markets. Watch out for manias and fads, and make plans to protect yourself when there is a lot of bad investing going on.

Contrarian Methods

Contrarian investing is the very heart of the search for something special. *Contrarian* means to go against the crowd, avoid the fads, and do not use the most popular investment methods. Once the crowd has adopted a stock or a method, then it is probably too late for the intelligent investor to expect to make much money in the same way. If everyone except you has already bought in, then the price is already too high. Who is left to support it with new buying?

The contrarian investor may look for the stock or the industry that has been widely neglected and unpopular for six months to a year. The idea is that when the crowd has run away from a company or an industry sector, then a lot of people may have sold too low. The price may become a bargain because the rats are leaving the ship. If an entire industry sector becomes unpopular, it is almost certain that there will be a good buy in there somewhere. Industry sectors exist because they are essential components of the economy. It is unlikely that all of the companies in a sector will go bad at once.

Contrarians usually have a lot in common with value investors. Both are likely to find their favorites among stocks with low P/E ratios or some other characteristics of relatively low price.

What kinds of things do contrarians buy or avoid? In 1991, they bought Chrysler at $12, when everyone said the stock was dead. In 1994, they sold it at $50. In 1993, they bought IBM at $50, when some seers were predicting the stock price would fall to $30. In 1997, they held the same stock priced at $170. Or maybe they sold it, since they were contrarians and everyone else was buying. In 1995, your contrarian probably liked Navistar at $12, and that one is looking pretty good (check your newspaper for NAV). In 1993, after the biotech fad had faded, the contrarian investor may have bought Amgen at $40. It was down from a 1992 high of $80. In 1996, she sold it at a split-adjusted price of $120.

Looks easy, right? Wrong. Being a steadfast and committed contrarian is the toughest role to fill in stock investing. The crowd is always turned against you, and the crowd sets prices. Contrarian investing requires that you stick to your guns and have faith in your decisions long enough for the true value of the company, or the mass error of the crowd, to become obvious. When the crowd changes direction, then you hope that your stock will correct to a fair value in the market.

I have been through a couple of those episodes. I bought Cree Research at $14, when it was falling from $25, and watched it fall as low as $6. I kept buying. It eventually went to $60 on a split-adjusted basis. But I stayed scared all the time. I bought Ford in 1991, when the world proclaimed that the American automobile industry was all washed up. Thank you very much. And more recently, I bought and held and bought more of Arcadia Financial as it crashed from $25 to $7. I think I understand what they are doing, and I like it, but it is a rough and lonely road.

Most investors and "experts" seem to agree that contrarian investing can be highly successful most of the time, if you do it right. The tough part is to make the right decision in the face of the crowd psychology and stick with it in the face of a long wait for the market forces to change. It is probably best for the individual investor to stay away from the practice until after you have developed more of a sense of the market and a tough skin to enable you to wait things out. *Smart Money* magazine regularly runs a column showing a stock that might be a good contrarian buy at that time.

Market Timing

Market timing is the practice of identifying and predicting market trends. More specifically, the timer wants to predict the turning points where a trend reverses. The timer will sell when the market, or a stock, approaches a high valuation before it falls back, and buy as it approaches or hits a low valuation.

I have said this before, but it is important. No market timing for us! Unless, unless, ah, perhaps, if you are very confident of your own ability to call the trends and the turns in the market. It is very difficult business. A friend of mine, of some experience in the field, goes even further than that warning. He says, "Expertise in market timing is not a virtue."[12] Few people are successful at market timing over a period of months. Only a very rare handful are successful at it over a period of years. If you must explore this topic,

---

[12] Haywood Spruill.

then by all means read Marty Zweig's book *Winning on Wall Street*. That is the best chance you will have to understand market timing.

Defensive Stocks

Any stock investor will at some time have to face up to a market that seems overpriced. Then we have to consider the possibility of an imminent decline in all stock values. One of the painful issues you have to deal with is that when the market starts a general decline, then your stocks will likely fall in price, too. Even if you bought a stock after thorough and insightful analysis, even if the P/E ratio is 10, even if the sales are growing at 20 percent a year, when the market is in a broad and general decline, then it is likely that your stock will fall too.

What can we do in those times to care for the PIG (protection, income, growth)? There are a few things that come to mind:[13]

- Sell your stocks? Perhaps, but this smacks of market timing. Frequently you will be wrong about the direction of the market. When you decide to reinvest, then there goes another round of brokerage fees.

- Buy conservative bonds? This may at least provide a steady income, with some possibility of capital gains.

- Stop buying stocks? Probably a fair idea, but it has some of the gambling-related odeur of market timing, too.

- Buy safer stocks! Ah, there is an idea!

What safer stocks? We would like to identify a class of stocks that are less likely to fall as fast as the general market. Some are less likely to fall as fast, and some will make your life easier even if they do fall. A class that usually fills those needs is the defensive stocks, including the high-yield stocks. What you are looking for here are some signs to help identify companies whose stocks will probably not fall as fast during a general market decline. Consider this as part of your diversification scheme. Even if you

---

[13] We could say, "Spring somewhat laboriously to mind," in the immortal words of Peter Ustinov.

want to buy growth stocks and small-cap stocks, a well-balanced portfolio will mix in a few that have some defensive characteristics.

We have already discussed the high-yield stocks. If a company was paying $1.20 annually in dividends per share, and if the company was solid, they probably would continue to pay the dividend while the market tumbled. If you owned 300 shares, then that would be $360 per year of income rolling along. If you wanted to practice conservative, long-term investing, then it would probably be just as well to ignore the share price fluctuations and continue collecting your dividends while waiting for the stock market to get well. With a sound and predictable dividend payment, you have another advantage, too. If most stocks are falling in price, then other investors might become disenchanted with looking for growth, and they would naturally be attracted to a better yield. Thus, your high-yield stock would become a desirable item. More buyers would be attracted to it, and the price would be supported better than the low-yield stocks.

The trick here is to identify those companies that will maintain a high yield during potential hard times. You might look for companies that have a long-term history of paying a high yield without reducing it. Look for those that have a manageable payout ratio. The annual dividends per share should probably be less than 75 percent of earnings. Look for companies in businesses that should stand up in case of a general economic slump.

That leads to the final idea: Look at the line of business and the history during previous economic down-turns. You can guess that some companies are going to keep business up even if the economy is slow—for example, grocery stores, drug companies, electric or gas utilities. Some may even improve their sales in a slump, such as the discount retail stores or bus lines. Previous market history has indicated that those industries are somewhat more defensive in nature.

Beat the Shorts!

This idea is a little off the wall. It is more like gambling than investing, but still an interesting idea. Short sellers are a class of speculators whose method is to invest against a stock, rather than investing in it. They are hoping to profit from a decline in the stock price, just the opposite from the rest of us. We will not do that; it requires much more experience and risk acceptance. What we can do, however, is use some public information about short sellers to try to improve our stock selection.

So what is the short seller? The short seller finds a stock that appears to be in trouble, a stock that he does not own. It might be in trouble because of some basic business problem for the company, or it might be simply that the stock has become overpriced in the market. For whatever reason, the short seller decides that the stock price should fall. The short seller will then borrow some stock, sell it, and plan to later buy the stock back to replace the borrowing.

Suppose that the stock of the Stiff Collar Company was selling at $14, which Roger thought was too high a price. Roger then might be a short seller if he borrowed 300 shares and sold them for $4200. Later, if the stock price fell to $8, he could buy back 300 shares for $2400 to replace what was borrowed. That leaves a profit of $1800 on a short sale of stock he did not own.

Short selling is highly risky business. If you sell short, you are betting against the market. If the original price was $14, then that means that most of the other investors who watched Stiff Collar thought that $14 was a fair price. You have to be willing to accept a high amount of risk to wager against them. And wager it is! For consider, instead of falling as you supposed, let us say that the price rose to $15, $18, $20. Now the original shareholder, who loaned her stock to you, wants it back to sell herself. You are then forced to buy back stock at a higher price. You buy back 300 shares at $20, which produces a net loss on the deal of $1800 (plus transaction fees).

We are not short sellers. That is grim business.

But we may have an opportunity to take advantage of the short sellers. In their search for something special, some investors like to look at the reported short selling in stocks and bet against the short sellers. Or, if not bet against them, use the reports of short sales to make better buying decisions. Here is the plan: Every short sale creates a future obligation for the short seller to buy back that stock. This is buying pressure that must be met some time in the future. After the short sale has been completed, it no longer creates downward pressure on the stock price, but creates a future upward pressure on the stock price.

Completed short sales represent opinions that the stock price should fall, and, at the same time, future buying that must support the stock price. The investor who can see that there has been a lot of short selling in a stock then knows that all of the short selling must be covered by buying in the future, and that will create higher prices.

Let us say that you have been studying Stiff Collar for six months, but you never bought it. Then, one day, you read in *Barron's* that there have been 2.5 million shares sold short. You may also know that the total number of shares in circulation is ten million. That means that 25 percent of the total shares must be bought back by the short sellers. That is tremendous buying pressure and should help to support or raise the price in the future.

Here we have a divergence of opinions and needs between the short sellers and those who like the stock. That's what makes the market go 'round. It is not wise to take the short selling as reason enough in itself to buy the stock, but it may be an additional piece of evidence to support the stock price, if you have a number of other reasons to be favorably inclined towards the stock.

As a final word of warning on the shorts: There is some well-reasoned analysis that seems to indicate that when a stock has been heavily shorted for a long time, then it really is in trouble and you should not buy it.[14]

Sectors

You may ask, "How can I keep up with all of the stocks and companies to know what to buy?" You can't! You don't need to. All you need to do is keep track of a sufficient number of them to find ten to fifteen good buys and avoid the losers. For that reason, it may be best for the individual investor to specialize in parts of the market and hope to acquire superior knowledge of those stocks. You can choose a sector, or two, or three, and work them to the limits of your endurance.

The first objection to this method is that you will sacrifice diversification that way. If you only buy financial companies' stocks, then you will not have safe and sound diversification. What you can do is pick a sector, or two, or three, to study for your own stock selections and buys, and use mutual funds to obtain adequate diversification from other sectors. Perhaps half of your investment funds go into stocks you select, and half go into four mutual funds that will improve your diversification. Here are a few reasonable choices.

Confine your own research to blue-chip, well-known companies. Also, buy three mutual funds: one that buys small-cap funds, one that buys long-term bonds, and one that invests globally. You might then find three or four good stocks and be able to follow their fortunes carefully, and have good diversification in your overall portfolio.

---

[14] See the column "Short Shrift," by Gene Epstein. *Barron's*, May 5, 1997.

Confine your own research to companies in the same area as your professional expertise, but use three or four mutual funds to round out the portfolio for good diversification. You should be better able than most professional investors to make good decisions about the stocks you are studying.

Confine your own research to companies in your own geographic area. You should have better and faster access to much of the critical business news for those local companies, particularly if you have a good local business newspaper. For example, in my home region, the Research Triangle Park, NC area, we have an outstanding business paper, the *Triangle Business Journal*, which is worth its weight in gold to stock pickers.

You might pick a particular market sector, such as computers or health care. You can see that there are many ways to reduce the scope of your own research to get an edge on the other analysts, using mutual funds to fill out the proper diversification that you need.

Recommended Further Reading

Band, Richard E. *Contrary Investing for the Nineties*. New York: St. Martin's Press, 1991.

O'Neil, William J. *How to Make Money in Stocks*. New York: McGraw Hill, 1991.

Schilit, Keith W., and Howard M. Schilit. *Blue Chips and Hot Tips*. New York: Prentice-Hall, 1992.

Steinberg, Jonathan. *Midas Investing*. New York: Random House, 1996.

Zweig, Martin. *Winning on Wall Street*. New York: Warner Books, 1990.

All men are liable to error; and most men are, in many
points, by passion or interest, under temptation to it.

—JOHN LOCKE, *AN ESSAY CONCERNING HUMAN UNDERSTANDING*

The Search for Good Information

This chapter deals with the question of information sources, which has been partially considered with every other topic thus far in the book. It needs to be brought together and summarized in one place.

Your success or failure as an investor will be directly dependent on the decisions you make. It is not a game of chance. Some people talk as if investing were a matter of luck, and those people are destined to be losers. You have the keys to success or failure in your own hands. That does not mean that everyone has the ability to make a lot of money in the stock markets. However, everyone can do one, or both, of these two things:

1. Stay away from the stock markets; or

2. Only buy stocks when you have done your homework.
   (Rule #1 says, "If you don't understand it, don't buy it.")[1]

The purpose of this book is to help you make intelligent decisions about those two items.

Before you can go very far in financial markets, you have to figure out how, when, and where you are going to find good information. This chapter will help with that. Just as in all the other subjects, you have choices to make. Some of the good sources of information might be too expensive for

---

[1] *The Small Investor.*

you. Some might be too advanced in terms of financial ideas. Some might be complex in terms of the way the information is presented. However, there are good, practical, and reasonably priced choices that will turn out to be helpful for you.

How to Use This Chapter

The material in this chapter is essential to using all of the ideas and methods in the rest of the book. The value investor may lean more on some sources and the income investor on others. You have to decide which will work well for you. Some sources, such as the *Value Line,* are well organized so that they may serve the needs of long-term or short-term investors. Some, such as *Zacks Analyst Watch* or *First Call Consensus Estimate Guide,* are more focused to the interests of investors who are willing to make more short-term trades, but they may still be of help to all of us.

The chapter is logically organized in six parts after this introductory section:

1. What kinds of information? (prices of stocks, company products, bond interest rates)

2. What sources? (newspapers, magazines, Internet, television)

3. Using your desktop computer

4. Online service providers

5. Internet sources and their individual features or problems

6. Financial software and data services

Recommendations or Not

In this chapter, I will mention many specific companies, publications, products, and services. Some will be clearly recommended for your further consideration. What about others? They fall into two classes:

1. Some are mentioned without any special recommendation; and

2. Some others are not mentioned at all.

In group 1—those that are mentioned in here—all of those products and services have some good features and some claim to your attention. If they don't get any special recommendation, it simply means that they possibly did not have any special stand-out qualities that demanded recommendation. Every product that I mention by name is a worthwhile source of information, if you learn to use it right and choose to use it. I have not specifically mentioned any products or services that are inferior.

In group two—those that are not mentioned at all—those products and services were not included for several reasons: Either I did not know about them, or I did not think the product was useful or worth the cost, or I did not take the time to evaluate them. If you hear about some sources of investing information that are not included here, then by all means check them out. There will be plenty of choices that I have not mentioned here that may deserve your attention.

Beyond that, obviously the whole Internet and online world is changing rapidly. Some of the resources that I like may be gone by next year. Some new superior services may be developed after this is written. It is worth your time and trouble to do some exploring and see what you can find.

What Kinds of Information?

Most of the work that you do in stock market investing will be spent in searching for information. There are many different types of information and various sources that suit one type better than another. It will help if we start by organizing the types of information you may need. All of this discussion should fit into context with the previous chapters. The rest of this chapter tells where you can look for help in each area.

Here are the principal types of information:

Information about individual stocks: When you study a single stock you want to know the price, the earnings, cash flow, market capitalization, and recent history of each of those. Some of the good sources are the *Value Line*, *Zacks Analyst Watch*, *Investor's Business Daily*, Standard & Poor's Reports on Demand, and the annual and quarterly reports from either the company or the SEC.

Information about individual companies: You want to know about their products and customers, their management and finances. Are they growing or retreating in their markets? Is the company a leader in its industry or an also-ran? For this you will use the annual and quarterly reports, the *Wall Street Journal*, daily newspapers' business sections, your local business newspaper, *Barron's*, *Forbes*, and *Kiplinger's* periodicals and others.

Information about industry sectors: It is not sufficient to study a single automobile company, no matter how good it may appear. You must look at it in the context of its peers and competitors. If the whole industry were exposed to some economic force, such as rapidly rising interest rates, then you would probably consider avoiding even the best of them. On the other hand, if one member of the industry looked like a good stock buy, then for much of the same reasons, their competitors might be as good or better. You should review the entire industry to properly understand your choices. These goals can be achieved by looking at specific industry analysis, or general broad business news. The sources will include the *Value Line* industry reviews, Standard & Poor's Industry Reports, *Forbes' Annual Review of American Industry*, *Barron's*, and specific industry trade journals.

Information about markets: You need to know what's happening. Is the general atmosphere bullish or bearish? Are the mutual funds still actively buying? Are individual investors active buyers or sellers? In this area, it is important to have timely news. That is where television excels. CNBC is dedicated to market news for twelve hours every business day. CNN brings us several shows dedicated to market news. The Public Broadcast System carries the *Nightly Business Report* every weekday evening and *Wall Street Week* on weekends. Other good sources would be *Investor's Business Daily*, *Barron's*, and Standard & Poor's *Outlook*. Nobody completely understands the markets; they are too complex; but these sources can help you to have a feel for what is going on.

Information about the economy: Where is business booming and where is it fading? What are prospects for new taxes or tax credits, and what impact will they have on specific industry sectors? All of the business and finance publications have much to offer. The most coverage of developing news will be in the daily publications—the *Wall Street Journal*, the *New York Times*, or your local paper. The better in-depth analysis of relationships and implications may be in the business trade periodicals, such as *Fortune*, *Forbes*, *Kiplinger's*, *Business Week*, or *Barron's*.

Information about trends: This area is wide open. Remember that the "experts" seldom reach any agreement about trends, so you can find almost any news or opinions that you may be willing to read. Most of the financial press will have irregular occasional articles where some wise guy is offering his or her latest interpretations of trends. These types of articles can be highly entertaining and provocative, provided that you read them critically. Not every opinion that gets into print is reliable. They should serve the useful purpose of stimulating new thoughts on how to understand the other information that you absorb.

Opinions and ratings: This is the stuff that dreams are made of. Ratings include the famous *Value Line* rankings of Timeliness and Safety, and the S&P ratings of the earnings and dividends quality of a common stock. They also include the buy, sell or hold recommendations that are so carelessly tossed about in the media.

The *Value Line,* Zacks, *First Call*, Standard & Poor, and many other sources will offer you a ton of ratings as to which stock or group of stocks is good to buy or to sell today. The good news is that these are usually credible opinions offered by serious professional analysts. They also give you some important information about the direction of thinking of other investors. The bad news is that none of those professional analysts know you, or your financial situation, or your current investments, or risk tolerance. The stock that looks like a good buy to someone else, may or may not be good for you.

What Sources?

There are good sources and bad sources, right? Maybe not. Maybe it would be more accurate to say that there are good readers and poor readers. Any source of information is a good source in the eyes of an alert and discerning reader; and any source is a stinging nettle to the naive. Don't believe everything you read, even in *Barron's*. Take the writers' or speakers' opinions as food for thought, not as the staff of life. Every bit of information you read or hear is history and subject to different interpretations.

Okay, so then, what sources?

Newspapers: The *Wall Street Journal, Investor's Business Daily*, the business sections of the major national dailies like the *New York Times* and the *Washington Post,* your local daily paper and particularly, your local business newspaper, if you are so lucky as to have one.

"If one eagle flies—it may go up; if two eagles fly—it may go down."

Magazines: Almost every periodical runs the occasional article on investing. Much of that is junk of a high order. Not everyone who can spell *invest* knows how to. Stick with the dedicated and professional periodicals of established reputation. They will give you more than you can absorb. Among them, check out *Forbes*, *Business Week*, *Smart Money*, *Kiplinger's*, *Money*, and *Worth* magazines.

Television: Watch CNBC sometimes. A couple of times, try to watch it for five or six hours in a day to get a feeling for the ebb and flow of the news and developments. Public television presents the *Nightly Business Report* and *Wall Street Week*. CNN has regular programs dedicated to financial news and investing. All of those are good if you want to see the news when it is hot. That's what television is good for, in case you had forgotten.

Brokers: Generally, the more you pay, the more you get. The full service brokers will offer more advice than you can deal with. It may be difficult to deal with. Don't believe everything a broker tells you unless you have developed a long-term, solid, trusting relationship with him/her. But they can provide plenty of good research. If you are considering a few companies, then certainly ask your broker what research they have available to give you on those companies, or their industry groups, or related companies.

Internet: The Internet is cheap and easy, if you like it. We will have much more on that later, but the essential feature is cheap access to tons of stories, opinions, and data on almost any company that you care to study. Much of that information is unreliable. Be an extremely discerning reader on the Internet, or using online services.

Gossip: Gossip is good. We all require a little healthy social intercourse. After all, just because we are interested in money does not necessarily make us misanthropes. However, very little of the gossip or loose talk that you hear is supported by credible research. If your co-worker just bought Dell Computer and is very excited about it, then fine—we wish her well. That does not necessarily become a good investment for you. Even if it is up 10 percent in the first week, it does not necessarily become a good investment for you. Be a critical listener and reader. Do your homework before you spend your money.

First hand investigations: Perhaps the best source of all. The greatest chance of finding something special is when you do your own research. Go somewhere that has not been visited by every analyst in Boston. Consider the products that you buy and enjoy. Look around. You may see something.

Business and investing news services: These include such services and products as software, data, and publications from the *Value Line*, a variety of reports available from Standard & Poor's, the *Morningstar Reports*, Zacks, *First Call*, and some of the better Web sites, like Shareholder Direct. If you start reading the financial literature, you will see ads for a variety of such products. Check them out. Many are educational and interesting. Some are rather expensive, depending on your perspective.

Using the Desktop Computer

I am writing to at least three distinct groups: those with no experience on computers, those with some experience but little technical knowledge, and those with good knowledge of computing. This chapter will totally ignore the technical issues and only deal with the issues of how well a system works and how easy it is to use. You may have a home computer and you may not. If you don't and have not been interested, this may be enough to get you interested.

There are several good ways to use a desktop computer. You may try one or all of them. To give an idea where we are going with this, let's lay out some of the options.

1. Buy software and data so that you can run your own stock screens and analysis. For example, *Morningstar*, Zacks, and the *Value Line* sell such products that we will consider later in this chapter.

2. Use an online content provider. That means a company that will let you dial into their computers to use a variety of information and services. For example, America Online has an array of services that include shopping and financial and investing forums, among others.

3. Use the Internet or Web, which incorporate thousands of sources. You can gain access to the Internet either through one of the content providers or by signing up with an Internet access provider. In that last class are AT&T WorldNet, IBM, Mindspring, and others.

If you don't know the Internet or the Web[2] yet, this may be a good time or a good reason to start learning. However, the challenge is that they are, to a large extent, set up to appeal to juveniles and people who don't value their own time very highly. If you begin exploring the Web, prepare yourself in advance for a great amount of aggravation and time spent fighting your way through what should be routine and easy tasks. Think of it as if every time you wanted to use your car it took five minutes to start, and the streets were frequently changed to one way, different ways, and every time you came to a stop sign, you had to watch a commercial before you could go ahead. Even as I write, just to do a careful job of presenting the options to you, I have six different accounts for Internet access, all with well-known companies. In my view, none of the six comes close to providing reliable, professional service. But I intend to keep using one of them

---

[2] *Web* is just a loosely defined term that means all the stuff that is out there in the Internet world.

anyway, because there are a few things (investment information) available on the Internet, or through the service providers, that I could not easily obtain elsewhere. You will have to be your own judge of whether it is worth the hassle.

Terminology
(Just in Case You Need the Primer)

By the end of this section, you should know the terms Internet, Web, Internet service provider (ISP), content provider, and resource. If you already know them, you might skip this section.

Think of the Internet and the Web as effectively the same thing.[3] You understand that there are telephones all over the world, and each of them would probably be answered by someone if you rang a connection to it. You could contact virtually any one of those telephones if you had the right number and were willing to pay for the connection. The Internet/Web is like that, except that instead of a person to answer at each number, there is a computer. The number you use to dial that computer is called its URL (universal resource locator). The URL works like a telephone number. The URL is one of those things that you see in advertisements and on business cards: www.goodnewslocator.com.

In order to use your home telephone, you have to have a local telephone company to connect you with the international telephone network through a local switch. Same deal for the Web. In order to use the Web, you need a local service provider who will provide you with a point of contact to the international computer network (the Internet). Examples of companies that might provide you local access to the Internet include IBM, AT&T, AOL, Mindspring, and others. Those companies are then called Internet service providers (ISPs)[4].

Each ISP may offer just three basic services, or they may choose to do more. The basic services are access to the Web, electronic mail (e-mail), and a personal Web site. The other (beyond basic) services might include investing information, games, news services, dating services, chat rooms,

---

[3] Some folks may say that is an oversimplification, but for our purposes, it is sufficient.

[4] Also, sometimes we say *access providers*.

forums, shopping services, travel services, and many other types of services that share the common trait of being largely dependent on information.

If the ISP chooses to offer some of the extra services, then we will call them a content provider. AOL is a content provider. AT&T and Mindspring are not. If the ISP does not provide extra services through their own computer site, then you can still get them through the Internet. The difference is that the presentation and organization by the content provider might be easier to use than searching for them on the Web. Think of it like shopping. If you need a coffeepot, then K-Mart is a good content provider. You can go to K-Mart and get a convenient choice of four or five brands. Without a content provider, you would have to search the Web, that is, contact each coffee pot maker individually to learn about their products.

Individually, those coffeepot makers would become resources. If you were an energetic and alert shopper, you might compile a list of preferred vendors who make most of the products you like to use. The same is true for us. A great many resources provide information of value to investors. They include Zacks, the *Value Line*, *Morningstar*, *First Call*, Dow Jones, Standard & Poor's, and Charles Schwab. In addition to those relatively well-known companies, there are a great many lesser-known resources that you may meet as you browse (you may say "surf") the Web. In the latter group, an outstanding resource is Shareholder Direct (URL = www.shareholder.com).

I wish I could just give you a good, complete list of resources, but things are changing too fast. The ugly side of the Web is that nothing is stable. For good references to new and revised resource sites, read periodicals like *Barron's* or *Smart Money* magazine, or just keep fishing around the Internet and see what you can find. This chapter will start you off with a partial list of resources.

The Online Content Providers

The content providers provide easy access to a variety of information and services through a single dial-in access point. You don't have to learn a lot of different URLs (Web addresses) or deal with the vagaries and inconsistency of accessing different sites on computers that have been set up differently. AOL is the most widely used content provider. They will offer you an account with access to good investing information for a low fee. The account will also enable you to find many other kinds of information and services, from computer games to cooking forums, but we will concentrate on the stock selection services.

Using America Online, you can access a group of services that they call their Personal Finance area. In Personal Finance, you could choose among sections dealing with:

- Financial News
- Financial Planning
- Mutual Funds Center
- Portfolios

- Stocks and Investing
- Tax Planning
- Quotes (stocks, bonds, and funds)
- Company Research

and several other titles.

By selecting Financial News, you would arrive in a section that included choices among Market News, Business News, The Economy, and *Investor's Business Daily*.

The *Investor's Business Daily* (IBD) section is quite useful. Last time I looked, it contained four choices that were of interest to stock investors: News, Market and Investing, Computers and Technology, and the Economy. The News section contained an excellent analytical story about the state of the long running financial expansion, and a story about recent earnings surprises from Kellogg's Corporation. The Market and Investing section contained another, more detailed analysis of Kellogg's. Computers and Technology contained a group of stories combining news and analysis. The Economy section had a report on their barometer of current business activity and analysis of the impact of new tax laws. Referring back to the beginning of this chapter, we looked at seven kinds of information that we wanted to find. That one area for IBD in America Online served all seven of them.

Returning to the Financial News and then into the Business News section, you would find a section on Company Research with quick and easy access to Stock Reports, which included three choices:

- Search the Database

- AAII[5] Special Screens

- Morningstar Menu

Under Search the Database, I entered the stock ticker symbol *BKS* to see recent information on Barnes & Noble. The screen that came back to me showed data that was more than a month old. That was not encouraging! It showed an old stock price, P/E ratio, and previous high for the stock. All of that information would have been potentially damaging to an investor who failed to notice the date of last update on the screen.

Returning to the Stock Reports section, I entered the AAII Special Screens area. That included a magazine article on finding stock market winners that was pretty good. It was also eight years old, but still pretty good. Going further into the AAII screens uncovered a set of stock screening tools. These are great.

AAII Stock Screening Tools on AOL

You recall from chapters 10, 11, and 12 that we had several stories of investors looking for stocks that would suit their own needs and criteria. They wanted to find stocks with high yield, low price-to-earnings ratios, or a combination of factors for value or growth. Many of the results in those chapters were based on manual searches through the *Value Line* reports or other written material. That may have been discouraging to you. It probably seemed like a lot of work. Now we can use this to illustrate some of the great power and usefulness of computer-based methods. Under the AAII Screens section in AOL, we can find tools to do fast searches of large data sets to locate good investments.

First, there is a section to screen for recent earnings surprises. This would be of interest to all stock investors, but particularly to those searching for

---

[5] *AAII* is the American Association of Individual Investors, an interesting and helpful organization.

growth candidates. With about one minute of work, I was able to produce the following list of companies that had positive changes in the analysts' estimates of their earnings.

Company (Ticker)	1 Month EPS Est. Change	Price Chg Over Last Qtr	Price Chg Over Last yr
Corel Corp (COSFF)	109.09	1.86	-36.80
Cabot Oil (COG)	26.00	-0.69	1.46
EXEL Ltd (XL)	10.56	22.04	46.27
Huntco Inc (HCO)	9.09	12.86	-26.00
Yellow Corp (YELL)	8.33	23.78	74.04
Seacor Smit (CKH)	7.48	-3.97	15.08
Micron Elec (MUEI)	6.52	-5.23	48.00
Consoldt Grph (CGX)	5.71	34.47	253.86
Allied Waste (AWIN)	5.45	105.50	85.14
Trico Marine (TMAR)	5.33	-11.03	89.85
McClatchy News (MNI)	5.33	19.89	29.55
Rohr Inc (RHR)	5.00	21.39	0.29
NABI (NABI)	5.00	0.00	-28.32
Ross Stores (ROST)	4.88	27.58	86.31
Perrigo Co (PRGO)	4.76	17.19	13.33
Kent Elec (KNT)	4.62	57.87	19.05
Logan's Rdhs (RDHS)	4.26	18.48	32.69
Albemarle Corp (ALB)	4.17	11.86	9.59
Cognos Inc (COGNF)	3.81	24.04	40.22
Ensco Int'l Inc (ESV)	3.70	0.12	51.72
USX-U.S. Steel Grp (X)	3.66	30.04	22.02
National Steel (NS)	3.64	108.90	48.81
MicroAge Inc (MICA)	3.60	36.15	34.85
Teradyne Inc (TER)	3.57	42.42	138.43
Provident Bksh (PBKS)	3.57	12.16	30.86

Reprinted by permission of the American Association of Individual Investors.

The left column gives the monthly increase, in cents, of the analysts' estimates of the annual earnings. The next two columns give the past quarter's and past year's changes in the stock price.

What about earnings? On this point, there was some confusion. The discussion of this screen said that the screen required increased earnings estimates for both the current and next fiscal years. The representation of the programmatic search criteria indicated that there had to be an increase for one or the other. This is a point of aggravation, but you could still use this data as a starting point for companies to consider. You would just have to consult more resources to clarify which earnings were actually being upgraded. This is a good illustration of an essential lesson: Don't expect the computer to do your thinking for you in making stock selection decisions. Use the computer for what it is good for, which is to search large blocks of data and find companies for your further consideration. Use your mind for what it is good for: discrimination and decisions.

With about thirty seconds' work, the next screen gave a list of companies with good dividend yield. The table shows the current and past five
years' yield rates and the five year earnings-per-share growth. The screening criteria here included several special considerations. One was that the
dividend had not been reduced any time in the past five years. Another was
that the current yield percentage was greater than the past five years average yield percentage. There were some other special considerations, but after
it was all said and done, you could safely conclude that these stocks would
have been worthy candidates for consideration by an income investor.

Company (Ticker)	Dividend Yield	5-Yr. Avg. Dividend Yield	5-Yr. EPS Growth
Friedman Ind (FRD)	4.7	3.8	26.7
Luby's Cafe (LUB)	4.0	2.9	7.0
Flamemaster (FAME)	4.0	2.9	-9.7
Superior Surg (SGC)	3.8	2.5	2.5
Weis Markets (WMK)	3.3	2.8	0.6
Enex Resrc (ENEX)	3.1	2.5	-37.7
Worthington (WTHG)	2.8	2.0	15.0
Kelly Serv (KELYA)	2.8	2.5	13.3
Federal Signal (FSS)	2.7	2.2	14.9
Standex Int'l (SXI)	2.6	2.2	16.0
Modine Manuf (MODI)	2.6	2.1	14.6
Nat'l Sanitary (NSSX)	2.5	2.3	6.4
Comm Systems (CSII)	2.5	2.1	12.7
Aceto Corp (ACET)	2.5	2.2	8.5
Trinity Ind (TRN)	2.2	2.0	23.9
Wellman Inc (WLM)	2.1	1.0	-10.7
Span-Am Med (SPAN)	2.0	1.7	-19.9
Bandag Inc (BDG)	2.0	1.3	3.8
Farmer Bros (FARM)	1.9	1.4	1.8
A Schulman (SHLM)	1.8	1.2	-0.4
Russell Corp (RML)	1.8	1.5	8.8
Astro-Med (ALOT)	1.8	1.1	-26.2

Reproduced by permission of the American Association of Individual Investors.

A third example of results from AOL/AAII is the following screen that
shows candidates for a value-oriented investor to consider. Again, it took
about thirty seconds to produce this list. In explaining this table, AAII goes
into some unnecessarily complicated contortions about why certain numbers should be adjusted or eliminated, but the final issue is that this gives
a good list of stocks for the value investor to consider. It was quick, easy,
and cheap to produce this list for AOL subscribers.

Another useful line of information is found by using the Historical Quotes
and Graphs section under the Company Research section. Again, with a few
minutes of work, I could retrieve and print out this graph of the performance

Company (Ticker)	P/E Ratio	5-Year Avg. P/E	Avg. P/E Valuation to Price
Rare Hospt1ty (RARE)	22.5	31.5	2.60
Hutchinson (HTCH)	12.7	19.9	2.57
Spec'l Devices (SDII)	13.6	31.1	2.53
Cooker Restrt (CGR)	14.4	29.8	2.44
Franklin Elec (FEP)	10.0	18.4	2.24
MA Jewelers (MAJ)	24.5	29.1	2.18
Tidewater Inc (TDW)	18.3	27.7	2.14
Trinity Ind (TRN)	10.1	21.3	1.99
Corvel Corp (CRVL)	16.8	27.3	1.95
Disc Auto Prts (DAP)	12.1	23.2	1.91
Micro Warehs (MWHS)	19.8	39.9	1.88
Tommy Hilfiger (TOM)	18.0	26.7	1.87
Harolds Stores (HLD)	16.8	21.5	1.84
Supertex Inc (SUPX)	15.2	23.6	1.82
AutoZone Inc (AZO)	19.4	33.3	1.82
Republic Auto (RAUT)	10.0	16.0	1.81
Durakon Ind (DRKN)	9.0	15.7	1.78
Empi Inc (EMPI)	16.2	25.0	1.77
World Fuel (INT)	13.2	19.5	1.74
Simpson Ind (SMPS)	10.4	18.8	1.73
SkyWest Inc (SKYW)	24.1	25.2	1.68
Amer Power (APCC)	19.1	27.3	1.67
Wausau Paper (WSAU)	14.2	22.6	1.64
Modine Manuf (MODI)	14.5	19.7	1.62
1st Team Sprts (FTSP)	19.7	26.3	1.62

Reproduced by permission of the American Association of Individual Investors.

of Pittway Corporation's stock (PRY). If a growth-oriented investor were considering Pittway as a good buy (as we saw previously), then it would be enlightening to see this visual representation of the stock price's past movements. Each vertical line represents the high to low price range for a week. The little crossing bar on each line is the closing price.

A world of good information is available through the AOL Financial News source. For one last example, I retrieved the details of earnings estimates for one more company by using the AOL access to the *First Call Earnings Estimates*. This kind of data should be of value to you any time that you are about to make a buy or sell decision on a stock. If you have been through a long study of one particular company, and are just about ready to make the commitment to buy the stock, then you should certainly take a little longer to at least consider the analysts' opinions about the earnings. In July 1997, for Arcadia Financial, the results came out as you see on page 282[6].

This does not by any means exhaust the information available from online content providers, but it should give you some ideas.

---

[6] This is only part of the *First Call* report on Arcadia.

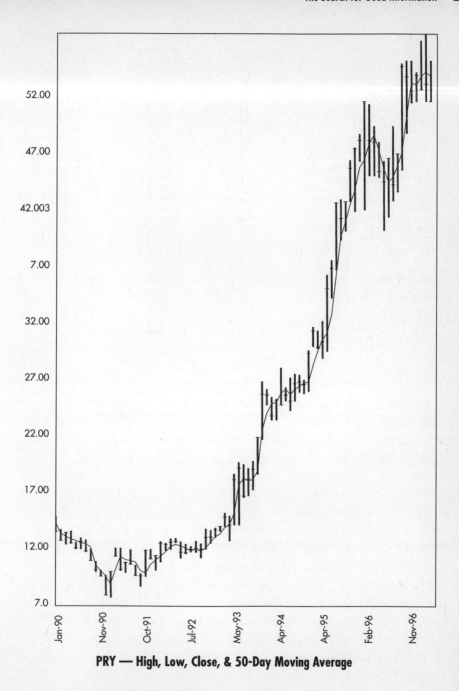

PRY — High, Low, Close, & 50-Day Moving Average

Reprinted by permission of America Online.

```
                    FIRST CALL EARNINGS ESTIMATES

AAC                      Arcadia Financial                  08/18/97
Industry: Fincl Svcs                              SIC:         6153
Latest Price: $8.94                          1997 P/E:         12.8
Analyst Recommendation: 3.0
```

	QTR Sep 97	QTR Dec 97	FY Dec 97	FY Dec 98
	---	---	--	--
CURRENT MEAN EPS	0.20	0.23	0.70	1.08
Number of Brokers	9	9	11	11
Median	0.20	0.23	0.70	1.20
Standard Deviation	0.02	0.04	0.07	0.39
Current High	0.25	0.30	0.81	1.50
Current Low	0.15	0.15	0.56	0.10
Year Ago EPS	0.44A	0.45A	1.65A	0.70
Current vs. Year Ago Change	-55%	-49%	-58%	54%
Report Date	wk/Oct 20	wk/Jan 28	wk/Jan 28	-

```
                EARNINGS ESTIMATE REVISION MOMENTUM
```

Up Revisions last 7 days	0	0	0	0
Up Revisions last 30 days	1	1	1	0
Down Revisions last 7 days	0	0	0	0
Down Revisions last 30 days	2	2	2	2

```
                EARNINGS ESTIMATES CONSENSUS TRENDS
```

Current Mean	0.20	0.23	0.70	1.08
7-days ago Mean	0.20	0.23	0.70	1.08
30-days ago Mean	0.20	0.23	0.70	1.16
60-days ago Mean	0.20	0.23	0.70	1.16
90-days ago Mean	0.19	0.23	1.05	1.13

Reprinted by permission of America Online and First Call.

The Internet and the Web for Stock Investors

This is REALLY a mix of good news and bad news! There is more good, informative, essential information available for free on the Internet than you will have time to read. There is more stupid, unreliable, dangerous trash mixed in with it than you will have time to sort out. In between those two extremes, there is plenty that may be useful or interesting, and at the same time may be poorly presented, or unclear, or mixed in with the bad.

The proliferation of junk on the Web creates an environment where serious workers don't want to spend their time. The situation is changing rapidly. By the time you read this, the Internet will be a different creature from today. I hope it is better and easier to use.

I hope that the Web and the Internet world environment are maturing. It appears so, but the pace of useful development seems slower than the generation of carnival-online. Thus, Gard's other law: Bad information drives out good information.

What kinds of bad information? Some of us are too quick to assume that whatever comes up on a computer screen must be accurate. It is not all accurate. For example, Bloomberg's Publishing has a Web site (URL = www.Bloomberg.com) that offers a pretty good collection of stock quotes, bond values, and market active traders for the day with current stock prices. But they also claim to have access to *Edgar*; when I tried it, it wasn't working. They claim to offer access to company news; when I tried it, it wasn't working. They do offer some nice charts of stock prices over a period of time.

For another example, AT&T has set up an Internet access service called AT&T WorldNet. In it you can go to a section called Business & Investing, and through there you can go to a section called Stock Quotes. In July 1997, I checked it for one particular stock that I was specifically interested in. They presented a screen that claimed to show the fifty-two–week price range, the P/E ratio, and the recent bid and asked prices. Both values given for range and P/E were wrong, and the values for the recent bid and asked prices were not available. In this business, accuracy and reliability are important. WorldNet didn't instill much confidence.

I am going to introduce a few of the best and a few more of the marginally useful Web sites. This is certainly not a complete guide to what you can find on the Web, because that has changed too much while this book was sitting in the store. If you are an Internet fan and know how to search

"Petro, your new browser came."

for good sites, then that will probably pay off in better investing decisions. Just be careful about how much of the stuff you believe. If you have not been an Internet fan, then financial information offers a new reason why it might be worth your trouble to get in and dig some. For the Internet novice or new Web crawler, you should be aware that there is just as much bad advice, poor presentation, and self-serving information in the Web as any other source.

All of the Web information is available through other sources, but it might take longer or cost more to gather. This book is not the right resource to teach you all about the Web. If you need that kind of instruction, find a friend, a class, or a good book on the subject.

EDGAR

Now for some good news: A huge resource of highly reliable, essential information is available, for free. The site is called EDGAR. It gives access to all of the financial reports filed by every publicly traded company listed on the American markets. The URL[7] is www.sec.gov/edgarhp.htm. Try this Web site first, then you will believe that the Web can help. It is maintained by the U.S. Securities and Exchange Commission. They require all financial reports to be filed with them electronically, so the data is timely. When you want to see the annual or quarterly financial reports of a traded company, the latest results will be in EDGAR. It also contains past reports. The SEC site also contains a lot of other interesting news; for example, newly proposed SEC regulations, and public and industry comments on those proposals.

The Dictionary of Financial Risk

This one is a horse of a hazel hue. It will be of no interest to some investors and immense interest to others. The URL is utah.e1.com/amex/findic.

This is an academic and specialized site that has a great list of financial terms explained in the sense that they are used among the academic-research community. For most of us, a better source is *Barron's Dictionary of Financial and Investment Terms*, found in your favorite book store. The Web site offers some ideas and an education that you will not find anywhere else.

---

[7] URL means universal resource locator. It is the name used for an Internet address.

Fun and Games, Bookstore, Market Data

The Marketing Direct Quotes site offers a lot. Part of it is unique and great, part is not so great. The URL is www.stockup.com.

They offer an online bookstore that maintains a fine list of available references in investing. They offer games and contests around the theme and practice of stock investing. You can, after some fashion, test yourself without putting any money at risk. (It's a clever game, but don't think that it really mirrors risk-oriented investing). They also have an excellent set up and access system. It's one of the easiest sites to learn and use.

Shareholder Direct

Another Web site that I find to be very high quality and useful is the Shareholder Direct service. The URL is www.shareholder.com.

This site offers financial reports and other notices from a group of companies. Each company gets its own area to present financial reports, biographical sketches of the management, job opening information, product information, general descriptions of the company and the business, or whatever else they like. There is considerable variation in what each client chooses to present.

What is consistent across the entire group is the quality of the individual company sites. Earlier, I said some disparaging things (for juveniles and people who don't value their own time) about the Internet in general. Well, Shareholder Direct is an exception that shows us the real hope for productivity and value in the Internet. If you want to get to know a company that you are studying, then the Shareholder Direct Internet site is an excellent place to start.

Financial Software and Data

There is one more good way to use your computer for stock research. Zacks, the *Value Line*, Standard & Poor's, and *Morningstar* will all sell you investment-research packages that include two parts:

1. A set of programs (software) that you load into your
   computer for analyzing data on stocks

2. A set of data on companies that may include their latest earnings, debt, sales, analysts' estimates, and numerous other types of information; the exact information that is used in each system varies from one provider to another

These systems, together with regular updating of the data used, may cost anywhere from a few hundred to several thousand dollars a year. The cost will also vary depending on how often you want to get updated data. Some people might think it is okay to get new data once a quarter, and others might want it available on call at any time. There would be a large difference in costs for those two kinds of service.

The *Value Line* Investment Survey for Windows

If you have a Windows-based computer and want to use it for investment research, there is an outstanding product available from the *Value Line* called the *Value Line Investment Survey for Windows*. This product will bring you a lot of data and a software system that will quickly apply a variety of search and presentation tools. It is available either with the 1700+ companies from the *Value Line Regular Edition*, or the 5,000+ stocks included in their *Extended Edition*. Their documentation and technical support service are superior[8] to *all* of the other technical products and services that I have used.

The system is designed to regularly update the data either by disc or by data transmission from the *Value Line's* computers. In addition to the data and software, it contains copies of the latest versions of their other publications that we have mentioned repeatedly throughout this book; they include: *How to Invest in Common Stocks*, and *The V/L Selection and Opinion*. It would be pointless to try to describe all of the features; instead, let's look at examples of the usefulness of the system.

If you have identified a single company that deserves close consideration, the *Value Line* system offers all of the following for immediate study:

1. General report of the company's current financial data

2. Historical report of ten years' financial data

---

[8] The documentation manual is a real book, written in clear English, and has several useful indices; the technical support line has always responded within one minute!

3. A ten-year graph of the growth of the stock price compared with the S&P 500 Index and the company's industry group

4. Analysis of their current business operations and prospects

5. Description of the business

6. List of mutual funds that have significant ownership of their stock

That collection of data and opinions does a lot for you. The principal tasks left to you in investigating the stock would be to check the very latest financial and news reports on the company (the *Value Line* may sometimes be a month or two out of date), and make your own judgment calls about the immediate prospects for their business development or competition.

In chapters 10, 11, and 12, we considered examples of investors looking for stocks with different points of emphasis and screening criteria. We will review those using the power and data available in the *Value Line* system.

The Income Investor

In chapter 10, the income investor, Eric, needed to find stocks that were not electric utilities, had P/E ratio less than 20, and yields above 5 percent. It took several hours of work to find a list of 26 reasonable candidates from among the 1700+ stocks in the *Value Line Regular Edition*. The following is a report that he could have produced using the *Value Line Investment Survey for Windows* in less than eight minutes,[9] searching a database of over 5,000 companies. There were 114 qualifying stocks found. This report shows thirty-seven of them, including some familiar names from before.

In addition to that, if Eric wanted to make a few little changes in the search criteria, then the following screening process could be completed in about one minute (really, this is not an exaggeration): Change the P/E requirement to less than 18, and also require that the past five years' average growth of sales should be at least 15 percent.

This produced the surprising result that only one stock out of the 5,000 passed that strict test in July 1997. It was Alliance Capital Management,

---

[9] That was starting from scratch to write the screening criteria; the actual computer search took less than three seconds.

Company Name	Ticker	Industry	Price/Earnings	Market Cap. $	% Current Yield
AGL Resources	ATG	GASDISTR	14.51	1162.00	5.44
ARCO Chemical	RCM	CHEMICAL	18.00	4382.72	6.17
Alliance Capital Mgmt.	AC	FINANCL	13.93	2800.28	7.32
Aquarion Co.	WTR	WATER	13.11	187.72	6.11
B.A.T Inds. ADR	BTI	TOBACCO	10.70	54338.60	6.57
Bay State Gas	BGC	GASDISTR	14.00	367.14	5.78
British Steel ADR	BST	STEELINT	5.93	5693.06	6.44
British Telecom ADR	BTY	TELEFGN	12.71	45208.72	5.81
Brown Group	BG	SHOE	14.20	309.93	5.81
Buckeye Partners L.P.	BPL	INDUSRV	11.89	599.32	6.51
CTG Resources	CTG	GASDISTR	13.33	232.61	6.94
Cascade Natural Gas	CGC	GASDISTR	16.66	161.10	5.93
Cedar Fair L.P.	FUN	RECREATE	14.05	1016.35	5.68
Chemed Corp.	CHE	DIVERSIF	13.05	369.96	5.74
Conn. Energy Corp.	CNE	GASDISTR	13.45	209.96	5.73
Ethyl Corp.	EY	CHEMSPEC	10.95	1051.19	5.63
Freeport McMoRan Res.	FRP	CHEMDIV	10.49	1455.04	10.52
G't Northern Iron	GNI	STEEL	9.60	92.25	9.75
Laclede Gas	LG	GASDISTR	13.35	410.41	5.64
MGI Properties	MGI	REIT	18.38	297.45	5.12
Merry Land & Inv.	MRY	REIT	16.76	820.82	7.21
National Presto Ind.	NPK	APPLIANC	18.66	286.76	5.43
New Jersey Resources	NJR	GASDISTR	14.72	583.40	5.11
New Plan R'lty Trust	NPR	REIT	17.55	1347.70	6.56
Ogden Corp.	OG	DIVERSIF	15.53	1019.38	6.09
Perkins Family Rest.	PFR	RESTRNT	8.14	113.58	8.18
Plum Creek Timber	PCL	PAPER	14.43	1400.97	6.37
Providence Energy	PVY	GASDISTR	14.77	103.30	6.04
RJR Nabisco Holdings	RN	TOBACCO	12.40	11195.65	6.02
Rank Group ADR	RANKY	ELECFGN	14.61	9851.84	5.02
Santa Fe Pac. Pipeline	SFL	INDUSRV	10.15	746.77	7.94
South Jersey Inds.	SJI	GASDISTR	13.60	247.48	6.26
TransAlta Corp.	TA.TO	CANENRGY	11.49	2696.02	5.79
U S West Communic.	USW	TELESERV	14.11	17597.77	5.85
UGI Corp.	UGI	GASDISTR	16.36	782.29	6.11
UST Inc.	UST	TOBACCO	11.83	5324.60	5.58
Washington R.E.I.T.	WRE	REIT	19.31	540.97	6.29

Reprinted by permission of the Value Line.

LP, an organization that provides investment advisory services to institutional clients.

The Value Investor

In chapter 11, the value investors Lillian and Richard searched for stocks that satisfied their individual criteria for value. There were two distinct phases to each search. First, they had to screen for some attractive candidates based on the financial data, and then they had to get down to the hard cases of decision making. For each of them, the screening process took several hours to review the 1700+ stocks in the *Value Line Regular Edition*. The decision-making process required much more time to find more complete data and reports on each of the five to ten companies that passed the first screens. The *Value Line Investment Survey for Windows* makes both of those processes quicker and easier.

Lillian's Search for Value

Lillian wanted to find stocks that satisfied these criteria:

1. The market capitalization should be $1 billion or less.

2. The P/E ratio should be 14 or less (based on current price and 1995 earnings).

3. The company reported a profit in 1993, 1994, and 1995.

4. The price-to-cash-flow ratio should be 5 or less (using current price and 1995 cash flow).

5. The total debt should be not more than 35 percent of capitalization (meaning the long-term liabilities plus shareholders' equity on the balance sheet).

6. The return on assets should be 12 percent or more.

7. The stock should improve diversification of her portfolio.

8. The company must offer products or services that she understands.

Using the V/L software, she could construct a screen (they call it a *filter*) to search for those companies among the 5,000+ stocks, and in about ten minutes, produce a list of fifteen companies that satisfied all of her conditions except the one on 1993, 1994, and 1995 profits, condition three. The software does not readily handle that test on past profits in the screening process. It took about another five minutes for Lillian to check the historical report for each of those fifteen companies and find that three of them failed one of the prior-year profit requirements. Based on July 1997 data, ten companies passed her test. In chapter 11, using earlier data, only three companies passed her tests, and three more came very close on the cash-flow test.[10]

The list of companies that pass a screen can be set up to show many different combinations of information, as shown below. Lillian's report included total return for 1994, 1995, and 1996, the industry group, market capitalization, price-to-sales ratio, price-to-book-value ratio, and the long-term debt ratio. A great deal more information was available for the clicking.

Company Name	Ticker Symbol	Industry	Price/Earnings Last 12 mo.	Beta	Div'd Yield
Ampco-Pittsburgh	AP	STEEL	11.64	.80	1.41
Bindley Western	BDY	MEDSUPPL	15.03	.80	.34
CTS Corp.	CTS	ELECTRNX	16.23	.65	.87
Carson Pirie Scott & Co	CRP	RETAIL	16.75	1.00	
Cleveland-Cliffs	CLF	STEEL	9.40	.90	3.01
Gehl Co	GEHL	MACHINE	10.93	1.15	
Genlyte Group	GLYT	BUILDING	12.50	.80	
Homebase Inc	HBI	RETAIL	3.92	1.20	
Kaman Corp.	KAMNA	DIVERSIF	14.36	.65	2.68
Mestek Inc.	MCC	MACHINE	12.80	.55	
Michael Foods	MIKL	FOODPROC	21.76	1.05	1.05
Mine Safety Applncs.	MNES	MACHINE	11.81	.30	2.00
Movado Group Inc	MOVA	INSTRMNT	18.48	.45	.41
Oglebay Norton Co.	OGLE	MARITIME	11.62	.35	2.80
Public Serv. (N.Mex.)	PNM	UTILWEST	10.83	.70	3.71
Roanoke Elec. Steel	RESC	METALFAB	10.02	.55	2.77
Slater STL Inc	SSI.TO	STEEL	10.00	.60	1.22
Springs Inds.	SMI	TEXTILE	15.09	.95	2.72
United Grain Growers Ltd.	UGG.TO	FOODPROC	15.00	.40	1.75
Virco Mfg Co.	VIR	FURNITUR	15.82	.65	.33
Zale Corp	ZLC	RETAILSP	15.95	.75	

Typical Value Line Results from a Filter

Reprinted with permission of the Value Line.

The system also helps with the final analysis and decision making by offering reports that describe the business and their prospects much more completely than the numbers alone. Here is one sample of the reports for First Brands Corp.

---

[10] There is one difficulty here—the *Value Line Investment Survey for Windows* price-to-cash-flow data only looks at the preceding quarter's cash flow. That seems to me to be inadequate since yearly cash flow should tell much more about the true financial condition of the company.

Value Line Analyst's Comments
First Brands Corp.

Ticker	FBR		Industry	Household Products

BUSINESS: First Brands Corp. develops, manufactures, and markets branded and private-label consumer products for the household and automotive markets. 1996 sales mix: plastic wrap/bags (Glad and Himolene) 65%; automotive specialty and appearance products (STP and Simoniz) 21%; pet products (Scoop Away and Ever Clean) 14%. Sold European Home Prods. 3/89; Prestone business 8/94. Purchased Forest Tech. Corp. 3/96. 1996 deprec. rate: 8.9%. Has about 4,200 empl., 515 shrhldrs. Officers/directors own about 4.8% of shares; Harris Assoc., 13.8%; Fidelity, 12.4%; Ariel Cap. Mgmt., 8.0% (9/96 Proxy). Chrmn., Pres. and C.E.O.: William V. Stephenson. Inc.: DE. Addr.: 83 Wooster Heights Rd., P.O. Box 1911, Danbury, CT 06813-1911. Tel.: 203-731-2300.

First Brands Corp. is having a tough time. The company has announced that its fourth-quarter earnings (years end June 30th) fell well short of the year-ago figure. The bottom-line pressure stems from promotional spending, lower orders by automotive-product retailers, and weak demand for plastic wrap and bags. Spending on advertising and promotions for new and existing products is slated to continue. Management has indicated it will continue promoting its brand names; and these expenses, without accompanying sales growth, will depress margins. Promotion may benefit the company in the long run in terms of maintaining its impressive market share, but it will hurt earnings for fiscal 1998. We are expecting a weak first quarter and a flat second quarter. The picture should improve some in the latter half of the year, when we estimate good year-to-year earnings comparisons. These increased profits assume unchanged raw- material costs and an improving sales mix. FBR also announced a restructuring program intended to reduce ongoing costs and improve operating efficiencies. After a non-recurring charge for fiscal 1997, the company expects to save about $4.5 million or $.07 a share annually starting in fiscal 1999. Wal-Mart's inventory reduction program will continue to hurt FBR for the next two quarters. Wal-Mart, which is the largest single retailer of FBR's automotive chemical products, is reducing its inventories, and that is resulting in volume pressure for the company's STP division. Previous inventory reduction programs have lasted between three to six months. Wal-Mart is also reducing in-store promotions, which will further trim sales. The Glad division is suffering from an industry-wide slump in demand for plastic wrap and bags. Sales in this division are currently little changed from a year ago, and this trend is likely to continue for at least the first half of fiscal 1998. The most recent twelve-week numbers indicate a significant sales slump for a major product, interlocking plastic bags. These shares are ranked Lowest for the year ahead. Investors should wait on the sidelines until FBR shows signs that its performance is back on track. Thomas M. O'Shea July 18, 1997

Reprinted with permission of Value Line Publishing, Inc.

The Growth Investor

The growth investor may have the hardest job of all in searching for candidates. The reason is that the basic historic data does not tell the whole story. It can't. If it did, then everyone would know about it, and the price would be bid to a fair level. But the growth investor can still get a lot out of the software.

If Carol was a fairly aggressive investor with a tolerance for risk, and was looking for a few new growth stock candidates, she might search the database using these criteria:

1. The market capitalization should be less than 200 million.

2. The five-year sales growth rate should be at least 25 percent.

3. The five-year EPS growth rate should be at least 25 percent.

4. The five-year book value growth rate should be at least 18 percent.

5. The *Value Line* projection of book-value growth rate should be at least 18 percent.

In not more than ten minutes, she could write the screen, search the 5,000 stocks, and discover that no stocks among the 5,000 satisfied these rigorous requirements. She could then easily modify the screen several times to discover that there were twelve companies that satisfied the first four conditions, but none of them had any projected book value growth rate from *Value Line*; and none of the twelve had any yield. She might have reasoned that the problem was that the first four conditions produced small companies with rapid growth over the past five years. Such companies are difficult to project in terms of future growth, and they are unlikely to pay any yield. She could then have modified her search in either of two directions. She might decide to simply stick with those twelve companies for further study, or she might decide to enlarge the market capitalization condition to allow up to $400 million. Suppose she did that. She could then modify the screen to include all five conditions above, with the market cap increased to 400 million, and rerun the screen in less than thirty seconds. Still no companies passed. After running several versions of this screen, she was learning a lot about the distribution of these statistics among the companies she wanted to review, and finally came up with the single candidate that satisfied these modified search criteria:

1. The market capitalization should be less than 400 million.

2. The five-year sales growth rate should be at least 20 percent.

3. The five-year EPS growth rate should be at least 20 percent.

4. The five-year book value growth rate should be at least 12 percent.

5. The *Value Line* projection of book value growth rate should be at least 12 percent.

The only company among the 5,000 in the *Value Line* database that satisfied all of these conditions in July 1997 was Thor Industries, the second largest manufacturer of recreational vehicles in the United States. It was then very easy, using the system, to review all of the current financial data for Thor, a description of their overall business operations, and the *Value Line* analysis of their prospects. This kind report is available for every company in the database.

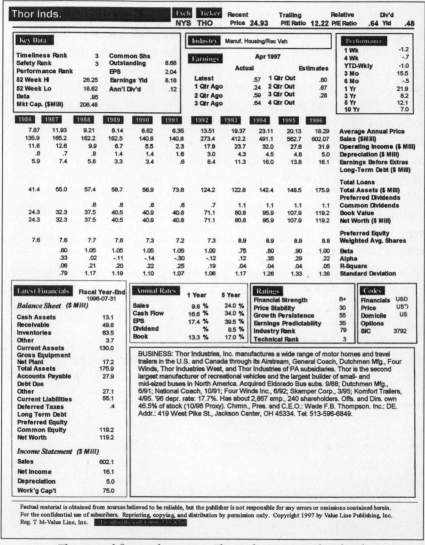

The general financial report on Thor Industries reproduced with permission from the Value Line Investment Survey for Windows.

All of this screening, modification, and data gathering could be completed in less than twenty minutes, with the result that she found a single sterling candidate among 5,000 companies. If one were trying to duplicate the work by reading reports, it is most likely that one would give up after the first twenty hours of work did not reveal a single company.

The preceding examples have illustrated only part of the power and ease of the *Value Line for Windows* product. For those who like to use the power of a desktop computer at its best, this product is well worth a close look.

Zacks Research Wizard

Zacks Investment Research has for years published *Analyst Watch*, a highly regarded summary of analysts' opinions about the prospective future earnings of publicly traded companies.

We should distinguish between two views of analysts' opinions. One view is the value of any individual analyst's earnings forecast. We know that such an individual's estimate is not to be taken as gospel, but merely is a reasonable guess into the future. The further out they try to forecast, the greater is the likelihood of error. However, the other view of the subject is the overall trend or consensus of all analysts' opinions. That can be, and is, reported with accuracy and timeliness by Zacks and *First Call,* and should be taken as a valuable indicator of one factor that can move markets or individual stock prices.

Keep in mind two factors that affect stock price changes. They are, first, the reality of what is happening to a company and, second, the market's opinions about what is going to happen. Some experienced investors would say that the only thing you need to be a successful investor is a reliable gauge of market opinions. That is what Zacks delivers in *Analyst Watch*. Substantial research, built up over many years, suggests that the direction and changes in analysts' consensus estimates of future earnings are reliable indicators of stock price trends.

Research Wizard is a combination of software, a database, and a regular data updating service to help the individual investor evaluate stocks. It offers these features.

1. **Zacks Company Reports:** A one-page summary of the latest key financial data, with charts of the stock prices and earnings history plus earnings forecasts.

2. **Zacks Easy Screen:** A one-page stock screening mechanism that allows the user to choose from among thirteen criteria and ask for stocks that fall within a certain highest or lowest value for each criterion; for example, you could ask for stocks that fall among the lowest 50 percent of all current market capitalization values. After the choice is made in all thirteen categories, the system screens through the database to present the stocks that satisfy the chosen criteria. This function is exceptionally quick and easy to use. Upon completing the search, the system presents a list, with key financial data, on all the companies that passed.

3. **Alert Reports:** A service that focuses on the main Zacks idea—earnings estimate changes and earnings surprises. The idea is simple: If analysts' expectations of earnings change, that will be reflected in the stock price. If a company significantly exceeds or misses analysts' earnings estimates, that will also be reflected in changes in the stock price. The data is somewhat more complex than the basic idea, and involves such things as the variability of analysts' estimates and the standard deviation of the previous trends in earnings. This information is very easy to obtain and use with the Alert Reports. Interpretation of the reports and making decisions will be considerably more involved.

4. **Screen II:** This is a far more detailed and feature-rich screen than the Easy Screen we mentioned above. It provides access to over 6,000 companies or 211 industry groups. It is more difficult to use than Easy Screen, but offers correspondingly greater possibilities to develop your own special criteria. It has one advantage over the *Value Line* screening functions in that, with Screen II, you have some choices to create your own calculations based on financial data. For example, *Value Line* does not offer a screening criteria based on the current price relative to the past year's cash flow. With Screen II, you can use that as a selection criterion. The *Value Line for Windows* product offers other features that are not in the *Research Wizard*.

Both of these software and database products can bring a lot of useful information within easy click. Both of them can serve as valuable tools to find many stocks that deserve your consideration, subject to your individual criteria for selection. The *Value Line* product puts somewhat more emphasis on reporting and analyzing a company's history, as seen through the eyes of their analysts and their rating factors. The Zacks product stresses the importance of the changes in the consensus estimates of all the analysts who follow each company and stock. Both of them provide data on approximately 5,000–6,000 stocks, and are quite easy to set up and use.

*Selecting and combining as he pleases, each
man reads his own peculiar lesson according
to his own peculiar mind and mood.*

HERMAN MELVILLE, *PIERRE*

Closing

So now you see, it is certainly as I advertised so many pages before: There are some stock-selection methods that make sense to you. There are some tools and ideas that could be of use to you. Decisiveness and the will to invest will have to come from within; I should not advise you on those, but the tools are within your grasp.

In this book, as well as in *The Small Investor*, I have tried to give you access to some of the basic ideas, language, and methods of investing. You should feel that you can confidently make your own decisions about whether to buy individual stocks. You should feel ready to talk to brokers, financial advisors, and market hotshots on their own terms and defend yourself and your point of view.

It is interesting that I write this closing in the middle of the worldwide market turmoil of the autumn of 1997. Within the past few months, all of the risks that we discussed have been fully illustrated in the heat of active daily trading. Fortunes have been made and lost. Truly, fortunes. Individuals have lost several hundreds of millions of dollars. Funds and institutions have lost hundreds of billions.

The tremendous bull market in American stocks of 1982 to 1997 may be coming to a close. The growth investors and their confederates the momentum investors may be in the difficult situation of reconsidering, perhaps abandoning, the methods that brought them great profits over the past few years. It is an interesting coincidence that, within the past two months, a news organization published the results of a nationwide poll indicating that individual investors on average were expecting over 30 percent annual returns from their investments going forward. The result defies credibility, but we must assume there was some logic in their polling methods, and some indication of investors' expectations. If indeed this cloud, too, has a silver lining, maybe it will be to shake some people back into reality.

The new risks and uncertainties that face income investors due to the changing behavior of the bond markets and the brave new world of deregulated utilities have forced us to reappraise the once serene practice of buying yield. The people who have doggedly stuck to value investing over the past two years may finally be seeing some vindication, and their chance to say "I told you so!" If we are truly headed for a bear market, they may not be hurt as bad as the others. Some consolation.

Are there any winners? Well, sure—the press, the prognosticators, and the contrarians. Turmoil is mother's milk to them. But among the individual investors, it is not clear. It won't be clear until we can look back on 1997 and 1998 from a safe distance. Doubtless, some will say, "Oh yeah, sure, I knew about that—I made 50 percent gain on oil" (or computers, or pharmaceuticals); "I knew exactly what was going on." That will be a lie. Nobody knows exactly what is going on. The smartest ladies and gentlemen in the business can only hope that they will have profitable investments more often than not, or at least that their gains on the correct moves will outweigh the losses on the others.

Will you be successful investing in the stock markets? No one knows. The future of any individual stock, or of the markets, is a mystery. It is brewed out of an ever changing turmoil of business activity and market psychology. None of us, nor any others, will ever be able to predict with certainty what next month holds in store for the markets. If anyone could, then he or she would do it, and all the rest of us would leave the markets, and there wouldn't be any more markets. Do not trick yourself. You will never buy or sell any stock with absolute certainty that you are doing the most profitable thing.

So what should you expect? Expect that you can find good information, that you can construct reasonable estimates of the condition of a company and the value of its stock. Expect that there are rational methods that have been tested and endorsed by many other investors and are accessible to you.

Do not expect to find an easy path to wealth. Do not expect to be right on all of your stock purchases. But expect that, with a fair amount of work and careful consideration of the evidence you find, you will make reasonable decisions about which stocks to buy or sell. You will then have as good a chance as the rest of us at turning a profit.

Glossary

The terms are defined here as they are used in this book. That allows some occasional differences from common English usage.

10K: A company's annual report to the Securities and Exchange Commission.

10Q: A company's quarterly report to the Securities and Exchange Commission.

401(k): Type of investment or savings account wherein workers may save part of their pay and invest it without current taxes on the pay or investment returns.

AAII: The American Association of Individual Investors.

accounts payable: Accounts that represent what a firm is currently obligated to pay.

accounts receivable: Accounts that represent money owed to a firm.

ADR: American depository receipt.

advisor: A person who helps with financial planning, usually a broker, investment advisor, financial planner, or insurance advisor; usually a professional in that business.

algorithm: A method of performing a calculation.

allocation: The process or results of dividing investment assets among different available choices such as stocks, bonds, mutual funds, or bank deposits.

American depository receipt: A security that represents foreign company shares of stock that are held in deposit by an American firm, usually a bank.

American Stock Exchange: The second largest stock exchange in the United States.

AMEX: The American Stock Exchange.

analyst: A financial professional who is employed to evaluate the potential risk, gains, or losses from financial investments.

annual reports: The reports issued by all publicly traded companies that show news and plans for current and future business operations, and descriptions of a company's financial condition.

arbitration: The process of allowing a neutral party to settle a dispute, usually instead of using the courts.

asset: Something of worth belonging to a company with a dollar value assigned to it.

average: In mathematics, it is the sum of a set of numbers divided by the number of values included; in the financial markets, it usually refers to a weighted average of stock or bond prices used as an indicator of overall market performance; for example, the Dow Jones industrial average.

balance sheet: A report that shows the dollar value of all of the assets and liabilities of a firm at a given date.

Barron's: A weekly newspaper published by Dow Jones that specializes in financial news and advice.

bear market: Any financial market during a period when prices are generally falling.

bears: Investors or analysts who predict falling prices for one or more types of assets, and/or sell some of their investments.

beta (ß): A number that is used to reflect the volatility of an investment; it is almost always used relative to the volatility of some appropriate market index; ß=1 for investments that fluctuate up or down as much as the relevant market index values; ß>1 means the investment is more volatile, and ß<1 means it is less volatile. Some investors or analysts use ß as a measurement of the historic risk level in the investment.

blue chip: A stock that is issued by a large and secure company, or a group of investments that concentrate in such stocks.

bond: An investment in the form of a loan, or the security (promise to repay) that represents the investment.

book value: (1) the value of a business asset as it is carried on the company's financial records; (2) one view of the value of a company seen as the total assets minus the liabilities of the firm; frequently divided by the number of shares of stock and referenced as the book value per share.

bottom-up: A practice of investing that begins by looking at specific details of individual companies' financial results before considering broader economic factors.

bourse: A stock exchange.

broker: A person who acts as a paid agent between buyers and sellers for securities sales, and is registered to conduct such business.

brokerage: The business or practice of buying and selling financial instruments for the public, for a fee.

bull market: Any financial market during a period that prices are generally rising.

bulls: Investors or analysts who predict rising prices for one or more types of assets, and/or buy investments.

buy and hold: An investment practice of buying stocks, bonds, or funds with the intention of holding for the long term.

capital gains tax: A tax that is paid on the gains from selling securities at higher prices than one paid for them.

capitalization: Total value of money committed to something (*see also* market capitalization).

cash equivalents: Assets (or the accounts showing those assets) that may be readily converted to a definite cash value.

cash flow: The changes in the cash account of a business during a fixed accounting reporting period; frequently, it is the earnings plus the depreciation.

Charles Dow: Founder of the *Wall Street Journal* and the Dow Jones industrial average.

churning: The practice of a broker producing a large number of trades for a customer's account with the intention of collecting excessive commissions.

closed-end fund: A mutual fund that does not promise to issue or redeem new shares at any time. The investment company sells a number of shares to begin business and then those shares are traded like stock. The price of a closed-end fund's share is determined by whatever willing buyers and sellers agree to in the markets.

CNBC: A cable news channel primarily dedicated to financial news.

CNN: A cable news channel devoted to news coverage.

commission: The sales fee paid to a person, usually a broker, who manages a trade for a customer.

common stock: The shares of ownership of a publicly traded company.

compound gains: The results of growth and profit over several periods of returns when each period's profit is reinvested to gain additional profits in the next period.

compound growth: Same as compound gains.

compound rate of return: The annualized rate of return on an investment that would have given a certain profit if it had been in effect over a certain time period. For example, if an investment returned nothing in its first year and 2 percent in its second year, then the compound rate of return would be close to 1 percent.

conservative book value: The result of computing the total assets minus the liabilities of a firm and subtracting the fair value of the liability for preferred stock.

contrarian: An investor who usually invests differently than most other investors.

correction: A short-term change in the trend of a market. So, a correction in a bull market would be a short-term decline.

crash: A sudden large fall in market prices.

Curb: A historical term for the American Stock Exchange still commonly used in casual reference.

current assets: Assets that should reasonably be expected to convert to cash within one year.

current liabilities: Liabilities that should reasonably be expected to be paid within one year.

current ratio: The current assets value divided by the current liabilities value.

debt: One party's obligation to pay some value to another party.

debt service: The process or plans that a company has for repaying its debt.

debt-to-equity ratio: The value of a company's total debt divided by the value of its total shareholders' equity.

decisiveness: The ability to make decisions and carry through to completion whatever actions may be indicated by the decision.

defensive stocks: Stocks that may reasonably be expected to lose value less than the market averages in a time of generally falling prices.

disciplinary actions: Actions such as fines, censures, or disqualifications that the regulatory bodies may impose on financial professionals or firms for improper business conduct.

discount broker: A broker, or brokerage firm, that usually charges relatively lower fees and delivers less individualized service to the investor.

distress sale: A firm's sale of assets when it is obliged to take almost any offered price.

diversification: The process, or the results of, allocating investment capital among different investments that might be expected to behave differently in various economic situations.

dividend: A portion of a firm's earnings paid out to the shareholders.

dividend reinvestment: The practice of using all dividends paid by a security to buy more of the same, or similar securities.

DJIA: The Dow Jones industrial average.

dog: A stock that has lagged behind some peer group in terms of price gains, frequently identified by its relatively high yield.

Dogs of the Dow: A group of dogs from among the Dow Jones thirty industrial stocks.

dollar cost averaging: A practice of investing a regular, fixed, predetermined amount in some security or mutual fund on a periodic basis.

Dow Jones & Co., Inc.: Publishes the *Wall Street Journal, Barron's,* and *Smart Money* magazine, and provides other financial information services.

Dow Jones industrial average: An index used to gauge stock market action, it is calculated based on the prices of the stocks of thirty large and well-established representatives of American business.

DRIP: A dividend reinvestment plan.

earnings: The profits earned by a company after taxes, interest on debt, depreciation, and dividends to preferred shareholders. The amount that represents profits to the common stock shareholders.

earnings per share: Earnings divided by the number of outstanding shares of common stock.

earnings report: A section of a company's financial reports that shows the revenues, expenses, other income, depreciation, taxes, and any other items necessary to calculate the company's earnings during an accounting period.

EBIT: Earnings before interest and taxes, also called gross profit.

EDGAR: A database with extensive data on companies and their financial reports that is available free to users of the Internet.

efficient market hypothesis: A theory, or any of various expressions and variations on the theory, that purports to show that individual investors can not expect to do any better than average by trying to select individual stocks with superior profitability prospects.

EMH: The efficient market hypothesis.

EPS: Earnings per share.

equity: A share of ownership in a company; usually represented by the stock.

fair price: A price that is agreed on for a sale between a willing buyer and a willing seller.

FFO: Funds from operations.

financial analysis: The practice or profession of identifying and explaining the most important data and influencing factors that may explain a company's financial situation, or predict changes in the financial situation.

financial data (or financial reports): The information that describes all of the assets and liabilities, the revenues and expenses, and the changes in those quantities for a company. Every publicly traded company is required to make its financial data available to the public (refer to EDGAR).

financial ratios: Any of a large number of ratios that may be computed using the financial data of a firm and then used in the financial analysis of the firm.

financial reports: Any or all of the reports that show and explain a company's financial condition and recent or expected changes in the condition.

fiscal year: A period of one year that a company chooses to use to report its annual operating results.

flexibility: The ability of an investor to buy and sell different kinds of investments and to move money among different kinds of investments.

full-service broker: A brokerage firm that offers research, advising, and other financial services, in addition to buying and selling in the financial markets.

funds from operations: Earnings reported by some industries, notably real estate investment trusts, that include only the earnings from normal ongoing business operations.

futures contract: A contract where a party promises to deliver for sale a specific amount of a particular good at a specified price on a future date.

GAAP: Generally accepted accounting principles.

generally accepted accounting principles: A set of guidelines that help accountants consistently and accurately report the financial situation of companies.

Graham, Benjamin: One of the pioneers of scientific, value-oriented investing, and author of *The Intelligent Investor* and co-author of *Security Analysis*.

greater fool: An investor who buys stock when it has already been overpriced in the markets.

gross profit: The profits left after all operating expenses have been subtracted from the revenue, but before the taxes and interest have been paid; also called EBIT.

growth: Increase in the share price of stock or the sales and earnings of a company.

growth company: A company with the quality of increasing sales and profits and probably increasing stock value.

growth fund: A mutual fund that tries to concentrate its assets in stocks of growth companies.

growth investor: An investor who tries to buy stock of growth companies.

growth stock: The stock of a company that is considered to be a growth company.

guru: One who claims to know more than the rest of us.

hedging: Investing in some securities, options, or futures with a view to balancing the risks in other investments.

income investing: The practice of buying stocks with higher-than-average dividend income.

income statement: Section of a financial report that shows the revenues, expenses, and earnings for a reporting period.

index: A calculated number that represents the price levels and price changes for a group of securities; for example, the Dow Jones industrial average, the Dow Jones utilities average, the S&P 500 average.

indexing: The practice of buying stocks in proportion to their weighting in one of the popular stock indices.

individual retirement account: An account that an individual sets up with a financial company for saving part of current income, while shielding the savings and/or earnings in the account from current taxes. The account is used for retirement support.

intermediate term: Time period for bond holdings of 2 to 6 years, or for stock holdings of 3 months to a year; these time limits are subject to varying interpretations by different investors.

inventory: The amount or the value of goods that a company has produced but not sold.

invest: To use one's money to earn more money by lending it, or buying securities that may produce future income or growth in market value.

investment club: A group (partnership) of private investors who agree to pool their investment capital and share the work and risk of investing through group analysis and discussion.

investment company: A company that owns and operates a mutual fund.

investor: A person who puts money at risk in financial markets in hopes of making profits.

IRA: Individual retirement account.

ISP: Internet service provider; for example, America Online or Mindspring.

large cap: A company, or its stock, for which the total market value of all the stock is above some high standard (perhaps 6 or 8 or 10 billion dollars); the standard is set differently by various commentators.

leverage: The use of borrowed money to run a business, or the ratio of borrowed money compared to the owner's equity.

liability: A debt or claim against the assets of a firm; for example, a bond sold by a firm represents a claim against the assets for both interest payments and final repayment, and this is a liability of the firm.

limit order: An order to a broker to buy or sell a security at the best price they can get above (for a sale) or below (for a purchase) some price specified by the investor.

liquidity: The ability to recover the cash value from an investment or other asset.

long-term debt: Debt that should be repaid over a period of several years.

mania: A period of excitement or public rush to buy stocks that causes prices to rise rapidly.

market capitalization: The total market value of all the stock of a company. This changes as the stock price changes.

market order: An order to a broker to buy or sell a security at the best price they can get in current market conditions.

market price: The price that is currently being accepted by both buyer and seller in the open markets; for a stock or bond, it is recognized as the price in the last sale of the security.

market rate: The interest rate that the bond markets impose on a bond, or group of bonds, to determine their current market price.

market risk: The risk that any stock price may fall simply because stocks in general are being sold at lower prices. Many professionals state that the market risk is the single greatest risk for all stock purchases.

market sector: A group of companies that have some common characteristics in their businesses or stocks; for example, the auto sector or the small capitalization companies.

market timing: The difficult and risky practice of trying to plan one's purchase and sale of stocks to take advantage of market trends and extreme values.

market trend: Any consistent direction of change in prices over a period of time.

markets: Organizations, places, or groups that are established for the purpose of buying and selling financial instruments.

mid cap: A company, or its stock, that has market capitalization within a range that is considered below large-cap stocks and above small-cap stocks. For example, some might say that stocks with market capitalization between $500 million and $5 billion are mid caps. The limits are set differently by various commentators.

modern portfolio theory: The idea that the main job of a money manager is to balance the volatility within the portfolio; *see also* the efficient market hypothesis, which is a related theory.

momentum: A tendency of a stock price, or a market average, to continue a trend that has been observed for some prior time period. Momentum is a device of speculation—some commentators believe it is real and some do not.

Morningstar: A firm that does extensive research on stocks and mutual funds, publishes their own periodical review of funds, and sells their research to the public or other firms.

MPT: Modern portfolio theory.

multiple: The price-to-earnings ratio of a stock.

mutual fund: A fund collected from the investing public by an investment company for the purpose of investing in stocks, bonds, other funds, or anything else that the investment company declares in the fund's prospectus.

NAIC: The National Association of Investors Corporation.

NASD: The National Association of Securities Dealers.

NASDAQ: The NASD automated quotation system, a computer network that provides brokers with information-management services for trading stocks of over 5,500 companies that are not listed on the major exchanges.

National Association of Securities Dealers: A self-regulating professional association of securities dealers.

near cash: Assets of a company that are believed to be convertible into cash at their reported value within a very short time.

net cash flow: The change in a company's cash account during a reporting period.

net worth: The value of the total assets minus the total liabilities of a firm; also referred to as owners equity or stockholders equity.

New York Stock Exchange: A stock exchange in New York City that provides registration and trading services for stocks of most of the largest American companies.

Nifty Fifty: The stocks of a group of blue-chip companies that were treated as if they were risk-free investments around 1970–71. They subsequently suffered very large losses in the bear market of 1973–74.

no-brainers: Investments that are made without due analysis of the risks; *see also* Nifty-Fifty.

NYSE: The New York Stock Exchange.

option: A contract that promises that the originator of the contract will buy (or sell) a specified number of shares of a security at a specified price within some time frame. The second party to the contract has an option, but not an obligation, to take the other side of the future transaction. The second party also has an option to let the contract expire with no action taken.

OTC: Over the counter.

over the counter: Term used to describe either markets away from regulated stock exchanges or the stocks that are traded in those markets.

panic: A period when investors rush to sell all of their financial assets and cause a rapid fall in prices.

payout ratio: The percentage ratio of annual dividends divided by annual earnings.

P/E: The price-to-earnings ratio.

penny stocks: Stocks that sell for very low prices, typically less than two dollars per share.

per share value: The result of any financial data divided by the number of shares of stock outstanding.

personal investment strategy: An individual investor's plan to allocate and manage investments to suit his personal needs and risk acceptance.

PIG principal: The idea that a stock investor's decisions should be guided by consideration of protection, income, and growth.

portfolio: The collection of investments owned by an investor, or a mutual fund or other organization.

preferred stock: A class of stock that may be issued by some companies that has provisions for a specified dividend rate and seniority over the common stock in case of distribution of the assets of the company. The preferred stock may commonly have various other provisions attached that distinguish its value from the common stock, such as voting rights or convertibility.

prevailing rates: The interest rates that the markets impose on a bond or group of bonds to determine their current prices.

price-to-cash-flow ratio: The stock share price divided by the annual cash flow per share.

price-to-earnings ratio: The ratio obtained by dividing the price of a stock share by its associated earnings per share (only makes sense if the earnings per share are positive, i.e. the company has some profits).

price-to-sales ratio: The stock share price divided by the annual sales per share.

principal: The dollar value of an investment.

publicly traded: For sale to the public through financial markets.

quick ratio: The result of dividing the total of cash and near cash assets by the current liabilities.

real estate investment trust: A company that raises money through stock or bond issues to use in real estate speculation or investments.

reality: There is no risk-free investment.

registered investment advisor: A person who has passed an examination on investment law and ethics, and has paid the SEC, and any state where advice will be offered, to register as an investment advisor.

REIT: Real estate investment trust.

retirement account: A savings account that is intended to provide income after the person retires.

return on assets: The ratio of annual earnings divided by the total assets of a firm.

return on equity: The ratio of annual earnings divided by the shareholders' equity of the firm.

return on investment: The ratio of the profits on an investment divided by the amount originally invested.

risk: The possibility of losing money in an investment, or any factor that might lead to the loss.

risk avoidance: The practice of buying investments for which the risks have been analyzed and found to be acceptable compared to the potential return on investment.

risk-free investment: A lie, a bad joke, a figment; there is no risk-free investment.

risk-oriented investment: An investment practice that recognizes and analyzes opportunities and risks to suit one's personal investment strategy.

risks in the economy: The risks attached to any investment that are caused by uncertainties in the economy.

Rogers, Jim: Money manager, finance professor, author of *Investment Biker*, and frequent commentator on CNBC.

Rukeyser, Louis: Avuncular host of the weekly public television program *Wall Street Week with Louis Rukeyser*.

rule of thumb on price: The idea (which is lacking in rigorous foundation) that a stock may be a good buy if the price-to-earnings ratio is less than the past few years' compound rate of growth per share. Sometimes, in place of the past few years' compound rate of growth, investors use the past year's rate, or a projection of the next year's rate.

Russell 2000: A group of stocks, or their associated price index, that includes 2000 small-capitalization stocks; this is a representative index for the values of all small-cap stocks.

S&P: Standard & Poor's company.

S&P 100: The 100 stocks with the largest market capitalization among the S&P 500.

S&P 400: The 400 stocks with the smallest market capitalization among the S&P 500.

S&P 500: A group of stocks, or their associated price index, that includes 500 large capitalization stocks; this is a representative index for the behavior of stock values for all large-cap stocks.

screens: Methods used to find stocks or bonds that satisfy specific conditions, frequently used with computers and data bases to select a few qualifying securities from among a large group.

SEC: The United States Securities and Exchange Commission.

secondary market: The market that deals with buying and selling bonds, or any security, after their original issue.

sector: A group of companies, or their stocks, that share some interesting attribute; for example, the automobile sector or the small-cap sector.

Securities and Exchange Commission: A Federal agency established by U.S. law for regulation of the registration and sale of securities.

security: Principally, a stock or bond, sometimes other types of financial instruments; anything that indicates ownership, right to benefits of ownership, or right to payment.

share: A part of the ownership of a company represented by the common stock; sometimes share and stock share or just stock are used synonymously.

short selling: The practice of trying to profit by borrowing a stock to sell at a high price, in hopes of buying it back later at a low price to redeem the borrowing.

small cap: A company, or its stock, for which the total market value of all the stock is below some standard (perhaps 300, 400, or 500 million dollars); the standard is set differently by various commentators.

split: The practice where a company chooses to increase their total number of shares by issuing new shares in proportion to those already out. Each stockholder gets the same proportional increase in shares held, and that is accompanied by a proportional decrease in the stock price, so the total value is unchanged.

split-adjusted prices: A calculated and hypothetical pre-split price for a stock share that has been adjusted to make it comparable to prices after the split.

spread: The difference between the offered and asked prices for a stock or bond.

Standard & Poor's: A securities analysis and research firm that publishes important reports and opinions on the value of stocks and bonds.

stock exchange: A business or association, or its physical presence, that is established to help people buy and sell stocks.

stop order: An order to a broker to sell a stock at market value if the price ever drops to some value specified by the investor; a stop order becomes a market order after the trigger price is realized in the market.

strategy: An investment plan to allocate funds among diverse investments over a period of time.

technical analysis: The practice of predicting price changes of a security, or group of securities, by analyzing prior changes and looking for patterns and relationships in graphs of price history.

technicians: Stock analysts who rely mostly on technical analysis.

timeliness (as used in the *Value Line*): A rating value (1 = best to 5 = worst) showing an opinion about the probable price performance of a stock over the next six to twelve months.

times interest earned: The ratio of earnings before interest and taxes divided by the annual interest owed.

top-down: A practice of investing analysis that begins with broad analysis of the complete economic conditions of the world, a nation, an industry sector, or some other large segment of business, and then tries to focus on specific companies that may benefit from economic trends.

total return: The total profits realized from an investment, including dividends, price appreciation, splits, or anything else that may be earned; usually expressed as an annual rate compared to the original purchase price.

trade: The act of buying or selling a security, or a term used sometimes to denote a short-term investment.

trader: One who buys and sells securities; sometimes used to connote an emphasis on short-term investing.

trading: (1) buying and selling financial instruments or securities; (2) frequent or short-term buying and selling.

transaction: Any purchase or sale of securities.

Treasury bills: Bonds issued by the U.S. Treasury that are due in one year or less.

TVL: The *Value Line*.

value: The concept of all the attributes of a stock, or a company, that make the stock a good buy at the current price.

value investing: An approach to stock selection that focuses on the price-related value attributes of the stock or the company before the long-term growth estimates.

Value Line: A publication of The Value Line, Inc. that provides data, analysis, and recommendations about stock investing.

volatility: The degree of price change in some specified time period; usually measured through the calculation of a quantity called beta (ß) relative to some specified market index.

volume: The number of shares traded within some specified time period.

Wall Street Journal: A daily newspaper published by Dow Jones that specializes in business news.

WEBs: A derivative securities class created by the American Stock Exchange for providing investors opportunities to profit from growth of foreign stocks.

weighted average: The result of assigning a weighting value to each number in a set; multiplying the numbers by their respective weights; summing the resulting products, and dividing that sum by the sum of the weighting values used.

Wilshire 5000: A group of companies, or their associated price index, that represents the majority of all firms traded in regulated American public stock markets.

WSJ: The *Wall Street Journal.*

yield: For a stock, the ratio of annual dividends divided by the stock price; for a bond, the rate of interest payments, which may refer to either current yield, yield to maturity, or coupon yield.

yield ratio (for a stock): The ratio of the annual dividend paid to its price.

Zweig, Martin: Authority on market history and market timing, author of *Winning on Wall Street;* frequent guest on *Wall Street Week* with Louis Rukeyser.

Index